Egypt & Nasser

Volume 1

1952-56

Egypt & Nasser

Volume 1

1952-56

Edited by Dan Hofstadter

FACTS ON FILE, INC.   NEW YORK, N.Y.

Egypt & Nasser

Volume 1

1952-56

© Copyright, 1973, by Facts on File, Inc.

Published by Facts on File, Inc.,
119 West 57th Street, New York, N.Y. 10019.

Library of Congress Catalog Card No. 74-154632
ISBN 0-87196-203-9

9 8 7 6 5 4 3 2 1
PRINTED IN
THE UNITED STATES OF AMERICA

CONTENTS

INTRODUCTION

GAMAL ABDEL NASSER PLAYED A UNIQUE role in Egypt and in the entire Arab world during the final 15 years of his life. He served almost as a flag around which not only Egyptians but most Arabs seemed to feel they could rally for various purposes—for war with Israel, for diplomatic dealings with the West (or East) or for regional planning.

To his fellow Egyptians, this charismatic leader embodied a people's yearning for national dignity and the poor man's hope for a life of relative plenty. To the people of all the Arab lands—from North Africa to Southern Arabia and Syria—Nasser personified the promise of a renewal of a Moslem unity and Arab grandeur that had been nothing more than a memory, although a vivid one, for half a millenium.

Nasser was the foremost leader of the diverse peoples who call themselves Arabs. Despite political and ideological differences that occasionally burst into bloody dispute among them, most Arabs apparently considered Nasser to be probably the only individual who could bring together a unified pan-Arabia capable of winning a respected place among the world's powers. There seemed to be evidence, too, that Nasser at times thought of himself as a world leader whose potential constituency might be greater than the United Arab Republic he had created or the pan-Islamic empire to which he almost overtly aspired.

Egypt (*Misr* in Arabic), or the United Arab Republic *(al-Gumhuria al-Arabia al-Muttahida)*, occupies a deceptively large corner of northwest Africa. In fact, townspeople and cultivators inhabit barely a 15th part of the land; the rest is desert. Only ponds of brine, brackish wadis and the rare camps of the Bedouin tribesmen relieve the arid wilderness, and the forages of these nomads recognize no international frontiers.

1

The settled, arable part—the Egypt of men—borders the northward-flowing Nile with savannahs and tilled fields as far as Cairo, where it fans into an ample delta. Many hundreds of moist grassmoors, lakes and streams water this delta, making it fertile enough to feed abundant marsh fowl and peccaries, as well as the bulk of the peasantry with their livestock.

Across the narrow isthmus that joins Africa to Asia is the Sinai Peninsula, also officially under Egyptian sovereignty. Since the Arab-Israeli war of June 1967 this desert has been occupied by the armed forces of Israel, and Israel also exploits the rich oil fields beneath the sand.

The 2 great Egyptian cities, Cairo and Alexandria, face respectively east and west. Alexandria *(al-Iskanderia)*, taking its name from the Greek emperor, was until 1957 a deeply European city—European in design, in culture and in the composition of its dominant merchant class. Many of Egypt's 100,000 Greeks lived in Alexandria, mingling with other trade-minded minorities—the Armenians, Jews, French and Italians. Most of this foreign colony was constrained to leave Egypt in 1957 as a consequence of Nasser's Egyptianization program. The largest community—the Greek—departed almost *in toto* for Greece under an agreement between Nasser and Greek Premier Constantine Karamanlis, while the Jews emigrated to Israel, Europe and Brazil.

More than 100 miles to the south, Cairo (in Arabic, *al-Qahira,* "the Conqueror") straddles the Nile and the large island of Gezira. Visitors arriving at Cairo airport and driving toward the administrative center through the elegant Heliopolis quarter see only the illusory facade of the city, the plush, ostentatious villas of pashas and beys chased away in the early phase of the revolution. These fading remnants of the British protectorate soon give way to the naked African metropolis with its narrow streets, dusty in summer, muddy in winter and always prodigal with beggars, mangomongers, water-sellers, street acrobats, bedevilled cyclists and hordes of beckoning dragomen. The people habitually dress in the pyjama-and-nightgown-like *galabeya*, which, apt as it is to ensare the wearer in train carriages or heavy machinery, has been officially discouraged by the revolutionary regime. Cairo, once abandoned every summer by the khedivial and royal courts for the breezier Alexandria, is the year-round capital of the post-1952 government. The administration, an enormous and imaginatively ramified bureaucracy, sits imposingly not far from the Nile Hilton, which has replaced the elegant old Shepheard's Hotel as the haunt of foreign diplomats, journalists and informers. Cairo also boasts Egypt's greatest mosques and the ancient Islamic university of al-Azhar.

Historical Background

The history of modern Egypt begins with Napoleon Bonaparte's capture of Alexandria in 1798. In a scheme reminiscent of an earlier conquerer, Alexander the Great, Bonaparte proclaimed his submission to Allah, his recognition of the Prophet and the concordance of French reason and Koranic religion in the belief in the equality of men.

The Mamluk (Mameluke) rulers of Egypt, scions of enfranchised slaves still enfeoffed to the Ottoman sultan in Istanbul, opposed Bonaparte at the battle of Ambalah, and Napoleon swiftly routed them. The Cairo populace at first rallied to Bonaparte; but when Britain's Nelson sank France's Nile fleet, and the French forces in Upper Egypt failed to secure the person of the chief Mamluk bey (the Amir al-Hajj Murad), the *ulama* (Moslem worthies) of Cairo provoked an insurrection. This Gen. J. B. Kleber promptly put down and, heedless of Moslem sensibilities, quartered his chasseurs and their mounts in the mosque of al-Azhar.

In the following 2 years the troops of 3 foreign powers, France Britain and the Ottoman Empire, engaged and counterengaged along the littoral of the Eastern Mediterranean. Gen. J. F. (Baron de) Menou, an eccentric French proselyte to Islam, recaptured and for a time held the loyalty of the Moslem masses. In Aug. 1801, however, a Turko-British expedition overwhelmed Menou at Alexandria, and the French quit Egypt entirely.

The tyranny of the Mamluks again oppressed all Egypt. Finally, on May 13, 1805, a delegation of the Moslem theological doctors of Cairo approached Muhammad Ali, an Albanian mercenary chieftain employed by the Sublime Porte,* bewailing the despotism of Khorshid the Mamluk. "Whom then will ye have?" asked the soldier-of-fortune. "We will have *thee*," the doctors answered, "to govern us according to the laws; for in thy countenance we see goodness and justice."

At first unsure of his power, Muhammad Ali temporized, abetting the influence of the Mamluks, many of whom kept palaces and seraglios in Cairo. But early in 1811 the Albanian invited all the Cairene Mamluks to the Investment of his son Tusun with a pelisse and the high command of an expedition against the Wahhabi heretics of the Najd. The gaudy cortege of the beys proceeded Mar. 1 to the citadel to take sweetmeats with Muhammad Ali and Tusun. While they shook with the bitter coffee, the gate closed behind them, and Muhammad Ali's retainers slaughtered them.

The extermination of the Mamluks and the accession of Muhammad Ali was considered in many ways a boon to Egypt. The Albanian pasha†, virtually independent of the Porte, restored public order, introduced European merchants, rebuilt Alexandria's harbor and the Mahmudiya Canal, join-

---

*The term Sublime Porte, a French transaltion of *babi ali*, refers to the high gate of the Ottoman sultan's palace in Constantinople at which justice was administered—and hence, by extension, to the palace and city themselves as the seat and capital of the imperial Turkish government, with sway until 1880 over most of the Balkans and North Africa as well as of the Middle East.

†The title *pasha* in this case means governor of a *pashalik*, or Ottoman province; but the title eventually became debased and was used as an honorific.

ing it to Cairo, and favored Western medicine and technology. But the pasha was no Egyptian, still less a man of the land, and the *fellahin*—the peasants fared ill under his rule. The British consul-general reported in 1838: "The government, possessing itself of the necessaries of life at a price fixed by itself, disposes of them at arbitrary prices. The *fellah* is thus deprived of his harvest and falls into arrears with his taxes, is harassed and bastinadoed to force him to pay his debts. This leads to deterioration of agriculture and lessens the production."

Senility overcame Muhammad Ali in 1847. His energetic son Ibrahim succeeded him but died the following year. After a brief interlude the *pashalik* of Egypt passed to Muhammad Ali's son Said.

4 months after his accession, Said in 1854 bestowed on a companion of his youth, Ferdinand Marie de Lesseps, a concession to dig the Suez Canal. To exploit the project, the French entrepreneur soon formed a consortium, the Compagnie Universelle du Canal Maritime de Suez (Suez Canal Co.), in which Frenchmen owned more than twice the shares held by Egyptians. In 1863, however, before excavation had begun, Said died, and was succeeded by the colorful Ismail Pasha, eldest surviving son of Ibrahim.

The widening American Civil War boded well for Ismail. As the Confederate South succumbed to the invading Union armies, Egyptian cotton prices soared, allowing Ismail to finance the labor to build the new canal. When it opened in 1869, Said spent £1 million on the dedication ceremony, which 6,000 guests attended, including the French Empress Eugenie, the Habsburg emperor and the Prussian crown prince.

The excavation of the 103-mile Suez Canal to a depth of 26 feet (now 42½ feet) and a width of 72 feet (now 197 feet) grew out of the 18th-century Franco-British rivalry for the trade of India and East Asia. Possible routes for a canal across the Isthmus of Suez, studied by Charles Lapère, a

French engineer, during Napoleon Bonaparte's occupation of
Egypt, had first come to de Lesseps' attention when he was
vice consul in Alexandria in 1832. De Lesseps in 1856 renewed his concession from the Pasha Said, in 1858 floated
the original Suez Co. issue of 400,000 shares at 500 gold
francs each and began digging operations a year later.

The Canal first admitted traffic Nov. 17, 1869. Prior
to its nationalization in 1956, the Canal was controlled by a
board of directors comprising 16 Frenchmen, 9 Britons, 5
Egyptians, one Dutchman and one American. A stock split
in 1924 had doubled to 800,000 the total number of shares,
each with a par value of 250 gold francs ($81.67). Some
2,000 to 2,500 shares were traded on the Paris Bourse in
1955 at prices ranging from $267.20 to $355.70 a share.

Disaster followed closely on this sumptuous dedication.
Described as giddy with new wealth and prestige, Taufiq
Ismail, the grandson of an Albanian ruffian, was said to have
come to fancy himself a Parisian *demi-mondain.* Never was
there a more generous prince than Ismail, *pasha* of Egypt;
inestimable were his lavish gifts to the courtiers. Incompar-
able was his sense of *noblesse oblige;* his Franco-oriental
manners charmed, soothed and flattered. In 1867 he won
from the Ottoman sultan the title of *khedive*, which recognized his and his successors' claim to the Egyptian throne by
right of primogeniture. But the ways of the *bourse* deceived
him, and his fiefdom on the Nile fell into the hands of European sharpers and confidence men. Between 1863 and 1878
the Egyptian foreign debt rose from £3 million to £68 million, the domestic debt from £4 million to £30 million. British Prime Min. Benjamin Disraeli in 1875 bought the Khedive's 176,602 shares in the Canal. In 1879 the great powers
of Europe pressured the Porte into deposing Ismail. The
British empress and the French president then became the
true rulers of Egypt.

Anglo-French dual control lasted from 1879 to 1882,
when a revolt of lower-echelon Egyptian army officers under

the nationalistic Col. Arabi provided the pretext for a British invasion. British troops decisively defeated Arabi's forces at Tel-el-Kebir in Sept. 1882 and invested Cairo. They were not fully withdrawn from Egyptian soil until 1954.

The British consul general, Sir Evelyn Baring—later Lord Cromer—ruled Egypt quasi-dictatorially until his retirement in 1907, despite Egypt's nominal adherence to the declining Ottoman Empire. British advisers controlled finance, the army, foreign affairs, agriculture and health; Egyptians retained power over local administration, justice, and the police. The economy improved enormously; the foreign debt was brought in rein; the Delta Barrage and the first dam at Aswan were built; the population doubled between 1883 and 1914. On the other hand, the lack of training of Egyptians for civil service posts caused great nationalistic resentment. *Bilharzia*, a hideous infection of the bloodstream by the eggs of a Nile mollusk, causing lifelong faintness and lassitude, spread alarmingly.

Finally, England, facing war with Turkey, Egypt's *de jure* master, unilaterally proclaimed a protectorate over Egypt Dec. 18, 1914 and declared martial law.

Political Tendencies

Between the 2 world wars, Egypt was a scene of great agitation. 2 days after World War I was over, Saad Zaghloul, the minister of education under Lord Cromer, presented Britain with a demand for independence. But the British Foreign Office, still pursuing the straightforwardly imperialistic policy of Lord Curzon, its secretary, remained unmoved. After several months of temperamental nationalistic provocation, the British military deported Zaghloul to Malta in Mar. 1919, along with 3 of his disciples.

The delegation (in Arabic, *wafd*) that Zaghloul had summoned to negotiate with the British, and which the British had declined to receive, gave its name to the great Egyptian nationalist party of the pre-1952 era. The Wafd party repre-

sented from 1919 to 1952 the most effective organized opposition to the British domination of Egypt.

Although Zaghloul remained in exile for 2 years, the
Wafd party never ceased its courting of the Egyptian populace. Zaghloul's following soon became so intransigent that
the British cabinet decided it had no choice but to offer
Egypt at least *pro forma* independence. Britain unilaterally
declared Egypt a sovereign state Feb. 28, 1922 and revoked
martial law.

Some Egyptians were said to be piqued by the paradox of
the United Kingdom proclaiming Egyptian sovereignty. Britain maintained a powerful presence in the officer corps and
diplomatic circles—not to speak of the Suez Canal, which
the British Royal Army still occupied. Moreover, although
King Fuad* had considerable powers under the new constitution of 1923, the *sirdar*, or commander-in-chief, of the Egyptian army was a Briton.

In Sept. 1923 Saad Zaghloul, newly returned from exile,
campaigned for the Wafd, gaining 188 out of 215 seats in the
Chamber of Deputies. In Jan. 1924 Zaghloul formed a cabinet and publicized his intention of ridding both the army and
the Canal of British troops and advisers. Throughout the
year Wafdist *provocateurs* incited riots, and in November Sir
Lee Stack, governor-general of the Anglo-Egyptian Sudan and
sirdar of the Egyptian army, was assassinated on a Cairo
street. 3 days later Gen. Lord Allenby, escorted by a regi-
ment of cavalry, handed Zaghloul a document in French
abusing the Egyptian cabinet, which it declared an object of
contempt by civilized humanity. Under this obvious threat,
Zaghloul resigned.

Nonetheless, Zaghloul continued to play a leading role in

---

*The last *khedive*, Abbas Hilmi II, a Turkophile, failed to regain Egypt
from his summer palazzo on the Bosphorus after the battle of Gallipoli.
The British in 1914, to replace him, created a sultan, Hussein, who
died in 1917. Fuad succeeded Hussein and became king (*malik*) in
1923.

Egyptian politics till his death in 1927. It was this magnetic Wafdist who actually formulated the policy that Gamal Abdel Nasser put into practice some 30 years later in 1956.

Nahas Pasha took over the leadership of the Wafd in 1927, soon appearing to be as ready to take umbrage as his fiery predecessor. At this critical point, however, King Fuad exploited the deadlock between the Wafd and the British: in a 1930 *coup d'état* he placed his man Ismail Sidky Pasha in power, then arranged Sidki's disgrace several years later. Fuad's preeminence allowed him to amass a gargantuan treasure, which was inherited by his only son, Farouk, on Fuad's death in 1936, along with a palace tradition of accommodating and often even manipulating both the British and the Wafd.

Nahas and the Wafd won a majority in the Chamber of Deputies in 1936 and formed a cabinet. Nahas Aug. 26 initialled the 1936 Anglo-Egyptian Treaty and 20-year military alliance, with great advantages for both Britain and the Wafd. A year later, after Egypt was already committed to Britain until the fateful year of 1956, a splinter party from the Wafd, the Saadists (named after Saad Zaghloul), gained power in a rigged election. Its leader, Ali Maher Pasha, was regarded as Farouk's puppet, and the palace attempted to rule through him until the coup of 1952.

Religion & Spiritual Outlook

It was during the British occupation before World War I that modern Egypt first caught fire with religious enthusiasm. Jemal al-Din al-Afghani, who taught in Cairo from 1871 to 1879, championed a new doctrine of Pan-Islamism, the belief in the political unity of the Moslem world (*dar al-Islam*). Afghani was soon succeeded by his gentle pupil, Muhammad Abdu, peasant, mystic and publicist. Abdu gave poetic and compelling utterance to the deep Arab nostalgia for the pristine ways of early Islam, thereby unwittingly paving the way for the fundamentalism of the 20th century secret society known as the Moslem Brotherhood.

The faith of Islam has deep roots in Egypt. Islam (from the Arabic *aslama*, to submit or accept) had penetrated Egypt in the 8th century AD and had spread—by word and sword—what Moslems regard as the final revelation of God's will, Allah's communications to the Prophet Muhammad (Mohammed). This man, an illiterate camel-driver, had received the holy book of the Koran (Arabic: *al-Koran al-Karim*, or "Venerable Speech") from an angel of Allah in a cave near Mecca in the Arabian Hijaz. Moslems recognize not only the authority of the Koran but also that of the Hadith (Arabic, *haditha*, to converse), the recorded sayings of the Prophet. Most Egyptian Moslems also accept the Sunna, a book of traditions of the Moslem community under the early caliphs (Arabic, *khalifa*, pontiff; literally, follower). The tenets of Islam, the so-called "5 Pillars," are the profession of the faith (*shahada*), fasting, prayer, almsgiving (*zakat*) and the pilgrimage to Mecca (*hajj*). It is said that to be a true Moslem one must testify to the unity of Allah in purity and candor with the phrase: *"la illah illa Allah, wa Muhammad Rasul Allah,"* "there is no God but God, and Muhammad is his Prophet"—a simple formula that can move the most hardened believer to tears. Almsgiving is largely attended to by the *Wukuf* (singular: *wakf*), state-recognized charitable foundations, for which there has always been a portfolio in the Egyptian cabinet.

From this ancient and colorful creed, fraught with prophecy, ecstatic companionship and the zeal to uproot iniquity, arose the most fanatical secret society of modern Egypt, the *Ikhwan al-Muslimin*—the Moslem Brotherhood. Conceived in 1928 by Dr. Hassan al-Banna, then an obscure scholar of Ismailia, the Brotherhood sought to replace the vanished fellowship of the Bedouin tribe with a new breed of warriors more suited to the town than to the desert, albeit armed with the same unswerving faith and not averse to treachery in the quest for the "true way." The righteous path of Dr. Banna, or the Supreme Guide as he was known, was soon teeming with young followers, to whom the new union of nostalgia for the Moslem past with hatred for foreign civil servants and cotton nabobs seemed to promise a forceful, effective way to remove the infidel occupier.

Banna's dream of a well-knit, modern Egypt in the semblance of an ancient Islamic theocracy attracted the devotees of both the scroll and the dagger, both the *ulama*, the Koranseekers of al-Azhar, and the bitter fanatics of the Cairene street mob. Striving at first to sustain the Egyptian masses through social welfare programs and agricultural cooperatives, the Brotherhood soon fixed on a more ruthless course. As the international crisis of the 1930s deepened, they dealt increasingly in intrigue and extortion combined with fanatic religiosity.

For a time in the 1940s this union of Western fascist-style ruthlessness and oriental blind faith seemed almost irresistible. The Moslem Brotherhood made inroads among all classes of Egyptians: functionaries, workers, peasants, the military, anti-British aristocrats who feared socialism. The commitment of the Brethren to conspiracy and assassination, however, provoked the Wafd government to seize 57 members in Alexandria in 1946. After the murder of a police chief in 1948, Premier Mahmoud Fahmy Nokrashi Pasha dissolved the Brotherhood, only to lose his own life to an assassin several days later. In 1949 the Supreme Guide, Dr. Hassan al-Banna, was himself assassinated. Dr. Banna was succeeded in 1950 by Dr. Hassan el-Hodeiby. But the ardent Hodeiby seemed little more than a pale reflection of the charismatic founder. The Brotherhood began to lose ground after the 1952 coup. It was construed as a political party and banned by the revolutionary government in 1954, although it still persisted in recent years.

Agricultural Background

During Farouk's reign it became apparent that, despite the threats of Britain and Israel, Egypt's principal problem was the utter impoverishment and degradation of its cultivating class, the *fellahin*.

The pervasive European influence of the 19th century had brought about a rapid modernization and expansion of Egypt's agriculture. Between 1880 and 1914 the major export crop, cotton, grew 2½ times in bulk and 4 times in market value. Great landowners accumulated enough investment capital to finance an entire European economic superstructure in the cities: a modern civil service, postal and sewage systems, banks, grand hotels for the tourist trade and cabarets for the gallicized cafe society. Unnoticed, the poor *fellahin* toiled on, unrewarded, gaining nothing, an ubiquitous, white-robed mirage.

By the mid-1920s Egypt's soil was virtually exhausted; the landed aristocracy imported chemical fertilizers, and a sharp fall in cotton prices caused a marked deterioration in Egypt's terms-of-trade. In the late 1920s and the 1930s the *fellah's* standard of living sank below the level of the prewar era.

In the beginning of 1952, the last year of King Farouk's reign, almost 6 million *feddans* of land (1 *feddan*=1.038 acres) were in cultivation, over half in the wet, fertile Delta, the rest divided evenly between Upper and Lower Egypt. The peasants of the Delta harvest crops 3 times yearly, the winter season (*shitwi*) yielding just under ⅓ of the annual produce, the summer (*saifi*) about 35%, the autumn (*nili*) about 17%. Winter brings the rich *busim* clover and the ordinary market vegetables, especially onions; *ful* beans, the national staple, grow beside patches of lentils, barley and the more exotic fenugreek, a leguminous herb of the pea family. The Ministry of Agriculture often imports wheat, but rice, a warm-weather crop, found its way into Egypt's export cargoes around 1956. Cotton is still king in Egypt. More than half the summer harvest is cotton, a crop bred for more than 50 years in Egypt; Egyptian cotton is the gentlest, strongest fiber in cultivation.

Meat, with the exception of fowl (the chickens, ducks and pigeons everywhere underfoot), rarely graces the ordinary Egyptian's table, although he sometimes enjoys kebab from a surplus cow or chops from a lame *gamoussa* buffalo.

In 1947, the average Egyptian peasant family required 3 to 5 *feddans* (3.1 to 5.2 acres) of land for subsistence, yet 70% of those who owned land had only one *feddan* or less. The average annual yield of one *feddan* fetched £E 30 ($86), while sharecroppers received a daily wage of 10 to 15 piastres (29¢ to 43¢). At the same time, 11,000 landowners, each with 50 *feddans* or more, held over 2 million *feddans*—more than ⅓ of Egypt's cultivated area. Moreover, most of the large plantations were held by absentee landlords living in Cairo, Alexandria or abroad. This situation became a major political issue within a year after the coup of 1952.

Postwar Developments

World War II ended with the Saadist Party dominant. Under the patronage of Farouk and despite the fierce opposition of the Wafd, the fascist "Young Egypt," the Moslem Brotherhood and the Communists, the Saadist government negotiated in 1946–7 a revision of the 1936 Anglo-Egyptian Treaty. British troops quit Alexandria and Cairo but remained in the Canal Zone despite violent popular outcry.

The contention between Egypt and Britain temporarily subsided with the advent of the state of Israel. Britain's mandatory rule in Palestine ended May 14, 1948. On the same day the Jewish National Council proclaimed the establishment of the state of Israel and the formation of a provisional government. Arab armies invaded Palestine the following day, May 15, in a determined effort to crush the new

Jewish state. The Israeli armed forces repelled the Arabs, and the fighting halted temporarily June 11 with the acceptance by both sides of a UN Security Council truce. Fighting resumed July 9 and was halted again by UN intervention 10 days later. Arab-Israeli clashes erupted several times thereafter but came to a full stop Jan. 7, 1949.

During the fighting, Egyptian troops at first claimed victory. While one force occupied the Negev and struck toward Jerusalem from Bethlehem, a 2d column engaged the Israelis at Ashdod, 20 miles south of Tel Aviv. But Jerusalem and Tel Aviv withstood the assault, and by Dec. 1949 Israeli armored forces had driven the Egyptians into the Gaza Strip and had even invaded the Sinai Peninsula.

By the end of the "Palestine War," Israel controlled more territory than had been alloted to it under the UN partition plan. The territories taken by Israel included the western Galilee, the city of Jaffa, the western section (New City) of Jerusalem and the corridor from Jerusalem to the coastal plain. The proposed Palestinian Arab state never came into existence; instead the Hashemite Kingdom of Jordan seized the territory west of the Jordan River and captured the Old City of Jerusalem, and Egypt seized the Gaza Strip.

Israel signed UN-mediated armistice agreements with the 4 Arab belligerents in 1949—with Egypt Feb. 24, with Lebanon Mar. 23, with Jordan Apr. 13 and with Syria July 20. But a UN Conciliation Commission (established Dec. 12, 1948) failed in efforts to translate the armistice into a stable permanent peace. Unreconciled to their defeat and to the existence of Israel, the Arab states embarked on a campaign of harassment against the new Jewish state. They proclaimed an economic boycott of Israel, and Egypt barred Israeli ships from the Suez Canal. The Arab refugee problem created by the 1948 war further exacerbated Israel's relations with the Arab states. Thousands of Arabs had fled Palestine in the wake of the fighting, and most of them encamped in crowded refugee centers in the Gaza Strip and in Jordan. The Arab states insisted on the return of the refugees to their former homes in Israel.

The Egyptian defeat in the "Palestine War" weakened King Farouk's position considerably, while imparting new strength to a clandestine antipalace movement in the army. At the same time, the war provided this movement's leader, Lt. Col. Gamal Abdel Nasser, with the opportunity to distinguish himself by his heroism in action. Within 3 years, Nasser replaced Farouk as Egypt's virtual ruler.

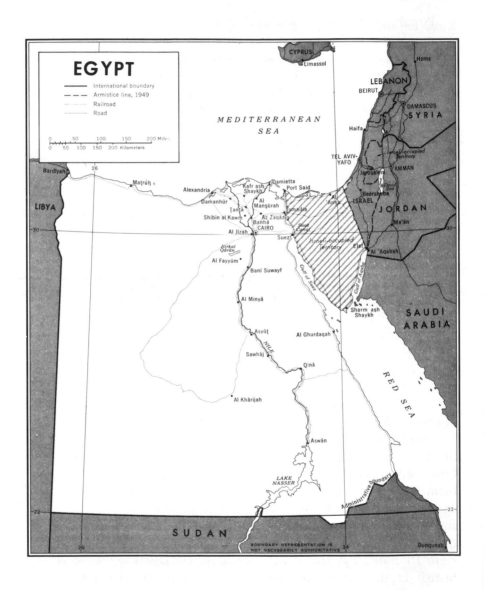

EGYPT

— International boundary
— — Armistice line, 1949
—·—·— Railroad
——— Road

0 50 100 150 200 Miles
0 50 100 150 200 Kilometers

MEDITERRANEAN SEA

CYPRUS
Limassol

Homs

LEBANON
BEIRUT

DAMASCUS
SYRIA

Haifa

Israeli-occupied Territory

TEL AVIV-YAFO

Jerusalem
AMMAN
Allenby Sea

Beersheba
ISRAEL
JORDAN

Ma'ān

Bardīyah
26
Matrūh

Alexandria
Kafr ash Shaykh
Damietta
Port Said

Damanhūr
Al Manṣūrah
Ismailia
Al 'Arīsh

Ṭanṭā
Az Zaqāzīq
LIBYA
Shibin al Kawm
Banhā
CAIRO

Al Jīzah
30
Suez
Suez Canal

Birkat
Qārūn
Israeli-occupied Territory
Elat
Al 'Aqabah
30

Al Fayyūm

Banī Suwayf
Gulf of Suez
Gulf of Aqaba

Al Minyā

Sharm ash Shaykh
SAUDI ARABIA

Asyūṭ
Al Ghurdaqah

Sawhāj
NILE

Qinā
RED SEA

Al Khārijah

Aswān

LAKE NASSER

Administrative boundary
22
22

SUDAN

26
BOUNDARY REPRESENTATION IS NOT NECESSARILY AUTHORITATIVE
34
Dunqunab

LAST DAYS OF FAROUK REGIME (JANUARY-JULY 1952)

Suez Canal Zone Clashes

Popular Egyptian feeling against Britain and foreign influence in general rose to a high point in Jan. 1952. The bitterness between Egypt and Britain centered around the Anglo-Egyptian Treaty of 1936, which stipulated a 20-year military alliance between Britain and Egypt, with British troops to be stationed in the Suez Canal Zone.

On the Egyptian side, the 1936 treaty had been the work of the nationalist Wafdist premier Mustapha el Nahas Pasha. But when the Wafd party and Nahas were returned to power in 1950 by a huge parliamentary majority, they viewed the treaty as out of date. By this time, both the premier, Nahas, and King Farouk were seeking (a) the departure of all British troops from Egyptian soil, (b) the release of £E450 million ($42 million) in wartime loans to England blocked in London (on account of British postwar bankruptcy) and (c) the transfer of the Sudan to the rule of the Egyptian crown.

The British, however, were concerned about the safety of the Canal and about Soviet intentions in the Eastern Mediterranean, and they remained strongly opposed to altering the Anglo-Egyptian Treaty. Nonetheless, after many warnings, Nahas Oct. 16, 1951 had unilaterally abrogated the treaty and demanded total British evacuation from Egyptian soil. Britain insisted that its troops would remain regardless of Egypt's action.

Incidents of British-Egyptian violence occurred daily in the Canal Zone during Jan. 1952. British troops backed by Cromwell tanks Jan. 12 fought off 100 guerrillas, many of them students. 12 guerrillas were killed, 15 wounded and 21 taken prisoner. Riots broke out in Cairo Jan. 14 and 15, and the British and American embassies were besieged until the police resorted to tear gas to drive off the attackers. At least 10 more Egyptians were killed in gunfights with the British in the Zone, and British troops Jan. 16 seized at

17

least 120 Egyptian policemen in antiguerrilla raids on Tel el-Kebir and el-Hammada.

Meanwhile, a crown prince, Ahmed Fuad, was born Jan. 16 to Farouk, 31, and his 2d wife, Queen Narriman, 18. In honor of the birth of the king's first son, the cabinet pointedly decreed a gift of $80,000 to be distributed among the families of "martyrs" killed in Suez clashes with the British. Britain announced that very day that it would release $28 million of Egypt's blocked wartime sterling balances in London, not the $42 million Cairo had demanded.

The British cruiser *Liverpool* fired warning salvos off Port Said Jan. 18 while British troops fought off an Egyptian guerrilla attack on a British camp. An American nun, Sister Anthony, was killed in Ismailia Jan. 19, possibly by a stray bullet, while Britons and Egyptians fought near her convent in a cemetery where guerrillas had stored ammunition. The British Jan. 21 intensified their efforts to round up Egyptian snipers in Ismailia.

Britain disclosed Jan. 23 that King Ibn Saud of Saudia Arabia, a supporter of Egypt in the Arab League, had offered to mediate the Anglo-Egyptian dispute over Suez and Sudan. His plan was said to call for an alliance between Arab and U.S., British, French and Turkish security groups, the arming of Arab states by Western powers and the policing of Suez by Egyptians and small international forces.

A clash, however, took place Jan. 25 between 1,500 British troops and a detachment of Egyptian auxiliary police. 42 Egyptians were reported killed and 58 wounded.

'Black Saturday' Riots

The day following the clash between the British troops and Egyptian auxiliary police was Jan. 26, 1952—later known as "Black Saturday." On this day an outbreak in Cairo began when a crowd gathered outside Premier Nahas' residence and demanded an Egyptian march on Ismailia. Then the demonstrators started to apply the torch to places identified with foreigners.

Millions of dollars worth of British, U.S. and French property in Cairo was destroyed as mobs went on a daylong anti-foreigner rampage of looting and burning. At least 67 persons were reported killed—mostly Britons, nearly all when they were trapped in buildings set afire by arsonists. Rioters started 150 fires, and many of Cairo's most famous establishments were burned out. Among Cairo establishments sacked and burned were Shepheard's Hotel, a luxurious showplace since 1891, often called the most famous hotel in the world; the British-owned Barclays Bank; the élite Turf Club; several department and clothing stores; many airline, oil and other company offices; and other clubs, theaters and restaurants operated by or for Europeans and Americans.

Nahas' government called out the Egyptian army to quell the riots. Farouk, who had conferred with U.S. Amb. Jefferson Caffery during the outbreak, signed a decree placing the entire country under martial law. Nearly all business places in Cairo were shut down and the city put under a dusk-to-dawn curfew. Troops fired into the air to disperse one mob of 20,000 persons.

By evening Farouk had appointed Nahas as military governor-general. Universities and schools were closed indefinitely, and rigorous press censorship was imposed. Nahas said in a radio speech Jan. 26 that the riots had angered him more than the British Army's killing of Egyptian police in Ismailia. He demanded public order during Egypt's "fight for freedom . . . against the occupant" (Britain). His social affairs minister, Abdel Fattah Hassan Pasha, charged that a "5th column, well organized and serving the British," had fomented the riots.

Maher Succeeds Nahas as Premier

Farouk dismissed the Nahas regime Jan. 27, 1952 on the ground that it had "failed to maintain security and order."

He awarded the premiership to Aly Maher Pasha, whom he called a man of "loyalty and efficiency" who could lead the country to its "goals of independence and unity."

Wafdists, who had been in power since Jan. 1950 and were often reported at odds with the king over how to deal with the West, agreed to support Maher when he said he would continue to press for British departure from Egypt. Maher won an overwhelming parliamentary vote of confidence Jan. 28 as the Chamber of Deputies and Senate extended martial law for 2 months.

Maher, 68, had been premier in 1936, when he restored order after a wave of student riots, and in 1939–40. A lawyer, ex-judge and one of Egypt's wealthiest men, Maher had held many cabinet posts in the 1920s and 1930s and was long a personal adviser to Farouk. After having been dismissed by the king as premier at British insistence in June 1940 for alleged reluctance to back up British actions against the Italians in Libya following Italy's entry into World War II, he was interned in 1942 and remained a prisoner for the duration of the war. Nahas, then premier, had arrested him to pacify the British. Maher said after he was released in 1945 that he would forget old disputes with Britain, and he called for Anglo-Egyptian friendship and internal Egyptian reforms.

The Maher cabinet: *Premier* and *Foreign, War & Marine Ministries*—Aly Maher Pasha; *Interior*—Ahmed al-Maraghi al-Mortada Bey; *Finance, Economy*—Muhammad Zaki Abdel Motaal Bey; *Social Affairs*—Mahmoud Hassan Pasha; *Agriculture*—Salib Sami Pasha; *Justice*—Muhammad Ali Namazi Pasha; *Public Works* and *Communications*—Hamed Suliman Pasha; *Education*—Abdel Khalek Hassouna Pasha; *Commerce, Industry & Supply*—Ibrahim Abdel Wahab Bey; *Moslem Charities* (Wakfs)—Saad el-Labban; *Health* and *Rural Affairs*—Ibrahim Shawky Pasha.

The Soviet press, which had been urging Arab countries to shun the West, denounced the cabinet change. The unofficial government daily *Izvestia* in Moscow charged Jan. 30 that the shift had been forced on Farouk by U.S. Amb. Jefferson Caffery.

Speaking in the British House of Commons Jan. 29, British Foreign Secy. (Robert) Anthony Eden had said: "From the earliest days of the tension in the Canal Zone, his majesty's forces in that area have at all times done their utmost to avoid conflict with the Egyptian authorities. The increase of terrorist activities, however, supported in many cases by detachments of the auxiliary Egyptian police, compelled his majesty's government to act if the security of the Canal Zone, of the British base, and of our forces themselves was to be preserved. I wish to give the House some account of the nature and activities of these auxiliary police. This force was not introduced into the Canal Zone until after the late Egyptian government had denounced the Anglo-Egyptian treaty of 1936 in October last. It was supposed to be charged with the task of assisting the regular police to preserve law and order. In fact, its energies were mainly directed to intimidating Egyptian labor employed by his majesty's forces, and later to conniving at and taking part in terrorist activities against our forces, many of which resulted in the deaths of British soldiers."

Eden also strongly reaffirmed "the ability and determination of his majesty's government to maintain their rights under the treaty of 1936, until such time as a new agreement to replace that treaty can be reached."

Cairo Police Chief Morah el-Holi Bey's dismissal because of the Jan. 26 riots was revealed Feb. 5. The government reported hundreds of persons arrested for the violence. (Maher meanwhile was attempting to work out a program of economic reforms to combat inflation and poverty.)

Peace Efforts

Premier Maher called in a British newsman Jan. 30, 1952 for an interview "as a gesture of friendship with Britain."

Maher told him that Egypt favored a Middle East defense command within the framework of the UN and would "consider any understanding Mr. Eden might propose." Maher also conferred with U.S., British, French and Turkish envoys in Cairo Jan. 30. He was said to have hinted that Egypt might join the Middle Eastern defense setup planned by those 4 countries if the British would first leave Suez and Sudan.

The U.S. had denied Jan. 29 that it was trying in a "formal sense" to mediate the Anglo-Egyptian dispute. But State Secy. Dean G. Acheson said Jan. 30 that the 4-power bid to Egypt on Mideastern defense was not a take-it-or-leave-it proposition and was open to negotiation.

Egypt's ultra-nationalist Moslem Brotherhood Feb. 4 declared itself opposed to an Egyptian defense alliance with the U.S., Britain, France and Turkey because "Islam forbids us."

Britain confirmed Feb. 5 that it was considering a plan proposed by Iraqi Premier Nuri as-Said Pasha to settle the Anglo-Egyptian dispute. Said's plan called for the restoration of peace in the Suez Canal Zone on the understanding that (1) British forces would withdraw but British defense installations would be maintained under arrangements made jointly by Britain and Egypt; (2) a new Arab security bloc would join with the West in pledging the defense of the Middle East; (3) the Anglo-Egyptian Sudan would decide its own political future in a free plebiscite without pressure from either Britain or Egypt. British Foreign Secy. Eden said that he would make every effort to negotiate a settlement with Egypt but that Egypt must take into account the "legitimate rights of both parties." Maher had said Feb. 1 that negotiation with Britain was the "only normal way to attain Egypt's aims," but he added Feb. 3 that settlement was "a long way off."

The Cairo Wafdist newspaper *Al Balagh* said Feb. 13 that Britain had "completely altered its stand toward the Egyptian question with the result that there is now every likelihood" of an early agreement on the Suez-Sudan dispute. Egypt disclosed by Feb. 14 that it had sent notes to Britain, the U.S. and 14 other countries apologizing for the Jan. 26 riots and indicating that some of the rioters had been involved in a subversive plot. (The curfew in Cairo had been moved back to midnight from 10 p.m. Feb. 10, Farouk's 32d birthday. Premier Maher had announced Feb. 9 that the regular Egyptian armed forces would take over the training of guerrilla "volunteers.")

Maher said in a note to British Foreign Secy. Eden Feb. 21 that scheduled Anglo-Egyptian talks would open in Cairo Mar. 1 in a "quick and decisive" effort to settle the Suez-Sudan dispute. He said Egypt would insist that the British leave Suez and permit the union of Egypt and Sudan. Maher apologized to the foreign powers whose nationals had suffered during the Jan. 26 disorders, and he established a fund of $14,350,000 (£E5 million) to compensate them, partially at least, for their damaged or destroyed property.

Tension between Egypt and Britain, as well as between the Wafd government and the king, continued, however, and the Egyptian premiership changed hands Mar. 1 for the 2d time in 5 weeks.

Governmental Instability

Ahmed Naguib al-Hillali Pasha, 60, a jurist famous in Egypt as a foe of governmental corruption, was named premier by King Farouk Mar. 1, 1952 after Aly Maher Pasha resigned. Maher reportedly had quit because the king wanted to suspend parliament for at least a month to prevent its Wafdist majority from interfering with Anglo-Egyptian talks and plans for economic and political reforms. The suspension was announced Mar. 2.

The new premier, an independent like Maher, had quit the Wafd in 1944 because of graft scandals involving it. He promised Mar. 2 to proceed with the British talks planned by Maher and to speed up reforms promised by his predecessor.

He named a nonpartisan cabinet whose chief members were holdovers from Maher's regime: Interior Min. Ahmed al-Maraghi al-Mortada Bey, Finance Min. Muhammad Zaki Abdel Motaal Bey, Commerce Min. Salib Sami Pasha and Foreign Min. Abdel Khalek Hassouna Pasha. The new government retained the martial law decreed after the Jan. 26 riots, and the Interior Ministry was empowered Mar. 5 to send agitators home if they were stirring up trouble in cities where they did not normally live.

In accordance with the new Premier Hillali's strategy of lowering the level of tension with Britain, preliminary Anglo-Egyptian talks began in Cairo Mar. 22 and were progressing by Mar. 29 toward a full-fledged conference on the Suez and Sudan dispute. Britain was said to have agreed in principle to withdraw its troops from Suez if the Egyptians accepted some other plan that would safeguard the Canal.

Meanwhile, King Farouk had dissolved parliament Mar. 23 to make way for new elections May 18. Parliament's majority Wafd party had declared its opposition to Hillali's regime. 2 leading ministers in the Wafdist cabinet of Nahas— Fuad Serag el-Din Pasha (Interior and Finance) and Abdel Fattah Hassan Pasha (Social Affairs)—had been arrested Mar. 18 during an official investigation of the Cairo riots of Jan. 26. Farouk extended martial law indefinitely Mar. 24.

In view of the continued resistance of the Wafd to the policy of the Egyptian crown, the cabinet decided Apr. 12 on an indefinite postponement of parliamentary elections so that Premier Hillali would have a free hand to revise Egypt's election laws and continue talks with Britain on the Suez-Sudan dispute. The antigovernment Wafd, the strongest party in the old parliament, issued a manifesto Apr. 15 accusing the government of collusion with the British.

Britain Apr. 5 released £10 million ($28 million) of Egypt's sterling balance in Britain as a "gesture of good will."

Trouble between the king and Egyptian government circles—notably with a group led by Ahmed al-Maraghi al-Mortada Bey, who had become minister of war and marine—was exacerbated by a quarrel about this time over how to deal with a seditious clandestine movement in the army. Mortada wanted general army reform, especially in view of revelations concerning corrupt war-profiteering during the Palestine War of 1947–8. Farouk preferred simply to arrest the suspected officers.

The general sense of Farouk's weakness was aggravated by alarming rumors. A National Broadcasting Co. report Apr. 28 that Farouk had been wounded in the thigh in an assassination attempt in March was denied by the Egyptian government Apr. 29 as an "utter fabrication."

Later, on the 16th anniversary of his accession to the throne, Farouk May 6 proclaimed himself a direct descendant of the Prophet Muhammad. He thus assumed the title El Sayed (descendant of the Prophet). This act further alienated Farouk from Egyptian Moslems, since, as a descendant of the Albanian soldier Muhammad Ali (pasha of Egypt 1806–49), he was not even of the same race as the Prophet.

In the meantime Hillali was failing to achieve a compromise with Britain. In a note handed to Britain May 20, Egypt rejected plans for settling the Sudan and Suez disputes. Moreover, Egyptian Foreign Min. Abdel Khalek Hassouna denied May 21 that Egypt had even set forth any counter-proposal to Britain.

In June the king came into open conflict with Mortada on the issue of the clandestine movement within the army. This movement (known as the Free Officers) had succeeded in electing a hero of the Palestine War of 1947–8, Gen. Muhammad Naguib, to the presidency of the Officers' Club in Dec. 1951, thereby defeating Farouk's own nominees.

Mortada's attempt to restrain the king from dismissing Naguib from the presidency of the Officers' Club led to the resignation of Premier Hillali Pasha June 28 after he had been in office 4 months. Hillali was unable to accept Farouk's presumed favoritism within the army, which he believed would hasten rather than check an uprising of the clandestine Free Officers.

Some observers argued that Hillali's professed intention of thoroughly investigating administrative corruption had incurred the fatal enmity of the mighty Wafd party, which, they implied, could exert sufficient pressure on the king to force a royal demand for Hillali's resignation. The London *Times* reported July 2, 1952 that while Hillali's official difference with the king came over a worsening economic crisis attributable to the Wafd, "his committees investigating administrative corruption threatened a widening group who had natural allies in the Wafd party."

Other reports from Cairo contended that Hillali's failure to win concessions from the British and his determination to hold general elections in October had caused a policy break with Farouk. A member of the outgoing cabinet told the press that Hillali also complained of U.S. interference in Egypt's domestic affairs. U.S. Amb. Jefferson Caffery denied the charge June 29.

The king June 29 appointed ex-Premier Hussein Sirry Pasha, 60, an irrigation engineer and political independent, as premier. The new cabinet, announced July 2: *Premier, Foreign Affairs, War & Marine—*Sirry Pasha; *Interior—*Muhammad Hashim Pasha; *State—*Karim Tabet Pasha; *Public Works* (Acting Finance Minister)—Naguib Ibrahim Pasha; *Rural & Municipal Affairs—*Muhammad Ali Rateb Pasha; *Education—*Sami Mazen Bey; *Agriculture—*Ali el-Kelani Bey; *Justice—*Ali Badawi Bey; *Wakfs* (Moslem charities)—Sheik Farag el-Sanhouri; *Commerce—*Abdel Moti Khayyal Bey; *Communications—*Hussein el-Ghamrawi Bey.

Sirry did not find it easier to deal with the king's attempt to break the clandestine movement in the army. Aware of the potentially superior power of the revolutionary elements in the army, he demurred at helping the king with his design and finally resigned after 18 days in office. Hillali returned to office for one day (22 July), after persuading Farouk to accept Mortada again as minister of war and marine. At the last moment, Farouk changed his mind and decided to sponsor his brother-in-law, Ismail Sharin, for the office. This last-minute nepotism was taken by the Free Officers as tantamount to a declaration of war.

NATIONALIST REVOLUTION & AFTERMATH
(JULY 1952-DEC. 1954)

'Free Officers' Overthrow Farouk

King Farouk I, 32, was overthrown in a military coup headed by Maj. Gen. Muhammad Naguib Bey, 51, a foe of Farouk's political policies and advisers.

The leaders of the coup, which took place July 23, 1952, forced the resignation of Premier Ahmed Naguib el-Hillali Pasha and the appointment of ex-Premier Aly Maher Pasha as Hillali's successor. Hillali, who had been premier Mar. 1— June 28, had been back in the premiership only one day as successor to Hussein Sirry Pasha, who resigned July 20.

Naguib proclaimed himself as the army's commander-in-chief in place of Gen. El Ferik Muhammad Haidar Pasha and sent troops to surround the Royal Palace and government buildings in Cairo. 20 high-ranking officers were arrested. Farouk was reported at liberty at the summer palace in Alexandria.

Naguib said in a nationwide broadcast July 23 that the coup was designed to eliminate from the government corruption and bribery, "the main reasons for our failure in the Palestine war" of 1948 and for "troubles in Egypt's political and economic life." His choice for premier, Maher Pasha, an independent ex-Wafdist and crusader against graft in government, had been premier Jan. 27—Mar. 1.

Naguib explained the purpose of the coup in this broadcast proclamation: "Egypt has undergone a critical time in her recent history. It has been a period of gross corruption and governmental instability, and these factors had a great influence on the army. People who received bribes contributed towards our defeat in the Palestine war. Traitors plotted against the army after the Palestine war, but now we have purged ourselves, and our affairs within the army have been placed in the hands of men in whose ability, character and patriotism we have faith. The whole of Egypt will welcome this news. No harm will be done to former military personnel who have been arrested. The entire army is working for the interests of Egypt within the constitution, and without any designs of its own. I appeal to all Egyptians not to resort to acts of sabotage or violence. Any such action will be met with unparalleled firmness, and the offender will be punished immediately for treason. The army will undertake responsibility for law and order in cooperation with the police. I want to assure foreigners of the safety of their lives and property, for which the army considers itself responsible."

The coup was originated by a clandestine movement of young, commissioned army men that called itself the Free Officers. According to Gamal Abdel Nasser's colleague Anwar al-Sadat (who succeeded Nasser in the Egyptian presidency in Oct. 1970), the Free Officers conspiracy had begun when British tanks invested the royal palace to impose a Wafd government in Feb. 1942. In his book *Revolt on the Nile,* Sadat stated that the officers first met in the Zamalek suburb of Cairo to discuss their objection to royal complicity with the British. The Free Officers group was reorganized in 1945 with Nasser as military director and Sadat as leader of nonmilitary members. The conspiracy then could already boast 5 extensive branches: security, propaganda, finance, terrorism, combat personnel. The last branch was a paramilitary wing within the army and national security forces. Heading all branches were Gamal Abdel Nasser and Abdel Hakim Amer. The group had no specific ideology beyond its dedication to the final expulsion of foreign occupation from Egyptian soil.

The Free Officers were approached by potential political allies at least twice: first, after World War II, by the Moslem Brotherhood, which insisted that Nasser take an unacceptable oath to the Brotherhood's "Supreme Guide," Dr. Hassan el-Banna, and later, in 1949, after the 1948 Palestine war, by King Farouk's secret police, also seeking alliance, to whom Nasser denied the very existence of a clandestine military society.

The Executive Committee of the Free Officers included the following in 1949: Gamal Abdel Nasser, Kamal el-Din Hussein, Abdel Hakim Amer, Hassan Ibrahim, Abdul Moneim Adbul Raouf, Salah Salem, Gamal Salem, Abdel Latif el-Boghdadi, Khaled Mohieddin and Anwar el-Sadat. Other important members not in the Executive Committee, were Zakaria Mohieddin, Hussein Shafei and Aly Sabry.

The Free Officers in 1951 undertook to train anti-British guerrillas operating in the Suez Canal Zone. In Dec. 1951 they persuaded a popular but politically moderate war hero, Gen. Muhammad Naguib, who had not previously been a member of the movement, to become their nominee for president of the Egyptian army's Officer's Club. Naguib was elected, thus securing the Club Committee for the Free Officers—to the king's great anger—without revealing the original membership of the secret organization. In Jan. 1952, after the "Black Saturday" riots, the Free Officers were said to have decided that the time for revolution had come. By July 1952 there were at least 1,000 members of the movement, although its leaders remained cleverly concealed behind Naguib.

After the revolution of July 23, 1952, the Free Officers, under Gamal Abdel Nasser, became the effective ruling body in Egypt. Naguib, although the nominal premier—later president, after the proclamation of the republic in June 1953—was actually directed by the Free Officers, by then called the Revolutionary Command Council (RCC). In the RCC meetings, Naguib still had only one vote, but he did not openly challenge Nasser until June 1953.

Farouk Abdicates

King Farouk abdicated the Egyptian throne July 26, 1952 at the insistence of Gen. Naguib. Farouk's infant son was designated his successor although the child was taken along by his parents when they went into 'exile in Italy. Farouk, accompanied by his son, ex-Queen Narriman and his 3 daughters by a former marriage, arrived in Naples and Capri July 29 on the government owned royal yacht *Mahroussa.*

The London *Times* presented this analysis of the immediate reasons for Farouk's overthrow: "King Farouk's fatal mistake was to surround himself with courtiers, some of foreign extraction, who used their positions to enrich themselves. There is no suggestion that he himself profited by the contracts which supplied the army with defective weapons and munitions for the Palestine war, but he was believed to have protected members of his entourage and army officers who did profit. . . . The arms scandal opened up a grave rift between the king and the army. The culminating blunder by King Farouk was to allow Hillali Pasha's first government to fall as a result of a sordid intrigue in which the court favorites and big business interests were involved. By the Egyptian army, the disappearance of Hillali Pasha in favor of Sirry Pasha's government was thought to mean that the influence of the palace and of Haidar Pasha, then commander-in-chief, would again be supreme in military affairs. The prime minister asked King Farouk to dismiss from the army Maj. Gen. Hussein Sirry Amer, a royal favorite against whom various charges had been made. The king would consent only if Naguib Bey too was dismissed. Sirry Pasha then resigned. A new government under Hillali Pasha was formed, but the younger officers had already decided to take matters into their own hands."

Before leaving Egypt Farouk proclaimed: "We, Farouk I, king of Egypt and the Sudan: Since we have always sought the welfare, happiness and advancement of our nation and desire our country to overcome the difficulties which it is facing in the present delicate circumstances, and in compliance with the wish of the people, we have decided to abdicate in favour of our son, Crown Prince Ahmed Fuad. We have issued our orders to His Eminence Aly Maher Pasha to act in accordance therewith."

The Egyptian government accepted the 6-month-old baby as king, with the Council of Ministers assuming the King's prerogatives until "the time comes to hand them over to a council of regency in accordance with the provisions of the constitution."

A Provisional Council of Regency for the infant king was selected Aug. 3 by the Maher cabinet and sworn in Aug. 5. The council comprised these members: (1) Prince Abdul Moneim, a 2d cousin of the ex-king, (2) Muhammad Bahi ed-Din Barakhat, an ex-Wafdist auditor general, and (3) Col. Muhammad Rashid Mohanna, the communications minister in Maher's cabinet.

Farouk told newsmen in Italy July 31: "I most sincerely wish good luck to those who have taken into their hands and on their consciences the task of governing Egypt. I wish them good luck because they will need it. I hope they will not think that to govern a country in these difficult days of world crises is so easy a task as, perhaps, those who are new to the game may believe. . . . My children are now all the kingdom that I possess. . . . It is untrue that I have brought from Egypt a fortune. Nor is it true that I have a fortune hidden away abroad. My wife, my baby son, and my 3 young daughters will live very simply."

The Egyptian government seized Farouk's property (estimated value: $287 million) Aug. 5 after cutting the annual royal salary from $280,000 to $100,000 Aug. 4. (Farouk said on Capri July 31: "I am no longer a rich man [but] by the standards of the very poor, I am still to be envied.")

The government admitted newsmen to Farouk's Abdin, Kubbeh and Montazah palaces Aug. 24 and revealed a collection of ornaments, art and museum pieces, including expensive jewels, pornographic paintings, Edwardian musical instruments, and modern gym equipment. A costly fleet of luxurious bullet-proof American and British autos was revealed when the 4th royal palace, Raseltin, was opened Aug. 26. Farouk's stamp collection, one of the world's most valuable, was evaluated at $16 million Aug. 25.

British Foreign Secy. Anthony Eden announced in the

House of Commons July 28 that the abdication of Farouk and the institution of a regency would not be cause for British intervention. But he also rejected the notion that the new infant king, Ahmed Fuad II, would have a legitimate claim on the Anglo-Egyptian Sudan.

After 6 meetings between Sir Ralph Stevenson, the British ambassador, and Premier Ali Maher Pasha, the British Embassy and the Egyptian government Aug. 6 declared "the earnest desire of the Egyptian and British governments that the closest possible touch and the friendliest relations should be maintained between them in the present critical situation."

Post-Coup Developments

A new cabinet was named July 24, 1952 by Premier Maher, who assigned to himself 3 portfolios—Foreign Affairs, Interior, and War & Marine. The other members of the cabinet were: *Finance*—Abdul Gelil el-Emary Bey; *Justice*—Muhammad Rushdi Bey; *Education*—Saad Labban Bey; *Social Affairs* —Zohair Garana Bey; *Commerce & Supplies*—Ibrahim Abdel Wahab Bey; *Municipal & Rural Affairs*—Abdullah Salem Bey; *Public Works*—Kamel Muhammad Nabeh Pasha; *Health*—Dr. Ibrahim Shawkry Pasha; *Wakfs* (Moslem Charities)—Fuad Sherin Bey; *Agriculture*—Alphonse Greiss Bey.

Naguib proposed Aug. 11 that parliamentary elections be held in Feb. 1953.

Naguib acted decisively in putting down riotous public disorders of the sort that had plagued the Nahas government in Jan. 1952. 567 men were arrested Aug. 14 after night-long rioting at the Kafr el Dawar cotton mills of the Misr Spinning Co. near Alexandria had caused 6 deaths. Army tanks and armored cars, directed by Naguib, subdued 6,000 workers demonstrating for "justice and higher wages." The area was placed under a state of emergency, and a military court was set up to "pass immediate judgment" on persons charged with inciting the riot. Naguib warned that "disturbances of public order" were considered treason, punishable by death.

Trials began Aug. 14 and Mustafa Khamis, 24, first worker to be tried, was condemned Aug. 18 to death by hanging. Naguib sent this message to the demonstrators: "Some persons without faith in God or country have succumbed to the intrigues of instigators, and will pay the penalty. The Prophet, after the conquest of Mecca, ordered that rioters who stood in the way of reform should be killed. We have, with God's blessing and the people's support, set foot on the path of reform. The armed forces, which carried out this reform in the name of the people and for their well-being, will always be vigilant to destroy anyone attempting treachery against the nation or the people. This criminal [Khamis] has caused the death of 3 soldiers and 3 civilians. He is a traitor to the nation, and it is only just to eliminate him from the nation."

Khamis and Muhammad el-Baqary, another convicted of leading the Alexandria cotton mill riots, were hanged Sept. 7 in Hadra prison in Alexandria.

A military court Oct. 1 sentenced 4 persons to 3-5 years imprisonment at hard labor for setting the Shepheard's Hotel fire in January. A 5th defendant was acquitted.

The new regime, handicapped in its economic plans by a shortage of monetary reserves, showed itself favorable to foreign capital investment. It altered the Company Law of 1947 by allowing foreigners to control up to 51% of the capital of new companies; the limit under Farouk had been 49%.

Among other developments in the new government's reform campaign: Naguib said July 3 that the army would give up control of civil affairs to concentrate on purging corruption from public life. Government employes were forbidden Aug. 3 to gamble. Premier Maher said Aug. 4 that more than 170 banned foreign publications would reappear in Egypt. The cabinet Aug. 4 approved the formation of purge commissions (composed of career judges) with "wide" investigation powers; civil servants were ordered to submit full statements on their incomes since 1939. Naguib told a women's suffrage leader Aug. 5 he would welcome women in the army but would not commit himself on votes for women.

Naguib asked for military aid from the U.S. or Britain Aug. 7. He warned that "I cannot say who will supply us if America and the Western democracies refuse us" arms and other modern weapons of war.

Premier Maher claimed to have asked the U.S. for police weapons for the maintenance of internal security. The request, he said, was made at an Aug. 26 conference with Naguib and U.S. Amb. Jefferson Caffery. But a U.S. State Department spokesman said Aug. 27 that the Caffery-Maher-Naguib conversations had centered on Point-4 aid to Egypt under a 1951 agreement. According to the spokesman, the U.S. had made police equipment available to Egypt several months previously but Egypt had not bought any.

Naguib-Wafd Showdown

Naguib had started the anticorruption crackdown late in July 1952. His most serious challenge ultimately came from the Wafd, many of whose members eventually fell victim to Naguib's punishment of alleged wrong-doing in government. The Naguib-Wafd clash resulted in the ouster of Premier Aly Maher and his Wafd cabinet.

Initially, the Wafd, the nation's ruling political party, had come out July 28 in support of Naguib's anticorruption campaign, and he was backed also by the Moslem Brotherhood, the Sudanese Independence Movement and the Arab League.

A number of ex-officials of sub-cabinet rank were interned July 28, and Naguib warned alleged grafters not to try to leave the country. Ex-army chief Muhammad Haidar was put under house arrest July 30. Peerage (titles of *pasha* and *bey*) was abolished July 30, and persons in jail for *lèse majesté* (offending the king) were freed.

7 purge committees received extraordinary powers (dis-

missal, arrest and enforcement of punishment) Aug. 12 to (a) investigate transactions of the War and Navy Ministries and particularly those connected with a 1948 defective-arms scandal, (b) look into reports of fraud in the procurement of government property, (c) probe abuses of public office, (d) investigate public construction contracts, (e) investigate the building of Alexandria's sewage system and (f) investigate foreign exchange and foreign barter in cereals and cotton.

Although Naguib was a conservative moderate, the Free Officers clandestine movement (which became the Revolutionary Command Council, or RCC), which Naguib represented, showed an increasing desire for radical reforms. In August Naguib attempted to force the major parliamentary parties to purge themselves of "evil elements"—grafters and corrupt politicians.

Egypt's 2d ranking political party, the Saadists, announced Aug. 28 that ex-Premier Ibrahim Abdel Hadi had been ousted as party president in a reorganization carried out in accordance with Naguib's demand for a clean-up in Egypt's political life.

Naguib began encountering considerable resistance, however, from the Wafd. Premier Ali Maher exemplified the Wafdists' tendency to belittle the RCC and its increasingly revolutionary ideas. Moreover, by the end of August it was evident that large numbers of Wafdists had run afoul of the government's anticorruption committees. The purge committee investigating the construction of Alexandria's new sewage system brought corruption charges Aug. 28 against Wafdist ex-Public Works Min. Osman Moharram and ex-Alexandria Municipality Director Muhammad Raafat. Ex-Premier Mustafa Nahas, leader of the Wafd, had called Aug. 23 for an end to army control of the government and a return to parliamentary processes.

In response to this open challenge from the Wafd, Naguib forced the resignation of Aly Maher's cabinet and assumed direct control of the Egyptian government Sept. 7 as premier.

Maher, who quit after the sudden arrests of 48 top political leaders early Sept. 7, said: "Gen. Naguib and myself felt present circumstances made it preferable that the authority should be concentrated in the hands of the armed forces." The army had criticized Maher's "lukewarm attitude" toward proposed reforms. Naguib was the only military man in the new government. Aides said that he would resign after the general elections, to be held no later than Feb. 1953.

Naguib, sworn in as premier by the Regency Council a few hours after Maher resigned, also took the post of war minister and named his chief political adviser, Soliman Hafez, as deputy premier and interior minister. Other cabinet members: *Foreign Affairs*—Ahmed Muhammad Farrag Tayeh; *Commerce & Industry*—Dr. Muhammad Ali Sabry; *Agriculture*—Abdel Aziz Abdullah Salem; *Public Works*—Mourad Fahmy; *Social Affairs*—Muhammad Fouad Galal; *Education*—Ismail el-Kabbany; *Communications*—Hussein Abou Zeid; *Municipal & Rural Affairs*—Abdel Aziz Aly; *Supplies*—Farid Antoun; *Justice*—Ahmed Housni; *Finance*—Abdel Guelil el-Emary (who had held the same post in the Maher cabinet); *Ministry of State*—Fathy Radwan, anti-British leader of *Watania* (Nationhood), the extreme nationalist party; *Wakfs* (Moslem Charities) —Ahmed Hassan al-Bakoury; *Public Health*—Dr. Nourreddin Tarraf. (The latter 2 were Moslem Brotherhood leaders.)

The U.S. State Department foresaw no change in U.S. policy toward Egypt and said Sept. 8 that it would support the Naguib government. Britain's "moderate optimism" about Naguib's reforms was reported "diluted by anxiety" over the appointment of leaders of the Moslem Brotherhood and other extreme nationalist groups to the cabinet.

All activities of Egypt's political parties were suspended for one month, during which they were to submit written statements of aims, finances and internal organization. This was done under a law that gave the Interior Ministry power to dissolve parties after the reorganization period. The Wafd, which had said it would not permit an investigation of its ranks, gave in Sept. 10 and agreed to reorganize for the first time since its founding in 1919.

Abdul Rahman Azzam had resigned as secretary-general of the Arab League Sept. 9 just before the League convened in Cairo to discuss mutual defense. Egyptian press circles asserted that he had resigned in accord with Naguib's wishes and indicated that Azzam had been mentioned in connection with a scandal over arms procurement for the Palestine war.

A number of persons had been arrested Sept. 7 by the army on charges of hindering the reform program. Those seized included: ex-Premier Ibrahim Abdel Hadi, the ex-Saadist party president; ex-Premier Ahmed Naguib Hillali; Wafd Secy. Gen. Fuad Serag ed-Din; Wafd Deputy Secy. Soliman Ghannam; ex-Public Works Min. Osman Moharram; the ex-cabinet member Ahmed al-Maraghi al-Mortada; Hamed Gouda, the Saadist vice president and ex-president of the Chamber of Deputies; ex-King Farouk's cabinet chief, Dr. Hafez Affifi, and his deputy, Hassan Youssef; Cairo Municipal Director Mustapha Fahmy; ex-Cairo Gov. Mahmoud Ghazali; Prince Abbas Halim, who offered Sept. 6 to distribute his land in excess of 200 acres to the poor, Prince Said Halim; Mustapha Sadek, ex-Queen Narriman's uncle; and Fouad Abaza, director general of the Royal Agriculture Society. Naguib said Sept. 8 that they would have fair hearings.

During September and October, the Wafd party—which never again gained enough power to form an Egyptian government—was reduced to an ineffective opposition. Mustafa Nahas, the party chief, announced Sept. 13 the provisional suspension of 3 important party members, Fuad Serag ed-Din, Osman Moharram and Soliman Ghannam. He also insisted that the Wafd had always really backed the RCC, since—as he put it—Egypt was "in dire need of such an operation to fight corruption and bring about sweeping reforms." The wafd submitted to Naguib's purge order Oct. 6 and accepted the resignation of Nahas and 6 other party leaders. Nahas was made the party's honorary president for life.

These 15 groups met the Oct. 8 deadline for the dissolution of political parties: the Moslem Brotherhood (which said Oct. 3 that it would keep out of politics), the Daughters of the Nile, and the National Feminist, Nile Democratic, *Fellah* ("Peasant") Socialist, New Nationalist, Democratic, Wafd, Liberal-Constitutional, Kotla, Saadist, Nationalist, Socialist, Labor and *Fellahin* ("Peasants") parties.

Naguib's program of purges was soon extended to the Regency Council. He announced the dissolution of the provisional Regency Council Oct. 14 and its replacement by a sole temporary regent, Prince Muhammad Abdel Moneim, one of the council's 3 members. The reorganization followed the dismissal that day of Col. Muhammad Rashid Mohanna, the regency's army representative, on charges of "overstepping the limits of his post."

In the final week of September the government purge had been extended to the diplomatic corps, the officer corps and the civil service. 5 ambassadors were dismissed Sept. 25, as well as 450 military officers of all ranks. The cabinet Oct. 23 suspended the Cairo and Alexandria municipal courts for a year.

RCC Consolidates Its Power

Another problem facing the RCC was the complicated one of its relations with Britain.

British War Secy. Antony Head declared during a visit to Egypt Sept. 21, 1952 that "to have a base in Egypt is absolutely vital strategically" for Britain and that there was "no alternative." This speech was criticized by Naguib Sept. 29. Naguib declared: "We shall have to show him [Mr. Head] that we can make the United Kingdom evacuate its forces willy-nilly from the Canal Zone."

Shortly thereafter, however, the British government attempted Oct. 9 to ease its tense relations with Egypt by releasing another £5 million ($14 million) from Egypt's blocked sterling balances in London as a goodwill gesture.

And Britain Oct. 10 announced the return to the Egyptian army of custody of the El Firdan bridge across the Suez Canal.

Egypt also made minor concessions. British Foreign Secy. Anthony Eden told the British House of Commons Nov. 6 that Naguib had agreed to compensate those injured in the "Black Saturday" riots of Jan. 26, 1952, that additional money had been raised for such compensation and that the victims and their relatives would themselves be allowed to present their claims.

By early Dec. 1952, it was reported, the army felt that it had achieved a relative degree of internal stability and foreign respect; and the RCC had gradually assumed virtually dictatorial powers.

Premier Naguib Dec. 10 abolished Egypt's "feudal" constitution and said that a "transitional government" would "uphold fundamental constitutional principles" until a new charter (possibly republican) was adopted. During a transitional period projected for the next 3 or so months, Naguib (representing the RCC) was to hold supreme executive powers wielded in accordance with the "spirit" of the constitution. These new ministers had been named to the cabinet Dec. 9: *Foreign Affairs*—Dr. Mahmoud Fawzi; *Municipal & Rural Affairs*—Dr. William Selim Hanna; *Commerce*—Dr. Bahgat Badawi; *Agriculture*—Abdel Razzak Sidky; *Social Affairs*—Dr. Abbas Ammar; *Supply*—Muhammad Sabry Mansour; *National Guidance*—Muhammad Fuad Galal; *Minister of State*—Fathy Radwan.

A general purge of corruption in public office, barring from political activity persons convicted of corruption or abuse of power, was decreed Dec. 21, 1952, retroactive to 1939.

Naguib launched a 5-year economic development plan Jan. 3, 1953 with the motto "Unity, Discipline, Labor." He said the plan would enable the government to build a greater Egypt and to raise the standard of living. The development plan, completed by the cabinet Dec. 31, 1952, authorized the establishment of committees to plan improvements in public services over 5-year periods. The committees were to work with a permanent Council for the Development of National Production, headed by ex-Finance Min. Hussein Fahmy. The release of an additional £10 million ($28 million) of Egypt's blocked sterling balances in London Jan. 2 was announced by the British embassy in Cairo Jan. 5.

The censorship in Cairo of outgoing and incoming news and other messages commenced Jan. 4 "to insure the security of the state."

25 Army officers and 15 civilians were arrested Jan. 14 as a "security precaution" against a possible plot to overthrow the Naguib regime, the government revealed Jan. 16. Among those held were: Col. Muhammad Rashid Mohanna, ex-Regency Council member; ex-Wafd Secy. Gen. Fuad Serag el-Din; Prince Abbas Halim, cousin of ex-King Farouk. A nationwide roundup of Communists began Jan. 17. By Jan. 20, 213 persons, including 49 Communists, were under arrest on charges of planning to foment unrest. Col. Muhammad Hosny el-Daman Houri Jan. 21 was condemned to death by firing squad for attempting to incite mutiny among the armed forces. He was sentenced by a special tribunal set up by Naguib Jan. 20 to try persons charged with "endangering the national security."

Naguib Jan. 16 had declared all parties dissolved, had confiscated their funds and had proclaimed a 3-year "transitional period," without elections, under his rule, to prepare for a democratic government. He charged that the political parties had been uncooperative with his reformist regime. The formation of new parties and all political activity by members of the former parties were banned. The Egyptian cabinet Jan. 17 extended Naguib's absolute powers to a full year and formally disbanded all political parties in partial accordance with Naguib's move. Naguib remained subject to RCC control, however.

A unique legal political party, the Liberation Rally, was founded by Naguib Jan. 23 during a public celebration in Cairo. Naguib introduced the party in a dedication speech in which he said: "We shall wage the battle of liberation, as other countries have done. Henceforth there shall be no treachery and no compromise. We have already removed the brand of dishonour and torn out the root of corruption in the government. Popular support for the new regime has been increasing daily, so that it now needs a body to organize the people, to foster their unity, and to co-ordinate the efforts of the workers. In the name of the Egyptian people . . . I announce the birth of the organization which will build our unity. I declare the birth of the organization which will struggle under a banner bearing the motto 'Unity, discipline and work.' We pledge ourselves in the sight of God to the service of the nation, offering our lives and property for the sake of the fatherland, and praying to God to give us strength for victory."

Naguib Feb. 10 issued a "constitutional proclamation" vesting the power to rule Egypt for 3 years in himself and a 13-man "Army Council of the Revolution." He promised a constitutional and democratic regime after the 3-year "transitional period." The decree also gave him the right to appoint and dismiss cabinet ministers, vested legislative power in the cabinet and authorized the cabinet and Army Council to act as a "congress." Naguib's proclamation said:

"With a view to bringing about stable conditions during the transition period, to defining the rights and duties of all citizens, and to promoting fruitful production and an improvement in the conditions of life desired by all, I declare in the name of the people that during the transition period the country will be governed according to the following principles:

"(1) The nation is the source of all powers.

"(2) All Egyptians are equal before the law and shall injoy equal rights and have equal duties.

"(3) Personal liberties and freedom of opinion will be safeguarded within the limits of the law, as well as ownership and the inviolability of the home.

"(4) Complete freedom of religion is guaranteed under state protection, provided that activities do not disturb public order.

"(5) The right of asylum is guaranteed to political refugees from abroad.

"(6) No tax may be imposed, nor any tax exemption granted, except as laid down by the law.

"(7) Judges shall be independent and will derive their powers entirely from the laws.

"(8) The leader of the revolution will exercise the power of supreme sovereignty; this will apply particularly to measures he may find necessary to protect the revolution and its aims.

"(9) These powers will apply to the right of appointing and dismissing ministers, who will have executive authority in their respective spheres of work.

"(10) The Council of the Revolution and the Council of Ministers will form a congress which will discuss the general policy of the state."

A decree enabling the government to proclaim a general mobilization in event of war or threat of war had been published Jan. 25.

The new regime also took action to exploit the growing U.S. interest in the Eastern Meditarranean. Egypt Feb. 23 announced an agreement with the U.S. for a joint survey of its industrial potential under the U.S. Point-4 aid program. The U.S. authorized $240,000 for the survey. Egypt and the U.S. Mar. 19 signed an agreement for $10 million in U.S. Point-4 aid. This was the largest single Point-4 project in the Middle East.

Agrarian Reform

A major reason for the July 1952 *coup d' état* was the desire for agrarian reform, one of the major issues on the RCC (Revolutionary Command Council) agenda. 5 proposals for land reform were submitted by Naguib to Premier Maher by Aug. 12, 1952. The proposals were that:

(1) No person or group would be permitted to buy more than 200 acres of land.

(2) No landowner with more than 200 acres would be permitted to acquire more land.

(3) The state would buy the surplus holdings in excess of 200 acres.

(4) The state would make cheap land available to land-less peasants.

(5) Peasants acquiring such land would not be permitted to resell it until it had been paid for (an anti-speculation proposal).

An RCC proposal published Aug. 12 suggested also that the government pay for expropriated lands in a period of 30 years; persons receiving land would repay the government in 30 annual low-interest installments.

At the time of Maher's resignation Sept. 7, press reports from Cairo intimated that Naguib had ordered the immediate implementation of the army plan for agrarian reform and that Maher had continued to block this implementation, while protesting the army's mass arrests of Wafdists and others.

In its first meeting Sept. 9 the new Naguib cabinet approved the army's land reform plan and a law for the compulsory reorganization of political parties to eliminate allegedly corrupt elements. The land reform law was the basis of Naguib's program to break the power of Egypt's landed class. The final legislation provided for:

(1) A limit of 200 acres per landowner, plus 50 additional acres per child, up to 2 children.

(2) A 5-year period of state redistribution of surplus land above the 200-acre limit.

(3) An impost 5 times the ordinary real estate tax on special holdings above the maximum limit.

(4) Direct sales from landowners to peasants with fewer than 10 acres at the time of sale.

(5) State-requisitioned land to be sold in lots of not greater than 5 acres.

(6) Agricultural cooperatives for holders with fewer than 6 acres.

(7) Payment for expropriated holdings with government bonds, redeemable in 30 years, at 3% interest per year.

(8) The implementation of the law under an Agriculture Ministry committee.

According to government figures, the law affected 2,115 estates, comprising in all about 1,100,000 acres, of which 731,000 acres would be expropriated for the distribution to *fellahin*. In defense of the land reform program, Finance Min. Adbel Guelil el-Emary reported that 65% of the land had been held by 6% of the owners, while the other 35% of the land was held by 94% of the owners, mostly *fellahin* with less than ½ acre apiece—an amount insufficient even for subsistence farming.

In a test of the government's agrarian policy, a wealthy landowner, Adly Seleh Lamloum, 23, was sentenced to life imprisonment at hard labor Oct. 5 after having been convicted of opposing the government program by force.

The first distribution of farmland under Naguib's land reform took place July 23, 1953 at the Nile delta town of Etay el Barud, where 1,200 acres were shared among 194 families.

As a result of its increasing influence, the U.S. Mar. 14, 1953 had formally joined Anglo-Egyptian talks in Cairo on the Suez Canal. U.S. State Secy. John Foster Dulles arrived in Cairo with Mutual Security Director Harold E. Stassen May 11 to begin a fact-finding tour of the Middle East.

Dulles indicated after a talk with Naguib that he upheld Egyptian sovereignty but favored the British position that British forces should be withdrawn gradually from Suez to insure its defense. The U.S. and Egypt signed 2 new agreements in Cairo June 18 for Point-4 aid to Egypt.

Anglo-Egyptian Agreement on the Sudan

The future of the Sudan had become a major issue for Egypt after World War II. Egyptians held that their control of the Sudan was vital for several reasons: (a) the possibility of Nile water diversion, (b) the threat of cotton competition, (c) the opportunity for Egyptian settlement in the Sudan as a result of the Gezira irrigation project (begun in 1925).

The Sudan had been under an Anglo-Egyptian condominium since 1899, but the frankest claim to Egyptian sovereignty over the Sudan was that made by King Farouk. (Some observers contended that, as the descendent of an Albanian, Farouk had no legitimate claim; it was held that a better one could have been made by the Arabian King Ibn Saud, whose ancestors of the puritanical Wahhabi sect of Islam had founded Khartoum in the early 19th century.) After the war Farouk had launched a campaign to have the unity of Egypt and the Sudan under his crown recognized *de jure* by foreign powers. By June 23, 1952 these 8 countries recognized Farouk as "king of Sudan": Jordan, Iraq, Syria, Lebanon, Saudia Arabia, Belgium, Pakistan and Greece. Italy became the 9th July 10.

After Farouk's abdication, the cabinet of Aly Maher said in a proclamation: "The Council of Ministers proclaims his majesty Ahmed Fuad II as king of Egypt and the Sudan and beseeches the Almighty that the country may enjoy during his reign the development, glory and happiness to which it looks forward. As from today the Council of Ministers has assumed under its own responsibility the king's constitutional prerogatives, in the name of the Egyptian nation, until the time comes to hand them over to a Council of Regency in accordance with the provisions of the constitution."

The British had entirely different plans for the Sudan and deplored all foreign recognition of Farouk's and Fuad's claim. Britain Apr. 2, 1952 had offered the Sudanese Legislative Assembly in Khartoum a constitution under which the Sudan would have a wholly-elected Chamber of Deputies and a 60%-elected Senate. The British governor general of the Anglo-Egyptian Sudan (then Sir Robert G. Howe) would be chief of state and appoint 40% of the Senate. The proffered constitution ignored Egyptian claims on the Sudan. A British Foreign Office spokesman said in London that the offer was "aimed at self-government of the the Sudan, not self-determination of the Sudanese."

The Sudanese parliament gave Britain a vote of thanks Apr. 23 for submitting the draft constitution but asked for an amendment giving Sudan the right to decide for itself whether to be independent or linked with Britain or Egypt.

In a concession to Sudanese desires, the British government approved of another version of a new Sudanese constitution. Announced Oct. 22, 1952 by British Foreign Secy. Anthony Eden, the draft constitution provided for Sudanese self-government in internal affairs. Britain and Egypt would keep responsibility for external affairs, Eden said. Eden told the House of Commons that Britain would begin early in November to curtail the powers of Sudanese Gov. Gen. Howe and would speed the establishment of a native parliament. He said that Britain still recognized Egypt's rights in the Sudan and hoped that Egypt would agree with the action.

Egypt objected to the new charter's provision that Sudanese elections be held under the auspices of the current administration. Expert Egyptians said that this would produce an anti-Egyptian vote. Leaders of the pro-British Sudanese Independence Movement were reported to have had a "friendly and preliminary" talk on the issue Oct. 22 with Egyptian Premier Naguib in Cairo.

Naguib, continuing negotiations with the Sudanese, contrived before the end of October to win the support of both the Umma (Nationalist) Party (pro-independence) and the National Unionist Party (pro-union with Egypt) by offering both sides the Egyptian leadership's pledge of respect for the right of self-determination for the Sudan. Naguib's mother was a Sudanese, and it was said that he believed himself and his new government popular enough with the Sudanese to guarantee a pro-Egyptian success in the event of a general election. Egypt and Britain at length were considered to be in official agreement on Sudan policy.

After months of negotiation, Britain and Egypt signed a pact in Cairo Feb. 12, 1953 guaranteeing self-determination for the Anglo-Egyptian Sudan by or before the end of a 3-year transitional period. A new dispute, however, arose from a broadcast in which Naguib warned Feb. 16 that he would repudiate the agreement if the Sudan attempted to join the British Commonwealth. He said that the terms restricted the Sudan to a choice between complete independence or union with Egypt and would bar Sudanese membership in the Commonwealth in either case. British Foreign Secy. Eden replied Feb. 17 that an independent Sudan would be free to "choose any form of association with any other state." He said that this had been made clear to the Egyptians Feb. 9.

The Sudan agreement took effect when signed Feb. 12 by Naguib and Amb.-to-Egypt Sir Ralph Stevenson. It provided for:

Self-government—A Sudanese parliament was to be elected within 2 months under the supervision of an international commission (composed of 3 Sudanese, an Indian, an American, a Briton and an Egyptian); a Sudanese government was to be formed and prepared for the assumption of full governmental powers under the guidance of a 2d commission (one Briton, one Egyptian and 3 Sudanese); a British governor general was to remain as the supreme constitutional authority during the transitional period with the assistance of a 3d commission (2 Sudanese, a Pakistani, a Briton and an Egyptian); the transitional period was not to exceed 3 years and to end whenever the Sudanese parliament wished to effect self-determination.

Self-determination—Egyptian and British military forces were to withdraw from the Sudan within 3 months after the Sudanese parliament's resolution effecting self-determination; that parliament was to call a nationwide election of a constituent assembly, which would decide the Sudan's permanent status. Britain and Egypt promised in the agreement to help enforce the constituent assembly's decisions.

Naguib said after the agreement was signed Feb. 12 that he hoped a "new page" had been "turned in the relations between Egypt and the United Kingdom . . . that restores confidence and augurs well for the settlement of other questions [chiefly, the British defense of Suez] outstanding between the 2 countries." He praised U.S. Amb. Jefferson Caffery for his aid in working out the Sudan agreement.

Egyptian Foreign Min. Mahmoud Fawzi, Ambs. Stevenson and Caffery and Indian Amb. Sardar K. M. Panikkar began talks Feb. 15 on the establishment of the commission to supervise Sudanese parliamentary elections.

Egypt Becomes a Republic

After 5,000 years of despotism or foreign rule, Egypt became a republic June 18, 1953.

A 5-man subcommittee of the Constituent Constitutional Committee had announced Mar. 24 that it unanimously favored the abolition of the Egyptian monarchy and the establishment of a parliamentary democracy. A special constitutional committee voted unanimously May 5 to give Egypt a republican form of government to replace the monarchy.

Egypt was proclaimed a republic June 18 with Premier Muhammad Naguib as its first president. He also continued as premier. The proclamation gave control of the government to Naguib and a 13-man "Army Council of the Revolution."

The proclamation, issued by the council, deposed 17-month-old King Fuad II, abolished all royal titles and ended the 148-year Muhammad Ali dynasty. It also promised a plebiscite at the end of a 3-year transitional period to determine "the shape of the republic" and to elect a new president.

Revolutionary Council leaders moved into key civilian posts in a cabinet reshuffle that accompanied the proclamation. Major changes: Lt. Col. Gamal Abdel Nasser was named deputy premier and replaced Soliman Hafez as interior minister in control of all police and internal security forces. Maj. Salah Salem succeeded Muhammad Fuad Galal as national guidance (propaganda) minister and took over the new post of minister of state for Sudan affairs. Wing Cmndr. Abdul Latif Boghdadi assumed the war and navy portfolios formerly held by Naguib. Maj. Abdel Hakim Amer succeeded Naguib as commander-in-chief of the armed forces. Communications Min. Hussein Abou Zeid and Works Min. Mourad Fahmy resigned. (Supply Min. Muhammad Ali Sabri Mansour had quit the cabinet June 15.)

The new cabinet was sworn in by Naguib June 19. Under Nasser's influence, the following were appointed later: *Public Works*—Ahmed el-Shurapaty (July 8); *Interior*—Lt. Col. Zakaria Mohyeddin (Oct. 5); *Communications*—Wing Cmndr. Gamal Salem (Oct. 5). The new cabinet was said to represent a major gain for Nasser. Long-time close associates of Nasser in the cabinet included Maj. Salah Salem, Wing Cmndr. Abdul Latif Boghdadi, Maj. Abdel Hakim Amer and Lt. Col. Zakaria Mohieddin.

Egypt unveiled its first paratroop battalion July 25 as part of a 4-day "liberation" celebration. A military review, featuring British-built jet planes, had opened the holiday July 23.

In addresses to celebrating Egyptians, Pres. Naguib said:

July 23—"The revolution" that had deposed Farouk was aimed at "that big enemy," Egyptians being "more convinced than ever that dignity and occupation by the usurper cannot go together." *July 25*—"Foreign occupation of our land must vanish from the whole Nile Valley or it will not be a true evacuation. . . . . Our safety in Egypt depends on the evacuation of the oppressor from the Sudan as well as from the [Suez] Canal."

The cabinet June 30 had approved a national financial austerity program, including cuts in government salaries and tax and tariff increases. Naguib cut his own annual salary from $17,340 to $8,670.

Egypt and the UN Relief & Works Agency agreed June 30 to start developing a 4-year agricultural project that ultimately might provide livelihood for 50,000 Palestinian refugees. The project, in the Gaza Strip and the northern coast of the Sinai Peninsula, was to get $30 million from UNRWA funds.

Official censorship of incoming and outgoing news dispatches and photographs ended July 3. The government retained some control over Egyptian newspapers.

'Traitors' Purged

The government announced Sept. 15, 1953 that it had uncovered an alliance between Egyptian "traitors" and "foreign imperialists" to overthrow the Naguib regime. A state of emergency was proclaimed throughout Cairo, and a nationwide "purge," with particular attention to the press, was promised. Armored cars were stationed near the British and U.S. embassies when the emergency was declared.

2 former premiers and 11 other former aides of ex-King Farouk were arrested Sept. 21 on charges of conspiracy against the Naguib government. They were held for trial before a new Revolutionary Tribunal, created to handle treason cases. The defendants were: Mustafa Nahas, leader of the dissolved Wafd party and premier 8 times (most recently

1949–52); his wife Zeinab; Ibrahim Abdel Hadi, Saadist premier 1948–9; Hafez Affifi, chief of Farouk's royal cabinet; Ibrahim Farrag, ex-minister of municipal affairs; Soliman Ghannam, ex-minister of commerce; Kamel el-Kawish, ex-governor of Cairo; Mahmoud Riad, another ex-minister of commerce; Lt. Col. Ismail el Meligy and Lt. Col. Saad el-Din el-Sumbati, former police officials; Abbas Halim, Farouk's cousin; Karim Tabet, Farouk's press adviser; Dr. Ahmed el-Nakib, Farouk's physician.

Ex-Premier Hadi, 57, was sentenced to death for treason Oct. 1 after a 3-day secret trial by the Revolutionary Tribunal. He was denied the right of appeal but told that the verdict and sentence were subject to review by the Revolutionary Command Council. The RCC Oct. 4 commuted Hadi's death sentence to life imprisonment.

4 politicians were hanged for treason: Mahmoud Sabry Aly Oct. 13; Ezzat Muhammad Bagheb, Alfred Ahmed Mikhail and Bulos Maximos Sweiha Oct. 17. Sentenced to life imprisonment were ex-State and Information Min. Ibraham Farag Oct. 6; Ahmed Nassif, ex-Justice Ministry official, Oct. 10; Karim Tabet, ex-press adviser to Farouk, Oct. 18. A 15-year sentence for implication in the Palestine War weapons fraud was given Col. Abdel Ghaffar Osman Nov. 7.

Wafd party leader Fuad Serag el-Din, 47, an enemy of the RCC, received a 15-year prison sentence from the Revolutionary Tribunal in Cairo Jan. 30, 1954 for corruption and abuse of power as a cabinet minister under Farouk.

(The RCC Nov. 8, 1953 had ordered the confiscation of all Egyptian property of ex-King Farouk and others of the former royal family.)

Suez Deadlock & Moslem Brotherhood's Dissolution

The 2 most serious challenges faced by the new Egyptian republic were probably the deadlock with Britain over the the Suez Canal Zone and the attempted overthrow of the

RCC by the Moslem Brotherhood under its "supreme guide," Dr. Hassan el-Hodeiby. The 2 problems eventually became entangled with each other and resulted in the outlawing of the Brotherhood.

Anglo-Egyptian meetings on the Suez issue were interrupted May 6, 1953 but were resumed more informally July 30 after the proclamation of the republic. Representing the British were Gen. Sir Brian Robertson, the British military commander in Egypt, and British Chargé d'Affaires Robert Hankey; Amb. Sir Ralph Stevenson was absent on sick leave. Egypt's new deputy premier and interior minister, Lt. Col. Gamal Abdel Nasser, had assumed control of Egypt's part in the talks and thus was virtually directing Egyptian foreign policy. Attending the talks with Nasser were Foreign Min. Mahmoud Fawzi, National Guidance Min. Salah Salem, Wing Cmndr. Latif Boghdadi, the war minister, and Maj. Abdel Hakim Amer, the Egyptian commander-in-chief.

The British attitude had been expressed May 11 by Prime Min. Sir Winston Churchill after the talks had been broken off: "Naturally we do not wish to keep indefinitely 80,000 men at a cost of, it might be, over £50 million [$140 million] a year, discharging the duty, which has largely fallen upon us alone, of safeguarding the interests of the free nations in the Middle East and also of preserving the international waterway of the Suez Canal. . . . Our hope is that negotiations will be resumed. In the meanwhile we may await the development of events with the composure which follows from a combination of patience with strength."

6 meetings took place during the summer of 1953, and the British embassy declared Oct. 4 that there was "no justication for excessive optimism." In England, at the Conservative Party conference in September, the possibility of permanently accepting the *status quo* had been discussed.

In the face of the deadlock, Nasser warned that the Egyptian people would "rally as one man to defend their independence and sovereignty." Maj. Salem declared Oct. 10 that it was "impossible to reach an agreement with the British side."

The bone of contention was the British desire to have the right, after their withdrawal, to reoccupy the Canal Zone in the event of an attack on British troops anywhere in the world. The Egyptians, however, said they were willing to consider such reoccupation only in the event of an attack on an Arab state or Turkey. After the final talk of a series of 15 during October, the British embassy and the Egyptian National Guidance Ministry declared jointly Oct. 21: "It has not been found possible to reach agreement at this meeting. A further meeting will be held after the position has been considered by both governments."

According to the RCC, during this period of Anglo-Egyptian talks on Suez, there was frequent contact between the British embassy and representatives of the extremist Moslem Brotherhood. Nasser later claimed to have protested the continuation of these contacts to the Brotherhood's "supreme guide," Dr. Hassan el-Hodeiby, as early as May 1953. Nasser apparently believed that the Moslem Brotherhood had repeatedly approached the British embassy with this compromise solution to the Suez question: If the British would aid the Brotherhood in its aim to overthrow the RCC and establish a theocratic regime under Hodeiby, the latter would submit the question of emergency reoccupation of the Canal Zone to the UN.

The Moslem Brotherhood was itself considered fanatically anti-British. Under the leadership of its founder and first "supreme guide," Dr. Hassan el-Banna (assassinated in 1949), it had sought the complete removal of the British and the establishment of a pan-Islamic state (*dar al-Islam*) under the rule of Banna as caliph (*khalifa*, successor). At first, then, it had supported the RCC because of its anti-British stand. The Brotherhood, however, soon came to feel that the

RCC was too secular a movement, and it resented Pres. Naguib's tampering with the officers of al-Azhar, the Koranic university, for allegedly political purposes.

Student members of the Brotherhood and student supporters of the Liberation Rally, the official RCC party, came to blows Jan. 12, 1954 during a Cairo University march to commemorate student "martyrs" killed by the British in the Canal Zone.

The government Jan. 13 proclaimed the dissolution of the Moslem Brotherhood. A state of emergency was announced Jan. 14, and 450 Brethren were arrested, including Hodeiby and the secretary-general, Abdel Hakim Abdin, as well as students, teachers, civil servants and members of the military. (149 Brethren were released Jan. 28 after questioning.)

Police searches Jan. 16 revealed a magazine of the explosive gelignite at the Helwan branch of the Brotherhood outside Cairo, and radio transmitters and receivers were found at a farm belonging to Hassan el-Ashmawi, a leading Moslem Brother. An RCC spokeman announced Jan. 17 that Hodeiby and his colleagues would be tried for conspiracy to overthrow the regime.

In explaining the forced dissolution of the Brotherhood, the RCC had stated Jan. 15 that Hodeiby: (a) had refused to support the revolution unless it be placed under strict Koranic law; (b) had presented unacceptable nominees to the cabinet after Nasser had offered 3 portfolios as a compromise; (c) had insisted that the Brotherhood have a veto power over all legislation after the dissolution of the political parties in Jan. 1953, and—this demand having been rejected by the RCC—(d) had instructed *agents provocateurs* of the Brotherhood to subvert Liberation Rally meetings and to organize paramilitary groups in the police, army and student organizations.

(As a struggle between Pres. Naguib and Deputy Premier Nasser came out in the open during February-September

1954, however, some analysts concluded that Nasser had dissolved the Moslem Brotherhood largely to prevent Naguib from allying himself with the followers of Dr. Hodeiby.)

Nasser Ousts Naguib

The RCC had originally announced that it would retain rule for a transitional 3-year period. Many of the older Egyptian political groups opposed this, and it was reported that in Feb. 1954 it seemed to Nasser and some of his colleagues that Naguib was disposed to side with these dissident groups, especially the Moslem Brotherhood. Bitter disagreements broke out between Nasser and Naguib in RCC meetings Feb. 22 and 23, and the cabinet Feb. 24 forced Naguib to resign.

Naguib's resignation as Egyptian president and premier was announced Feb. 25 by the cabinet and Revolutionary Command Council in Cairo. The announcement said that Naguib, 37, had quit Feb. 22 after the Council had rejected his demand for "absolute autocratic authority." The communiqué said that Vice Pres. Nasser, 37, had replaced Naguib as premier and that the presidency would be filled by an election. Nasser, the statement said, had been picked to lead the 1952 revolt against ex-King Farouk's regime with Naguib "presented to the world" as leader.

Nasser proclaimed a state of emergency in Egypt Feb. 25 to guard against disorders. Naguib was placed under house arrest to prevent him from trying to start a movement to regain power. The new regime said it would continue moderate policies toward the West.

Nasser's assumption of the premiership put him into opposition with forces still more powerful than he. Maj. Khaled Mohieddin of the RCC, the commander of the tank corps and a leading backer of Naguib, threatened Nasser and the RCC headquarters Feb. 27 with a tank assault unless Naguib was restored to the presidency.

Initially, a compromise was reached. The presidency was returned to Naguib, but Nasser was retained as premier. After continuing pro-Naguib pressure from some of the Moslem Brotherhood, Wafdists, Socialists and others, however, Naguib was reinstated as premier and RCC chairman Mar. 8— only 9 days after he had resumed the presidency. Nasser stepped down to his old post as deputy premier and vice chairman of the RCC (vice president).

The government had announced Mar. 5 that an election would be held in July for a constituent assembly to serve as a parliament while a constitution was being drafted. The RCC Mar. 25 announced its intention of relinquishing power. Sovereignty was to be transferred July 24 to the constituent assembly to be elected June 18. Hence, the government-sponsored Liberation Rally (the sole legal political party) would be dissolved and replaced by the old parties.

Both Nasser and his friend Maj. Salah Salem absented themselves from the meeting at which this decision was adopted. Whereas Naguib and his followers apparently felt that the nation would not accept prolonged military rule, the Nasser faction of the RCC followed an increasingly tough line against a return to the old days of parliamentary squabbles.

Nasser's supporters in the RCC and in the trade unions— especially the Cairo transport workers' union—protested Mar. 27 against the proposed return to a parliamentary regime. A general strike began and spread across the Nile Delta area, paralyzing transportation and the production of cotton, the country's major export crop. Naguib agreed Mar. 28 to cancel the decisions of Mar. 25, and he collapsed of exhaustion the following day.

Maj. Khaled Mohieddin of the tank corps resigned from the RCC and reportedly went into exile.. 16 army officers— all but one belonging to the tank corps—were put on trial in Cairo June 5–22; 13 were sentenced to imprisonment or dismissal from the army, 3 were acquitted.

In a new attempt to suppress the old political parties, the RCC decreed Apr. 15 that any member of the Wafd, Saadist or Liberal Constitutional parties who had been a cabinet minister between 1942 and July 1952 would be deprived of all political rights for 10 years. The council also began a purge of allegedly corrupt press elements Apr. 16 by dissolving the Egyptian Press Syndicate.

Deputy Premier Nasser, still leader of the ruling military junta, replaced the ailing Naguib Apr. 18 as premier of Egypt. Naguib retained the figurehead post of president. Nasser's cabinet, also installed Apr. 18, was substantially the same as Naguib's. 8 members of the RCC received or retained ministries. 5 ministers who had backed Naguib's fruitless efforts to end military rule resigned Apr. 17. The new cabinet: *Foreign Affairs*—Dr. Muhammad Fawzi; *War & Marine*—Lt. Col. Hussein Shafei; *Interior*—Lt. Col. Zakaria Mohieddin; *Finance*—Abdel Hamid el-Sherid; *National Guidance and Sudanese Affairs*—Maj. Salah Salem; *Municipal & Rural Affairs*—Wing Cmndr. Abdel Latif Boghdadi; *Communications*—Wing Cmndr. Gamal Salem; *State Ministry for the Presidency of the Republic*—Cmndr. Hassan Ibrahim; *Justice*—Ahmed Housni; *Health*—Nourreddin Tarraf; *Wakfs* (Moslem charities) —Sheikh Ahmed Hassan el-Bakkour; *State Ministry*—Dr. Fathy Radwan; *Commerce & Industry*—Dr. Hassan Marei; *Supply*—Guindi Abdel Malek; *Education*—Dr. Muhammad Awad Muhammad; *Agriculture*—Dr. Abdel Razzak Sidky; *Public Works*—Ahmed el-Shurapaty; *Social Affairs*—Maj. Kamal ed-Din Hussein; *Finance* (deputy minister)—Abdel Moneim el-Kaissouni; *Commerce & Industry* (deputy minister)—Muhammad Abu Nosseir; *Sudanese Affairs* (deputy minister)—Col. Abdel Fattah Hassan.

Throughout the summer of 1954 Naguib retained a certain amount of influence as president. The old political parties supported him, as did the Sudanese (whom the Egyptians tried not to affront). Naguib had lost his supporters among the officers of the tank corps, but strong paramilitary elements in the Moslem Brotherhood swung over to him late in the summer as a result of Nasser's Suez negotiations with the British—which, they charged, had become "heretically" compromising.

The RCC July 8 had restored the legitimacy of the Moslem Brotherhood. Observers speculated that the militancy of the Brotherhood would strengthen Nasser's hand with the British, making him appear subject to extreme internal anti-British pressure. The conclusion of the Anglo-Egyptian agreement on Suez July 27, however, provoked fierce enmity from the Brethren, one whose members denounced the government as "heretics who do not comply with the teachings of the Koran." This charge, in a sermon at the mosque of Tanta, provoked violent riots there Sept. 10.

As Premier Nasser was addressing an audience in Alexandria Oct. 26, a Moslem Brother, Mahmoud Abdel Latif, fired 8 pistol shots at him. A light-bulb above the premier was shattered but he continued his speech. A Cairo mob put the Brotherhood's central offices to the torch Oct. 27, and the government Oct. 29 banned the Brotherhood for the 2d time and arrested its "supreme guide," Dr. Hassan el-Hodeiby.

The RCC removed Naguib, 53, from the Egyptian presidency Nov. 14 on grounds that he had plotted with the Moslem Brotherhood against the life of Nasser. Hindawi Duweir, a Brotherhood leader in a Cairo suburb, had testified at a trial Nov. 11 that Naguib had agreed to make a radio speech and "calm the population" if Nasser were assassinated. The government also reported Nov. 14 that Youssef Talaat, leader of a secret order of the Brotherhood, had been arrested and had confessed that Naguib had approved the plot to kill Nasser.

Nasser assumed the functions of the presidency Nov. 17. The Egyptian government assured Sudanese leaders Nov. 21 that Naguib, a Sudanese, would not be tried for his alleged plotting to overthrow Nasser. The attempt on Nasser

Oct. 26, it was said, had furnished him with a pretext for finally removing the last vestiges of Naguib's power. Thereafter Naguib remained under house arrest in Zeitoun near Cairo for over 15 years.

The Egyptian government Dec. 7 executed by hanging 6 Moslem Brotherhood leaders condemned by a military court in Cairo Dec. 4 for plotting to assassinated Nasser and seize the country. Those executed were Mahmoud Abdel Latif, who had fired at Nasser in Alexandria Oct. 26; Youssef Talaat; Sheik Muhammad Farghali; Ibrahim Tayeb; Hindawi Duweir and Abdel Kader Oda. The death sentence of Hassan el-Hodeiby, the Brotherhood's supreme guide, was commuted Dec. 4 to life imprisonment by the RCC.

Anglo-Egyptian Agreement on Suez (July 1954)

Anglo-Egyptian negotiations on the evacuation of British troops from the Suez Canal Zone had been broken off Oct. 21, 1953. They were reopened in Cairo July 10, 1954 and produced an accord that same month. The chief negotiators were British Amb.-to-Egypt Sir Ralph Stevenson and Egyptian Premier Gamal Abdel Nasser. Nasser and British War Secy. Antony Head initialed an evacuation agreement July 27.

The arrangement provided for: (a) Britain to withdraw all its forces within 20 months; (b) Egypt to turn over sections of the Zone to the British in the event of foreign aggression against Egypt; (c) Egypt to give "most-favored-nation" treatment to overflights and servicing of the Royal Air Force (RAF); (d) respect for the Constantinople Convention of 1888 (signed by 9 European powers, including Turkey, but not by Turkey's vassal, Egypt) guaranteeing international freedom of navigation through the Canal.

British Foreign Secy. Anthony Eden declared July 28 in Britain's House of Commons: "It is the conviction of the government that this agreement will preserve our essential requirements in this area in the light of modern conditions.

We are convinced that in the Middle East, as elsewhere, our defense arrangements must be based on consent and cooperation with the peoples concerned. I would like to take this opportunity of reaffirming the government's intention to abide by the terms of the Tripartite Declaration of May 2, 1950, relating to peace and stability between the Arab States and Israel. I have discussed this with both the French and American governments and find them both equally determined to uphold this declaration. It is our hope that it will now be possible to establish our relations with Egypt on a new basis of friendship and understanding. Her majesty's government believe that this is also the intention of the Egyptian government. The agreement should thus contribute to a reduction of tension throughout the Middle East as a whole."

Public satisfaction in Egypt was overwhelming—with the exception of the Moslem Brotherhood, whose members called the agreement too comprising. Nasser heralded the agreement as "the biggest single achievement in Egypt's national aspirations to date." He added: "We want to get rid of the hatred in our hearts and start building up our relations with Britain on a solid basis of mutual trust and confidence, which has been lacking for the past 70 years."

Throughout the West and in Commonwealth countries the reaction was favorable. But Israel expressed apprehension that the new Egyptian control of the Canal might enable Egypt to block Israel-bound shipping. Israeli Premier Moshe Sharett predicted in Tel Aviv July 28 that the Anglo-Egyptian agreement would work "an important change in the balance of power between us and the [Arab] world around us." He said: "Egypt will be tested by the way she uses her great national asset [the Suez Canal]—which in truth is an international asset—and the new position of strength which is about to fall to her share after such a prolonged struggle. We have heard threats of aggression from the lips of Egyptian leaders which justify the deepest concern and require from us the greatest watchfulness. The granting of a new position of strength to Egypt, without any obligation on her part to regularize her relations with Israel, is liable to be interpreted and actually to serve as a spur to aggression. We stand prepared and watchful, and we shall constantly strengthen and perfect our defense forces to meet any emergency. . . . Israel hopes that every nation may achieve its rightful aspiration to complete freedom and independence—yet not in order that it should foment strife, increase enmity, and plot aggression against a neighboring state."

The mutual distrust between Israel and Egypt increased sharply during 1954, providing the context for an arms race and cold war penetration into the Middle East.

THE COLD WAR & EGYPT (1954-6)

Israeli-Egyptian Tension

Incidents of violence between Israel and the surrounding Arab states, especially Egypt, rose sharply in 1954. During March, violent incidents occurred on all of Israel's borders but the Lebanese.

Meanwhile, Egypt told the UN Security Council Mar. 13 that it would not give up its practice of halting Israel-bound ships in the Suez Canal unless the Council acted on alleged Israeli truce violations. Dr. Mahmoud Azmi, the Egyptian delegate, said that the Egyptian restrictions on shipping in the Suez Canal and the Gulf of Aqaba were an exercise of the right of visit, search and "possibly seizure" and did not constitute a blockade. Russia used its 59th veto in the UN Security Council Mar. 29 to kill a New Zealand resolution calling on Egypt to stop interfering with Israel-bound shipping in the Suez Canal. The vote: 8 for, the Soviet Union and Lebanon against, Nationalist China abstaining.

In another UN action involving Egyptian interests, the Security Council was also asked to take up a Mar. 28-29 incident in which 9 Jordanians were killed and 19 wounded in an Israeli attack on Nahhalin, a village 8 miles southwest of Jerusalem and 1½ miles from the Israeli-Jordanian armistice line. Israel was condemned for the raid "in the strongest terms" Mar. 30 by the UN Mixed Armistice Commission, then consisting only of the chairman, U.S. Navy Cmndr. Elmo H. Hutchison, and 2 Jordanian delegates. Israeli members had boycotted the commission since Mar. 23.

The Nahhalin attack took place less than 2 weeks after 11 Israelis, including women and children, had been killed Mar. 17 in an Arab ambush of a bus on a Negev road 95 miles north of Elath. Only 4 passengers survived. One survivor said: Machine-gun fire halted the bus, killed the driver and most of the passengers; armed "Arabs in khaki" examined each body and "if they saw signs of life . . . shot the victims

65

at close range"; the survivors pretended to be dead. Israel asked the UN Israeli-Jordanian Mixed Armistice Commission to investigate the attack immediately. It said the ambush was a "warlike act" for which "the government from whose territory this unit of murderers was sent forth" was responsible. (The Jewish Telegraphic Agency reported from Jerusalem that the raiders had been identified as Jordanians.)

The Security Council reported its discussion of Middle Eastern tension Apr. 8 as Israeli-Arab clashes increased. Israel, Egypt and Jordan all had reported border incidents to the UN Mixed Armistice Commission during the preceding week. The session had been called Apr. 5 by Soviet Deputy Foreign Min. Andrei Y. Vishinsky, Council president for April, to consider Israeli and Lebanese charges. Lebanon, acting for Jordan, complained Apr. 1 against Israel over the raid on Nahhalin. Israeli Amb.-to-UN Abba Eban contended Apr. 7 that the Israeli-Jordanian truce machinery had suffered "a complete organic breakdown." He said that Soviet vetoes of Security Council resolutions criticizing Arab states indicated that the Council could take only actions "congenial to Arab opinion." Eban told newsmen afterwards that since 1949, Arab raiders had killed 500 Israelis and that Israelis were becoming less willing "to suffer. . . without response." (UN Secy. Gen. Dag Hammarskjöld had said Mar. 25 that he had given up efforts to arrange direct high-level Israeli-Jordanian peace talks because Jordan insisted that the [Palestine War] Armistice Commission was the only "appropriate" channel for negotiations.)

Delegates of the U.S., Britain, France, Holland and Turkey expressed support in the Security Council Apr. 8 for Israel's demand that the Council review the entire question of Middle Eastern tension. Lebanon, supported by the Soviet Union and Nationalist China, demanded that the Council confine itself to Jordan's complaint against the Israeli attack on Nahhalin. Arab representatives indicated

Apr. 12 that they would agree to a general debate if the Council first condemned Israel for the Nahhalin incident.

After a month of procedural argument, the Security Council voted May 4 to permit general debate on the Israeli-Jordanian border situation. The vote on the Brazilian-Colombian resolution was 8 for, Lebanon and the USSR opposed, China abstaining. The Arab countries had threatened to quit if full debate were permitted but, after the Council voted, Dr. Charles Malik of Lebanon said that the Arabs would not withdraw. He later introduced a resolution condemning Israel for the attack on Nahhalin and calling for a UN economic and diplomatic boycott of Israel. (Israeli-Jordanian border incidents continued into the summer. The UN truce organization's chief, Maj. Gen. Vagn Bennike, reported July 11 that it had been impossible to determine which side had started an outbreak of fighting in Jerusalem June 30–July 2 but that both Israel and Jordan had broken the truce.)

Incidents on the Israeli-Egyptian front, meanwhile, had grown frequent, and this situation underscored the anomaly of Egypt's military administration in the Gaza Strip. While Egypt had not formally annexed the area since coming into control of it during the Palestine War, Cairo Jan. 2, 1954 had issued a new law granting more self-government and freedom of religion to the strip's permanent residents and Arab refugees than they had hitherto enjoyed under Egyptian military rule. The area's population, 70,000 when the British Mandate over Palestine ended in May 1948, had been swollen by the influx of more than 200,000 Palestinian Arab refugees after the 1948-9 war.

The Egyptian-Israeli Mixed Armistice Commission censured Israel Apr. 4 for 2 attacks on Egyptian military posts in which 3 Egyptian soldiers were killed and one wounded. The raids reportedly had been mounted in reprisal for a clash between Egyptian and Israeli troops Mar. 25 near Kisufim

on the Israeli side of the Strip. Israel had reported one of
its soldiers wounded and another captured in the incident.
2 Israeli soldiers were wounded in a new incident near
Kisufim Apr. 6, reportedly by an Egyptian patrol. The
Mixed Armistice Commission, boycotted by its Egyptian
members, condemned Egypt Apr. 11 for 4 truce violations
near Gaza Apr. 8-9 in which one Israeli civilian was killed
and 5 wounded. Both Israel and Egypt were censured by the
commission Apr. 29 for clashes along the Gaza Strip Apr.
25-26.

As with those on Israel's Jordanian border, incidents
along the Gaza Strip's frontiers continued into the summer
of 1954. The Mixed Armistice Commission July 16 again
censured both Israel and Egypt for 3 truce violations in the
Gaza area. The most serious incident had occurred July 10,
when 6 Egyptians and one Israeli were killed in the storming
of an Egyptian outpost by an Israeli unit, reportedly in reprisal for an earlier Egyptian attack. As with the Israeli-
Jordanian strife, moreover, border incidents in the Gaza
Strip area continued to escalate through September. The
Egyptian press Aug. 30 reported a Gaza Strip raid in which
armed Israelis had killed 15 and injured 22 persons in the El
Boreig Arab refugee camp. Israel Sept. 26 alleged 16 instances of Egyptian aggression within the past 6 weeks and
charged Egyptian forces with the deaths of 4 Israelis and the
wounding of 5.

Many observers expressed a belief that the increase in
incidents of Egyptian and Israeli mutual military provocation
had resulted from the Anglo-Egyptian Suez agreement. This
agreement had erased much anti-Western sentiment among
the Arabs, and many Israelis suspected that it might pave the
way for an Arab military pact linked to NATO and dangerous
to Israel's security. According to this view, Israel had entered
1955 in a mood to show Egypt that it was ready for any stiff
new military confrontation.

Following the Anglo-Egyptian agreement on Suez July

27, 1954, Egypt's economic blockade of the Suez Canal Zone base was lifted, permitting British troops to buy Egyptian products for the first time in 2 years. But Egypt continued to forbid Israeli shipping—or any cargo ships bound for Israel—access to the Canal, in which it had imposed a total blockade with respect to Israel in Jan. 1954.

Egyptian Premier Nasser said in Cairo Aug. 3 that Egypt would welcome U.S. military aid in strengthening its armed forces and that he assumed that the U.S. would aid Egypt in the event of attack "by some other power."

Britain lifted its 3-year embargo on the sale of arms to Egypt Aug. 30 but asked for Egypt's assurance that any British arms Egypt might buy would not be used for aggressive purposes. The Egyptian commander-in-chief, Maj. Gen. Abdel Hakim Amer, said that he accepted the British offer "without reluctance because we have no intention to attack Israel or any other country."

Israeli Premier Moshe Sharett said Sept. 1 that his government was ready to meet any movement toward peace with Egypt. But if Egypt wanted war, "we are also ready to meet that," he told the Knesset (parliament) in a foreign policy debate. Israel's controversey with the U.S. and Britain, Sharett said, was "severe and bitter" because "in practice they encourage the aggressor to pursue aggressive designs." He also said that his government was "interested" in friendship with the USSR if it were "possible to attain it" but that "real friendship" was impossible as long as Russia isolated Soviet Jewry from Israel and accelerated "the race to appease" the Arab states. The Knesset voted confidence in Sharett's foreign policy, 54–9.

Egypt Reacts to Baghdad Pact

6-year-old plans for a Mediterranean and Middle Eastern defense agreement under Western auspices finally came to fruition early in 1955, when Iraq agreed to conclude a mutual security treaty with Turkey. They soon were joined by Iran,

Pakistan and Britain in what came to be known as the Baghdad Pact.

Egypt's reaction was immeditate. Maj. Salah Salem, the minister for national guidance (propaganda), visited Damascus and announced there Feb. 27 the drafting of a new Arab military defense treaty excluding Iraq to supplant the Arab League's 1950 collective security pact. The new treaty was signed by Egypt and Syria Mar. 2; by Mar. 8, Saudi Arabia and Yemen had also adhered. Lebanon and Jordan, however, both traditionally pro-Western in outlook, adopted a neutral position between the 2 axes—Iraq-Turkey-Iran-Pakistan and Egypt-Syria-Saudi Arabia-Yemen.

In further reaction, Egypt began to form even more cordial ties with communist nations and to negotiate for Soviet-bloc weapons.

The idea of such a Mediterranean arrangement as the Middle East Treaty Organization (METO)—as the Baghdad Pact was formally known until 1959*—had been first proposed by Turkish Foreign Min. Nejmeddin Sadak in Paris Feb. 17, 1949 after the Western powers had rejected Turkey's request for membership in the newly formed North Atlantic Treaty Organization (NATO) because of Turkey's geographical remoteness from the North Atlantic area. The Western Big 3 commanders of NATO, U.S. Gen. Omar N. Bradley, British Field Marshall Sir William Slim and French Gen. Charles Lecheres, discussed with Turkish Premier Adnan Menderes and his principal cabinet ministers in Ankara Oct. 12–15, 1951 Turkey's wish to enter NATO. All parties concluded that the establishment of a Middle Eastern command was a "necessary and useful" first step toward the creation of wider diplomatic-and-military arrangements.

As the 1951 Ankara talks were going on, Turkish Amb.-to-Egypt Sayed H. F. Tugay, U.S. Amb. Jefferson Caffery,

---

*When it became the Central Treaty Organization (CENTO).

French Amb. Maurice Couve de Murville and British Amb. Sir Ralph Stevenson visited Egyptian Foreign Min. Muhammad Salah ed-Din Pasha in Cairo Oct. 13 and invited Egypt to become an equal partner with the Western Big 3 and Turkey in the prospective Middle Eastern command. But Egyptian Interior Min. Fuad Sirag ed-Din Pasha announced Oct. 15 that the Egyptian government had decided to defer further consideration of the proposal until Egypt's differences with Britain had been settled. Turkey and the Western Big 3 went ahead without Egypt.

Before Egypt could take any unilateral action on the matter, however, it reportedly received further diplomatic warning (Mar. 23, 1954) that the Soviet Union would consider "unfriendly and even hostile" the creation of any Western-sponsored Middle Eastern defense pact of Arab states.

More than 5 weeks after Britain and Egypt had initialed the Suez evacuation agreement, the Egyptian Revolutionary Council Sept. 2, 1954 issued to foreign newsmen a "background paper" in which the Council took the position that Egypt, while preferring to ally itself with the West rather than the Communist world, was still not ready to adhere to the projected Middle Eastern defense pact, which to the Egyptian people would smack of colonialism. The Council at the same time declared that Egypt looked on the USSR as the only major threat to Middle Eastern sovereignty. The Egyptian press learned of the paper's contents and reported on the matter Sept. 3. Premier Nasser thereupon formally denied the existence of such a paper—a statement that Western observers interpreted as designed solely for Egyptian ears.

Turkey's charter-member participation in the projected defense alliance worked against any attraction that such a plan might otherwise have exerted on most of Turkey's former vassals. Syria opposed such a group from the outset. Egypt remained cool toward it, and neither Saudi Arabia nor

Jordan could be persuaded that its best interests lay within such an organization. Iraq became its only non-Turkish convert west of the Caspian Sea.

Gen. Nuri as-Said, premier of Iraq, announced Jan. 12, 1955 that Iraq would soon adhere to a mutual security treaty with Turkey similar to those already in existence between Turkey and Pakistan (signed in Apr. 1954) and Turkey, Greece and Yugoslavia (signed in Bled, Yugoslavia Aug. 6, 1954). (Both Greece and Turkey had joined NATO Feb. 18, 1952.) Nuri and Turkish Premier Menderes Jan. 14, 1955 said in a joint communiqué: "Turkey and Iraq have decided to conclude a treaty to bring into effect, and to expand as soon as possible, cooperation for the stability and security of the Middle East. The signatories will undertake to cooperate, in conformity with the right of legitimate defense under the UN Charter, against any aggression which may be made against them from within or without the region—that is, from any quarter—in accordance with the right of legitimate self-defence as stipulated by Article 51 of the UN Charter. The Turkish and Iraqi governments believe that such a treaty will serve to establish security in the Middle East in a manner conforming with the UN Charter. Therefore they deem it useful and necessary that other like-minded states, taking into consideration their geographical position and the means at their disposal, should join this treaty. Consequently, before the treaty is drawn up, Turkey and Iraq will remain in close contact with those states which express a desire to act in concert with them, and will make every endeavor to persuade those states to sign the treaty simultaneously with them. Should this not prove feasible, they will continue to make the same efforts after the treaty has been signed."

Maj. Gen. Muhammad Rafiq Arif, the Iraqi army chief of staff, had asserted Jan. 13, after the treaty announcement, that Iraq hoped to receive larger allocations of U.S. military equipment, including jet aircraft.

Iraq's plan to form an alliance with Turkey aroused the

opposition of Egypt and other members of the Arab League and its 1950 Arab collective security alliance. Egyptian Premier Nasser Jan. 16 called a conference of Arab premiers to consider what Egypt termed the threat to Arab unity posed by the Iraqi-Turkish decision.

Turkish Premier Adnan Menderes visited Iraq and Lebanon Jan. 6–18 in an effort to bring both nations into a Middle East collective security system not based on the Arab League. A joint Lebanese-Turkish communiqué Jan. 18 indicated that Menderes had not immediately succeeded in bringing Lebanon into the Iraqi-Turkish alliance but that talks would continue. (In a policy statement Dec. 27, 1954 Menderes had in effect rejected Egypt's proposal that Turkey join a regional alliance connected with the Arab League. He offered Jan. 18, 1955 to visit Cairo in an attempt to secure Egyptian participation in the Iraqi-Turkish alliance. An Egyptian announcement Jan. 20 said Premier Nasser would be unable to meet with Menderes in Cairo or Turkey.)

Nasser presided in Cairo Jan. 22 at the opening meeting of the conference he had called. The meeting was attended by the Syrian, Jordanian, Saudi Arabian and Lebanese premiers. (Iraqi Premier Said declined to attend on the ground of illness.) An Egyptian Foreign Office spokesman said Jan. 22 that Egypt opposed the Iraqi-Turkish treaty because "Iraq has put new responsibilities on her partners in the Arab collective security pact without first consulting them."

Maj. Salah Salem, the Egyptian minister for national guidance, asserted at a press conference Feb. 7 that the signing of a Turkish-Iraqi defense treaty would force Egypt to denounce its commitment to the Arab League collective security pact.

Egypt, Syria, Lebanon, Saudi Arabia and Yemen had signed the League's collective security pact in Cairo June 17, 1950. Jordan finally adhered to it Feb. 16, 1952. No report of Iraq's adherence circulated in the West, but in an official statement Jan. 18, 1955, the Iraqi government professed itself a signatory.

Under the arrangement's terms, an attack on any member of the Arab League was to be considered an attack on all members, obliging them to aid in defending the state under attack. Since both Iraq and Egypt were members of the League, any aggression on Iraq would require Egypt to provide military assistance. Hence, the operation of a mutual security treaty between Iraq and Turkey might obligate Egypt to go to the aid of Iraq after Turkey, a non-Arab state, became subject to foreign aggression. According to the Egyptian view, expressed by Maj. Salem, an Iraqi-Turkish mutual security treaty would in effect commit Egypt to the defense of Turkey in the event of war, thereby also allying Egypt with Turkey's Western allies, the U.S. and Britain.

It was Egypt's position, then, that no member of the Arab League had the right to make an alliance with a non-Arab state. In the event of such an alliance as the one planned between Iraq and Turkey, Egypt was ready to leave the Arab League and sign a new mutual defense treaty with all other sovereign Arab states except Iraq.

Over Egyptian objections, Iraq Feb. 25, 1955 signed with Turkey the "Turkish-Iraqi Mutual Cooperation Treaty," soon referred to simply as the Baghdad Pact. The Pact contained these provisions:

Article 1. Consistent with Article 51 of the UN Charter, the parties will cooperate for their security and defense. Such measures as they agree to take to give effect to this cooperation may form the subject of special agreements with each other.

Article 2. In order to ensure the realization and effect application of the cooperation provided for in Article 1, the competent authorities of the parties will determine the measures to be taken as soon as the present pact enters into force. These measures will become operative as soon as they have been approved by the governments of the parties.

Article 3. The parties undertake to refrain from any interference whatsoever in each other's internal affairs. They will settle any disputes between themselves in a peaceful way in accordance with the UN Charter.

Article 4. The parties declare that the dispositions of the present pact are not in contradiction with any of the international obligations contracted by either of them with any 3d state or states. They do not derogate from, and cannot be interpreted as derogating from, the said international obligations. The parties undertake not to enter into any international obligation incompatible with the present pact.

Article 5. This pact shall be open for accession to any member-state of the Arab League or any other state actively concerned with the security and peace in this region and which is fully recognized by both of the parties. Accession shall come into force from the date on which the instrument of accession of the state concerned is deposited with the Ministry of Foreign Affairs of Iraq. Any acceding state . . . may conclude special agreements, in accordance with Article 1, with one or more States parties to the present pact. The competent authorities of any acceding State may determine measures in accordance with Article 2. These measures will become operative as soon as they have been approved by the governments of the parties concerned.

Article 6. A permanent council at ministerial level will be set up to function within the framework of the purposes of this pact when at least 4 Powers become parties to the pact. The council will draw up its own rule of procedure.

Article 7. This pact remains in force for a period of 5 years, renewable for further 5-year periods. Any contracting party may withdraw from the pact by notifying the other parties in writing of its desire to do so 5 months before the expiration of any of the above-mentioned periods, in which case the pact remains valid for the other parties.

Article 8. This pact shall be ratified by the parties and ratifications shall be exchanged at Ankara as soon as possible. It shall come into force from the date of the exchange of ratifications.

In a correspondance designed to elucidate further the provisions of Articles 1 and 2, Turkish Premier Adnan Menderes and Iraqi Premier Nuri as-Said publicly affirmed that "this pact will enable our 2 countries to cooperate in resisting any aggression directed against either of them and that, in order to ensure the maintenance of peace and security in the Middle East region, we have agreed to work in close cooperation for effecting the carrying out of the UN resolutions concerning Palestine."

Menderes later added in the Turkish National Assembly: "We see in Turkey, as in Iraq, full unanimity concerning the usefulness and necessity of the pact. The only shadow comes from the opposition of some Arab countries, but we do not lose hope and we are not irritated by unjust attacks. We want to collaborate with all Arab countries, including Egypt."

Speaking in the Iraqi Chamber of Deputies, Nuri as-Said formally invited Britain, the U.S., Iran, Pakistan and Afghanistan to join the Baghdad Pact. In Apr. 1955 Britain did adhere to the pact (terminating the earlier Anglo-Iraqi Treaty of 1930) and evacuated its troops from the Habbaniya and Shuayba airfields, thereby greatly increasing its popularity and influence in Iraq. Soon Iraq and Pakistan also adhered, and the U.S. began sending military equipment and missions to pact members.

U.S. Deputy State Undersecy. Loy W. Henderson said at the opening session of the Baghdad Pact Council in Teheran Apr. 16 that the U.S. would join in the alliance's economic and military aid programs. He did not refer to invitations to full U.S. membership extended Apr. 16 by Premiers Nuri as-Said of Iraq and Hussein Ala of Iran. Henderson, chief U.S. observer at the METO Council meeting, implied that Egyptian opposition to the pact weighed in the U.S. decision not to accept membership. "It is our sincere desire to retain close, friendly and effective ties with other nations in the area," he said.

Preconference reports from Teheran Apr. 14 had indicated that pact members were pressing for U.S. funds to cover projects involving more than one nation, rather than single-nation aid allotments common hitherto. Eisenhower Administration sources said in Washington Apr. 15 that special economic aid planned for the METO nations would be geared to foreign aid requests than before Congress, which included $100 million for a regional Middle East fund.

The METO Council Apr. 17 approved plans to pool police resources in a combined drive against subversion in member states. A communiqué issued in Teheran Apr. 18 said that the METO Council had voted to accept U.S. participation in the pact's Economic Committee as proposed by Henderson Apr. 16. The U.S. delegation Apr. 19 agreed to establish a military liaison office at METO permanent head-quarters, take part in work of the Anti-Subversion Committee and share the cost of a METO secretariat. (Washington reports Apr. 5 had said that International Cooperation Administration officials had requested the doubling of aid appropriations for the Middle East, with most of the $884,318,000 sought for Middle Eastern aid to be earmarked for Baghdad Pact nations. Britain was reported Apr. 10 to have offered in the Economic Council in Teheran to provide $700,000.)

Despite his official neutrality, Premier Nasser soon began to strengthen his ties with the Communist bloc. Nasser Aug. 9 accepted an invitation to visit the USSR in 1956. Egypt also announced Aug. 9 that Communist China had placed an order for more than 28 million pounds of cotton, valued at about $9.8 million, in addition to normal purchases of 17.1 million pounds made earlier in the season (ending Aug. 31).

Nasser announced Sept. 27, 1955 that Czechoslovakia had signed an agreement the previous week to exchange all kinds of Czechoslovak-manufactured arms in return for Egyptian cotton. Egypt, meanwhile, informed Britain that Egypt had decided to accept a Soviet offer of arms aid. Speaking at a military exhibition in Cairo, Nasser said: The Czechoslovak agreement was on "a purely commercial basis" and "will not create Russian or Czechoslovak influence in the Middle East or Egypt." "We will never attack or threaten anyone else, but the Western powers have refused to give us arms for defense." Egypt had first applied to the West for the weaponry, "but all we got were demands." Egypt had rejected offers of Western arms "at the expense of our freedom," and the U.S. and Britain were annoyed "at our success in procuring arms."

U.S. sources at UN headquarters in New York said Sept. 27 that the U.S. had rejected an Egyptian request in June for jet bombers, heavy tanks and artillery and naval craft because the U.S. feared that such heavy equipment would alter the balance of forces in the Middle East. In 1954 Egypt had declined to sign a mutual-security agreement with the U.S. under which U.S. arms could not be used for aggression.

U.S. State Secy. John Foster Dulles and British Foreign Secy. Harold Macmillan asserted in a joint statement in New York Sept. 28 that the U.S. and Britain "have for some time been in close consultation with each other [and] with other governments" regarding "arms supply policies in the Middle East." The U.S. and Britain were in "complete harmony" on the subject and based their policies "on the desire, on one hand, to enable the various countries to provide for internal security and for their defense, and on the other, to avoid an arms race which would inevitably increase the tensions in the area."

A British spokesman said that the USSR was included in the reference to "other governments" and that the joint statement was made "to correct the false impression that the U.S. is going to offer arms to Egypt to forestall the USSR in supplying them." The spokesman also denied reports that Britain had protested "such action by the U.S."

George V. Allen, U.S. Assistant State Secretary for Near Eastern, South Asian and African affairs, left Washington by air for Cairo Sept. 28 for talks with Nasser. (He also was scheduled to visit Lebanon and Greece "to discuss current problems.")

State Secy. John Foster Dulles, who returned to Washington from New York that day, said Allen's trip was "only a more or less routine visit." Dulles said he had discussed the sale of arms to Egypt in a talk with Soviet Foreign Min. Vyacheslav M. Molotov in New York Sept. 27 "as part of a general review of world matters." Dulles said at his news conference Oct. 4 that he had told Molotov that, "from the standpoint of U.S. relations with the USSR, such delivery of arms would not contribute to relaxing tensions." In a press statement, Dulles said: "It is difficult to be critical of countries which, feeling themselves endangered, seek the arms which they sincerely believe they need for defense. On the other hand, I doubt very much that, under the conditions which prevail in the [Middle East] area, it is possible for any country to get security through an arms race."

Dulles said Oct. 4 that there was a "better understanding" between Egypt and the U.S. as the result of talks in Cairo between Nasser and Allen. But Dulles also said that "we have no reason to believe" Egypt would not carry through its arrangement with Czechoslovakia. He declined to say whether the U.S. might provide arms to Israel to balance Soviet-bloc arms to Egypt.

Nasser, in an interview with Kenneth Love of the *N.Y. Times* Oct. 5, said that Egypt had informed the U.S. in June that it would seek Soviet-bloc arms if the U.S. would not supply them. (U.S. State Department officials said they had heard of no such alternative in June.) Nasser said the U.S. apparently had thought Egypt was "bluffing," but "I needed the arms and I had no alternative but to supply myself from the East." Nasser said he had learned through sources in Western capitals of arms Israel had "contracted to receive in the next 10 months." Remarking that Israel had bought French Mystère jet fighters, Nasser said: "So now we will be meeting Mystères with MiGs. This is better than meeting Mystères with nothing."

Nasser had told a graduating class at the Egyptian military academy Oct. 2 that Egypt had intercepted British and French documents listing Israeli purchases of heavy arms from the U.S. and Britain. Nasser said Egypt had a document stating that Britain believed that Egypt had no aggressive intentions but doubted that Israel had similar peaceful aims. Nasser called the West's arms policy in the Middle East "a big deception." (British and French officials declined comment on Nasser's statements.)

The Baghdad Pact, seen as essentially a cold war response to Soviet postwar penetration of the Mideast, was considered not unlike the earlier Marshall Plan in Turkey and Greece. The Pact's concept was simple: to range a "northern tier" of anti-Communist states all the way from Greece to Pakistan. The new cold war line of defense would include not only the adherents to the Pact—Turkey, Iraq, Iran and Pakistan—but also other states with traditional ties to the West, such as Greece and Jordan.

Apparently, the British Foreign Office had believed that the signing of the Anglo-Egyptian Suez agreement in July 1954 would bring Egypt close enough to Britain to allay Egyptian suspicions of a new Anglo-American bloc of influence in the Mideast. The new treaty, however, isolated the militarily strongest state in the area, Israel. Particularly galling to Israel was the alliance of Turkey, a state hitherto friendly to Israel, with an Arab state, Iraq—especially as Turkey began to follow, at least in public pronouncements, the Arab line on Palestine. The Israeli Foreign Ministry Feb. 26, 1955 described the pro-Western Pact as "hostile to Israel" and "Likely to encourage Arab belligerency towards Israel and to foment aggressive Arab ambitions." Israel Mar. 3 officially asked Britain and the U.S. to clarify the "anti-Israel aspects" of the Baghdad Pact.

By this time Israeli-Soviet relations, which had been amicable at the time of the creation of the Jewish state in 1948, had deteriorated disastrously after the revelation in 1952 of alleged anti-Semitic developments in the USSR. Israel began to acquire arms as rapidly as possible from a 3d party—France, which still had a strong Mediterranean sphere of influence extending from Lebanon to Morocco, as well as a strong and rapidly growing military aircraft industry.

Bandung Conference

One of Nasser's declared aims was to strengthen the ties between Egypt and other nations that were neutral or tended toward *de facto* neutrality in the cold war. He pursued this aim from the Balkans to Indonesia.

A conference of Afro-Asian nations was held in Bandung, Indonesia, Apr. 18–24, 1955. The Bandung Conference, organized by Indonesia (then a neutral power under Pres. Sukarno), brought together representatives from 28 African and Asian countries. Concern was expressed over 3 major issues: (1) the increasing pressure of large pro-Western alliances such as the Southeast Asia Treaty Organization (SEATO) and the Baghdad Pact (METO); (2) Communist China, which, it was felt, should be accorded more recognition as a new world power; and (3) the persistence of colonialism, especially French colonialism in Algeria. Whereas the USSR was censured for its role in eastern Europe, Communist China's prestige was significantly boosted by the Bandung Conference. The Egyptian and Communist Chinese governments tended to view each other favorably in 1955 and later during the Suez crisis of 1956–7.

Israeli-Egyptian Antagonism Intensifies

The continuing mutual distrust between Egypt and Israel resulted in active antagonism again in the summer of 1954, but only after Egypt's takeover of the Canal Zone did matters escalate into an unmistakable crisis.

Tensions were brought to a head by 2 incidents. In the first, the Israeli freighter *Bat Galim* attempted Sept. 28 to pass through the Canal in a test of Egyptian intentions and was detained by the Egyptians. In the 2d incident, an Israeli military unit of about 2 platoons entered the Gaza Strip Feb. 28, 1955, surprised an Egyptian garrison and ambushed a truckload of troops brought up to the garrison's relief. 42 Egyptians were killed and 31 wounded; Israeli casualties were 8 killed and 13 wounded. Israel termed the raid an act of retaliation for earlier Egyptian provocations and said that the Israeli unit involved was pursuing an Egyptian unit that had crossed the border and fired on an Israeli patrol.

Despite Israeli protests, Egypt kept the freighter and did

not release the crew until Jan. 1, 1955. In a UN Security Council debate in New York Dec. 7, 1954, Egyptian Amb. Omar Loutfi announced that Egypt would continue to refuse Israel passage through the Canal. He justified this position with the assertion that Egypt was entitled to such a course by a self-defense provision of the Constantinople Convention of 1888.

Units of Egyptian and Israeli forces had become involved in a number of shooting incidents beginning Sept. 28, 1954 along the Gaza Strip and Negev Desert border areas. Mutual alarm over the situation led both sides Oct. 4 to agree to the UN's revival of the Israeli-Egyptian Mixed Armistice Commission, which subsequently looked into such incidents late in October as the sabotage of an Israeli water pipeline near Mefalsim in the Negev and 2 shooting episodes in the Gaza Strip. After the appointment of Maj. Gen. Francois X. Giacomaggi of France as the Mixed Armistice Commission's chairman Dec. 3, the 2 sides agreed to cancel 30 Egyptian and 20 Israeli complaints as settled. The commission Dec. 13 censured Egypt for 6 other violations and Israel for one.

In the first reported border incident between the 2 countries in 1955, an Israeli soldier was killed and 2 other wounded Jan. 21 in an Egyptian attack on an Israeli military outpost in the Negev. In the 2d such incident, an Israeli tractor driver and 2 Arabs were killed Jan. 24 in a *fedayin** raid from the Gaza Strip. These 2 incidents led to a shooting skirmish between Egyptian and Israeli forces Feb. 1. Egypt complained Feb. 2 that an Egyptian soldier had been killed and 2 others wounded by an Israeli patrol that had crossed the truce line in the Gaza area. Both Israel and Egypt were censured by the commission Feb. 3 for the affair.

4 Egyptian soldiers were wounded in Rafa Feb. 22 by Israeli mortar fire; Israel insisted that its forces had fired after

---

*Suicide squads, commandos; usually Palestinian Arab guerrilla organizations in current parlance.

Egyptian soldiers had violated the truce line and fired on an Israeli patrol inside Israel. In 2 incidents reported Feb. 26, an Israeli cyclist was ambushed by *fedayin* raiders and an Israeli patrol killed another infiltrator from the Gaza Strip on Israeli territory.

Nasser apparently resolved to assume a full war footing after the Israeli raid Feb. 28 in the Gaza Strip. Iraqi Acting Foreign Min. Burhanuddin Bashayan assured the Egyptian government Mar. 2 of Iraq's complete willingness to furnish any and all military aid requested by Egypt, some of whose ministers had alleged that Iraq had incited the Israeli attack. Nasser warned in Cairo Mar. 3 that his country was prepared to give the Israelis "a harsh lesson" if "they want a battle." He said Egypt was "not counting on the Security Council" because it "has helped the Israelis to attain their objectives."

The Egyptian-Israeli Mixed Armistice Commission in Jerusalem decided by a 2–1 vote Mar. 6 that the Israeli army had committed an act of "brutal aggression" by its "pre-arranged and planned attack, ordered by Israeli authorities," against an Egyptian army camp in the Gaza Strip Feb. 28. The commission's UN chairman, Gen. Giacomaggi of France, and its Egyptian delegates outvoted the Israeli delegation in adopting the resolution to condemn Israel. Giacomaggi's abstention on Israel's countercharge that the Gaza battle grew out of an Egyptian ambush of an Israeli patrol Feb. 28 had the effect of defeating it. Israel announced an appeal to UN Truce Supervision headquarters in Jerusalem.

An Israeli spokesman Mar. 1 had listed 40 armed encounters, 27 Egyptian raids into Israel (in which 7 persons died and 24 were wounded), 26 condemnations of Egypt by the commission for these raids, several instances of sabotage (including the destruction of Israeli water pipelines) and no Israeli incursions into Egypt since Sept. 1954.

The UN Security Council had agreed unanimously Mar. 4 to recall Canadian Maj. Gen. Eedson L. M. Burns, chief Palestine truce supervisor, from Jerusalem to report on the

Gaza incident. All Council delegates except the USSR's indicated in statements Mar. 4 their belief that Israel was to blame for the battle. Selim Sarper of Turkey, Council president during March, called on the Israelis and Egyptians to abstain from further fighting so as to avoid a possible major flareup of violence in the Middle East. (16 wives and children of UN truce supervisory personnel were moved from Gaza to the Arab section of Jerusalem Mar. 5 for fear that they might be injured by anti-UN Arab demonstrators in the Gaza sector.)

The Israeli-Egyptian Mixed Armistice Commission Mar. 7 upheld Israeli complaints that Egypt had provoked 2 incidents that had preceded the Gaza raid: the killing of an Israeli in Rehevot Feb. 25 by 3 armed Egyptian border violators and Egyptian troops' firing Feb. 22 on an Israeli patrol that was questioning a large group of Arab civilian grass-cutters who had crossed the Gaza Strip frontier. An Israeli patrol was rebuked by the commission for opening fire on an Egyptian army post across the border Feb. 22.

Gen. Burns Mar. 11 rejected the Israeli appeal of the Mixed-Armistice Commission's decision that Israel was to blame for the Feb. 28 attack near Gaza. U.S. State Secy. John Foster Dulles indicated Mar. 15 that the Gaza incident had caused the U.S. to postpone a pledge of aid to Israel in the event of an Arab attack. Israel was condemned by unanimous Security Council vote Mar. 29 for the Feb. 28 attack. The U.S. joined other Council nations in rejecting Israel's argument that the attack was a justifiable retaliation for harassment by Egyptian infiltrators. Council members also deplored a raid Mar. 24 on an Israeli wedding party in Patish, for which the armistice commission had held Egypt responsible Mar. 27. An Israeli farmhouse in the Negev 7 miles from Egyptian-held territory had been bombed Mar. 15 and one man wounded by attackers thought to have come from the Gaza Strip.

Israel charged before the Security Council Apr. 6, 1955

that Egypt had started a new series of border incidents that threatened the 6-year truce Israeli authorities charged that Egyptian forces had loosed a 2-hour mortar barrage on Israel's settlement of Nahal Oz in the Negev Apr. 3, killing 2 Israeli soldiers and wounding 16 (2 Egyptian soliders were also killed). But the Egyptian-Israeli Mixed Armistice Commission condemned both Israel and Egypt Apr. 9 for the battle.

Burns warned both countries Apr. 10 that the Gaza incidents had "resulted in a deteriorating situation [that] can and should be ended." Israel asked the Security Council Apr. 11 to speed consideration of its complaints against "Egyptian assaults." The Council had suspended consideration of Israel's latest complaint pending a report from Burns.

Mortal violations of the Israeli-Egyptian truce continued to occur, and the 2 sides fought a 2-hour battle near Kisufim May 21.

Israel and Egypt were urged by UN Secy. Gen. Dag Hammarskjold in appeals he sent June 5, 1955 to exercise restraint in the Gaza area and to support Burns' efforts to reduce tension. Egypt June 6 announced its rejection of a UN proposal that Egyptian and Israeli officials negotiate directly, instead of through the UN armistice agency, to end Gaza clashes. U.S. Amb.-to-UN Henry Cabot Lodge Jr., acting as Security Council president for June, sent letters to both countries June 7 urging that they cooperate "promptly" with efforts by Burns to restore order in the Gaza area.

Israeli Premier Moshe Sharett said June 17 that Israel would welcome the establishment of a kilometer-wide mine zone along the Gaza Strip, fenced in by barbed wire and patroled by joint Israeli-Egyptian units, as Gen. Burns had recommended Mar. 17 to the Security Council. Sharett maintained that only such a drastic arrangement could interdict the area to Arab marauders. His statement represented a reply to a proposal by Egyptian Premier Nasser June 5 that a demilitarized zone be established around the Gaza Strip.

With Burns as chairman, Egyptian-Israeli meetings were begun in Gaza June 28 in an effort to negotiate an end of Gaza-Strip fighting. But the talks were suspended June 29 in failure to reach agreement on an agenda. The talks were resumed July 6 on the Egyptian-Israeli border after the conferees agreed on an agenda proposed by Burns. An Israeli delegate said that the agenda was similar to the one rejected the previous week by the Egyptians. Egypt and Israel reached agreement on a preamble for a security arrangement July 14.

The talks were adjourned for 3 weeks while Israeli representative Yosef Tekoah and Jordanian representative Hazem Nusseibeh conferred on the renewal of the Jerusalem military commanders' communications agreement and its extension to include the entire frontier between Israel and Jordan. Israel and Jordan reached such an agreement Aug. 4.

Meanwhile, Israeli Defense Min. David Ben-Gurion July 24 publicly offered to meet with Nasser or "any Egyptian statesman" in an effort to help pacify the Egyptian-Israeli border. His overture was apparently ignored, and saboteurs July 25 demolished an Israeli waterpipe junction near Kisufim.

Egyptian-Israeli truce talks on the Gaza Strip were resumed Aug. 8 but became bogged down over Egyptian insistence on retaining the UN as an intermediary in the talks. Israel Aug. 15 reported that an Israeli patrol had driven off Egyptian armed infiltrators found 8 miles inside Israeli territory.

Egypt announced Aug. 24 that it was quitting the talks with Israel because of Israeli "aggression" against an Egyptian post near Mefalsim in the Gaza Strip Aug. 22. Egypt's decision was given to Burns, who was visiting Cairo to discuss details of the deadlocked talks. Israel and Egypt accused each other of provoking the Aug. 22 incident in order to sabotage the Gaza talks. Israeli officials said their troops had crossed the armistice line and stormed the Egyptian post after Egyptians had attacked a routine Israeli patrol-convoy of 3 vehicles. One Egyptian was killed. The breakdown of Gaza Strip peace talks Aug. 24 was followed by a week of Israeli-Egyptian fighting. Jet fighters clashed over Gaza Aug. 29 in what was believed to be the first such incident since the 1949 armistice. Israel said 4 Egyptian planes had been driven off after entering Israeli air space, while Egypt said 2 Israeli planes had dived over an Egyptian town in the Gaza zone.

Egypt agreed Aug. 31, 1955 to a cease-fire proposed by Gen. Burns. Less than 24 hours later an Israeli army unit raided the Khan Yunis military camp 4 miles inside the Gaza Strip, killing 25 *fedayin*, 10 Egyptian soldiers and 19 others and wounding 50 persons in reprisal for terrorist raids. Israeli casualties amounted to one soldier killed and 8 wounded. 2 Israeli jets intercepted 4 Egyptian ones north of the Gaza Strip Sept. 1 and shot down one. The Israeli Foreign Ministry asserted that Israeli troops had attacked an Egyptian military camp that had been a base for terrorist squads that had killed 15 Israelis since Aug. 25. Israel called on Burns to "obtain the assurance of the Egyptian government that it accepts full responsibility for these acts and that it is ready to give guarantees" for an immediate end to hostilities.

The U.S. Sept. 1 indorsed calls for a cease-fire. State Secy. Dulles and State Undersecy. Herbert Hoover Jr. said they expected both sides to be able to reach an understanding–which they did Sept. 4. The Sept. 4 agreement was broken the same night when an Israeli patrol entered Egyptian territory between Khan Yunis and Rafa; at least 2 Israelis were killed in shooting which followed. The Israeli army announced Sept. 5 that the patrol had "lost its way and crossed the line" by mistake.

Israelis and Egyptians met in Jerusalem Sept. 5 at a meeting of the Mixed Armistice Commission, but the 15-hour session produced no meeting of minds on how the Gaza Strip clashes had begun Aug. 22. The UN Security Council in New York Sept. 8 approved, by 11–0 vote, a U.S.-British-French resolution directing both sides to cooperate on achieving the tighter border controls recommended by Gen. Burns. The 3 powers acted after Burns Sept. 5 had submitted a report to the UN on 10 days of clashes that had caused at least 70 deaths. Burns recommended the establishment of a kilo-meter-wide (1,093 yards) "effective physical barrier" be-tween Israeli and Egyptian forces as the "only" way to avoid further clashes.

U.S. Pres. Dwight D. Eisenhower's Administration had fol-lowed the Gaza Strip strife with increasing concern. State Secy. Dulles had made the U.S. diplomatic stand on the issue of boundaries one of the points of a program for "stability, tranquility and progress in the Middle East" that he had pro-posed Aug. 26 in a speech before the Council on Foreign Re-lations in New York. He said: As fixed by the 1949 armis-tice agreements, Israel's boundaries "were not designed to be permanent frontiers in every respect"; they partly "reflected the status of the fighting at the moment." "In spite of con-flicting claims and sentiments, I believe it is possible to find a way of reconciling the vital interests of all the parties. The U.S. would be willing to help in the search for a solution . . . ." "At a time when a great effort is being made to ease the ten-sion which has long prevailed between the Soviet and Western worlds, can we not hope that a similar spirit should prevail in the Middle East? That is our plea."

Dulles said in his news conference Aug. 30 that he had re-ceived unofficial reports that the USSR had offered military equipment to Egypt and other Arab countries. He said such action would not contribute to the easing of tension discussed at the Big 4 summit meeting in Geneva. He said that the U.S. and Britain had urged Israel and Egypt within the past 48 hours to avoid force in the Gaza area.

The Middle East's reaction to Dulles' proposals took a month to become clear. The first Arab comment came in a Radio Cairo broadcast of Aug. 29 that denounced the "Dulles plan" as an attempt "to deliver the Arabs to the mercy of Is-rael." The Egyptian Foreign Ministry announced Aug. 31 that representatives of the Arab states would meet in Cairo to discuss the U.S. plan after special U.S. Amb. Eric A. Johnston, then in Cairo, completed a Middle Eastern tour.

Israel's first official reaction to the U.S. proposals came Sept. 6, when Israel asked the U.S. State Department for an explanation of "frontier adjustment" and other details. Israel called the U.S. plan "constructive." Israeli Premier Moshe Sharett said in an interview with the British United Press Sept. 11 that Israel was willing to discuss certain mutual border adjustments with its Arab neighbors but was not prepared to make unilateral concessions of territory, particularly in the Negev. In Sharett's view, Dulles had appeared to "make the fixing of boundaries a condition that must come before the conclusion of the defense treaties, which he himself regards as urgently needed." But the existing armistice lines, "whatever technical or other demerits they possess, have at least the inestimable advantage of being agreed upon, whereas any agreed correction of these lines in the near future is highly problematical, if not illusory," Sharett observed. He said that "the Negev was of particular importance to Israel both for its mineral wealth and for the "supreme value" of Eilat (Elath), its southern port on the Gulf of Aqaba (which the Israelis called the Gulf of Eilat). "That foothold on the Red Sea is of far-reaching significance to Israel and invests with the same quality of decisive value any part of the land bridge between it and the main body of the state's territory," Sharett declared.

Israeli Amb.-to-U.S. Abba Eban Sept. 11, with the authority of Premier Sharett, commended Dulles' "realistic and imaginative approach" to the Middle East problem but said that it was "acutely discouraging to read Mr. Dulles' paragraph on frontiers." Eban maintained that the Israeli government considered the existing truce lines between Israel and the Arab states as having "more solid attributes" than Dulles' speech had indicated. The lines had existed by international agreement and arrangement for 7 years "in recognized integrity" even though hostilities had occurred from time to time; they were "vastly superior to any imaginary line which does not have the tradition of stability or the virtue of reality," he said. Both Israel and the Arab states had agreed not to change the lines except by agreement. None of the parties had invoked the armistice procedure for change; all were more likely to prefer the existing lines to a quest for a new agreement, Eban said. Anyhow, "there can be no question of unilateral concessions by Israel to the Arab states. . . ."

Eban argued that what could be "a fitting subject for the tripartite agreement . . . [of May 25,] 1950 [between the U.S., Britain and France—against the violation of frontiers and armistice lines] cannot be an unfitting subject for a treaty engagement today." Moreover, even the advocates of a new boundary agreement did not propose any drastic alterations, he asserted. "How, then, could an adjustment, which admittedly would be only minor in character, be so momentous as to make all the difference between the application of a treaty solution and its denial?" Eban asked. There was "nothing intrinsically tense" about the shape of the existing truce lines; tension would result rather from the relationship between the governments on either side of the line, he maintained.

It was "the foundation of Israel's position," Eban said, that "we will explore every road of progress towards the liquidation of conflict between the Arab states and Israel. While being ready for mutual adjustments of the boundary line, we shall accept no unilateral territorial concessions for ourselves, just as we have demanded nothing from our neighbors. Mr. Sharett's statement on the Negev is an absolutely fundamental and immutable part of our policy. Now that there is an important willingness in principle for the leaders of the United States to engage themselves by a treaty to thwart aggression in our area, we urgently advocate that this priceless stability be conferred upon our region now and not be lost through association with unattainable conditions." Eban declared that Israel and the U.S. had drawn closer together in this "memorable discussion" but that much work remained to be done before the promise incorporated in Dulles' statement could effect a lasting peace and genuine security for the Middle East.

Israel, in a letter to the UN Security Council Sept. 28, 1955, protested Egypt's ban on Israel's use of the Suez Canal as violating international law, the 1949 Egyptian-Israeli armistice and previous Council resolutions. Israel said it would protect its right to free passage "at whatever time and by whatever methods" it deemed necessary. Israel was building a port at Eilat on the Gulf of Aqaba to stimulate trade with East Africa and the Far East. But Egypt, Jordan and Saudi Arabia also bordered on the gulf, and Egyptian guns dominated its only navigable entrance. Israeli Premier-designate David Ben-Gurion had announced Sept. 25 that Israel would seek talks with Egypt on Aqaba when Eilat port facilities were nearing completion. He said the completion of the port would be the "first job" of his new government. (Ben-Gurion had been called on by Israeli Pres. Izhak Ben-Zvi Aug. 18 to form a new government.)

Israeli Amb.-to-U.S. Eban, speaking in the UN General Assembly's general debate Oct. 3, called on the big powers to avoid disturbing the military balance in the Middle East. Quoting from Soviet Foreign Min. Vyacheslav M. Molotov's statement in the UN Sept. 23 that the UN's primary objective must be the ending of arms races, Eban said: "It is unfortunate that a few days later an armament race was stimulated in the Middle East." Eban said that the purchase of arms was a sovereign nation's right but that there also were political and moral implications. He asked whether "Israel, or indeed any state in like circumstances," would be expected "to wait passively while a hostile neighbor, asserting or practicing a state of war, strengthened himself for the decisive blow." Eban was followed to the UN rostrum by Syrian chief delegate Ahmad el-Shukhairy, who declared: "We accept no intervention, no observation, from any side in the exercise of our right to build up our defense." Conceding that excessive arms threatened peace, he said that to be under-armed invited aggression. He suggested an international arms pool, under UN control, to effect a just distribution of arms among the "haves" and "have-nots."

Israel and Egypt had withdrawn their forces from the demilitarized zone of El Auja in the Negev Oct. 2 in compliance with an agreement worked out by UN truce chief Burns. Israel had entered the 95-square-mile triangle Sept. 21, charging that Egypt had 2 military positions in the zone. 2 Egyptians were wounded as the Israelis moved in. Israel claimed sovereignty over the area; Egypt and said neither side had sovereignty. An Egyptian force Oct. 26 drove Israeli border police from the zone, killing one Israeli, wounding 3 Israelis and capturing 2.

An Israeli army unit Oct. 27 raided Kuntilla on the Sinai Peninsula well inside the Egyptian frontier, killing 10 Egyptian soldiers, taking 20 prisoner and destroying 17 army trucks.

Ben-Gurion returned to office as premier Nov. 2, 1955 and told the Knesset in a general policy address: "The forays from the Gaza Strip alone caused 153 Israeli casualties in killed and wounded during the first 9 months of 1955. The Egyptian representatives at the UN have openly declared that a state of war continues between Egypt and Israel. The government of Egypt has violated basic international law governing the freedom of shipping through Suez, on which there was also a specific resolution of the Security Council. Thus Egypt now seeks to seal the Red Sea route against Israeli vessels. . . . This one-sided war will have to stop, for it cannot remain one-sided forever. The government of Israel is ready faithfully to respect the armistice agreements in all their terms and details, preserving them in the letter and the spirit. But this duty is also binding on the other party. An agreement which is violated by the other side will also not be binding on us. If the armistice lines are opened by them to saboteurs and murderers, they will not be found closed to our defenders. If our rights are assailed by acts of violence on land or sea, we shall reserve freedom of action to defend those rights in the most effective manner. We seek peace—but not suicide."

The most severe Israeli-Arab fighting since the 1949 armistice broke out at the strategic El Sabha post in the El Auja-Nitsana demilitarized zone during the night of Nov. 2–3. The post had been claimed by both Israel and Egypt. The Egyptians said the post changed hands twice during the night, and both sides claimed that they were in control of it Nov. 3. The Israelis said that they had killed 50 Egyptians and captured 40; the Egyptians said 70 of their men were killed or missing. An Israeli spokesman denied an Egyptian claim of 200 Israeli dead. (Israeli casualties were put later at 5 killed and 8 wounded.) Mortar and artillery fire continued through Nov. 4, but a UN official said that "nothing serious happened."

(Israeli and Egyptian forces also clashed along the Gaza Strip border Nov. 4 and 5, but no casualties were reported.)

Nasser told a *N.Y. Times* reporter in Cairo Nov. 3 that Israel's forces "attacked ours, thus determining the answer" to Ben-Gurion, who had asked Nov. 2 for Israeli-Arab negotiations. Nasser said: "Hardly 10 hours passed since . . . [Ben-Gurion] posed to the world as a peace-loving man before he ordered his troops to march on El Sabha inside Egyptian territory."

In New York Nov. 3, UN Secy. Gen. Dag Hammarskjöld expressed "grave concern" to Israel over its action in the outbreak. He submitted truce proposals to both sides without disclosing them publicly. The proposals were submitted after Hammarskjöld conferred with representatives of the U.S., Britain, and France and with UN truce chief Burns, who then returned to Jerusalem.

U.S. Asst. State Secy. George V. Allen conferred separately in Washington Nov. 5 with Israeli Amb. Eban and Egyptian Amb. Ahmed Hussein, both of whom assured Allen that their respective countries had no aggressive plans. A State Department statement issued after the talks deplored the "resort to force for the settlement of disputes" and declared that

the U.S. "strongly supports the UN's efforts to acheive settlement by peaceful means, especially the current proposals of
Gen. Burns." The State Department noted reports that UN
observers under Burns had been "prevented from carrying out
their assigned functions." The U.S. asked that these observers
"have full liberty to perform their peaceful functions."

It was reported in Washington Nov. 7 that the U.S. had
decided to sell Israel "significant" amounts of arms. Israel's
request for U.S. arms was reported Nov. 17 to total less than
$40 million, or substantially less than half the value of Egyp-
tian arms purchases from the Soviet bolc. Israel reportedly
has asked for at least 40 late-model jet planes, antisubmarine
vessels, heavy tanks, antitank guns and antiaircraft weapons.

Israeli Foreign Min. Moshe Sharett told the National Press
Club in Washington Nov. 21 that Israel, like "any other nation," would take arms from the Soviet bloc if its survival
were at stake in "a very tight corner." But, he added, the
question "hardly arises," since the U.S. was under a "moral
obligation" to counterbalance Communist arms sales to Egypt.
Sharett pledged that Israel would not "launch an offensive
war no matter what the provocation might be." Peace in the
Middle East must be based on "maintenance of the *status
quo*," he said.

Meanwhile, the U.S. and Britain had begun actively seeking to bring about a settlement of the Israeli-Arab border disputes. U.S. State Undersecy. Herbert Hoover Jr. read at a
press conference in Denver Nov. 9 a statement on the Middle
East by Pres. Eisenhower, who was recuperating there from a
heart attack. The President said that "recent developments
have made it . . . imperative that a settlement be found." The
statement reaffirmed U.S. support for the UN's truce efforts,
which had "already contributed so markedly to minimize
violence in the area." "I hope that other nations of the world
will cooperate in this endeavor, thereby contributing significantly to world peace," it continued. The repeated hostilities
"inevitably retard our search for world peace," Eisenhower's

statement said. "Insecurity in one region is bound to affect the world as a whole." The statement said: "While we continue willing to consider requests for arms needed for legitimate self-defense, we do not intend to contribute to an arms competition in the Near East because we do not think such a race would be in the true interest of any of the participants." The U.S.-British-French declaration of May 1950 "still remains our policy."

An offer to mediate was made Nov. 9 by British Prime Min. Sir Anthony Eden, who said that he and his government "are available to render any service" in bringing the Israelis and Arabs to an agreement. Speaking before the annual Lord Mayor's banquet in London, Eden said "the stark truth" was that both sides "must make some compromise" if they "want to win a peace which is in both their interests." Eden noted that the Arabs "take their stand on the 1947 and other UN resolutions. . . . They said they would be willing to open discussions with Israel from that basis." The Israelis, he said, stand "on the later armistice agreement of 1949 and on the present territories which they occupy." Eden asked if the gap was "so wide that no negotiation is possible to bridge it." "If there is anything, anything that we can do to help, we would gladly do it for the sake of peace." Eden expressed regret that the USSR had injected into the "delicate" Middle East situation "a new element of danger" by delivering weapons "to one side only."

Israeli Foreign Min. Sharett told U.S. State Secy. Dulles Dec. 6 that Israel was willing to discuss some "minor mutual adjustments" of borders but that Israel took an "irrevocable stand" against making territorial concessions. Sharett told newsmen later that he had told Dulles that he saw no improvement of peace prospects in the Middle East, but "if there is willingness on the Arab side then there will be peace."

Israeli sources in Washington disclosed Dec. 19 that Israel, in response to U.S. State Department urging, had recapitulated previous offers of concessions to draw up a 7-point

peace plan: (1) Israel would open natural lines of communication between Egypt and Lebanon to all forms of Arab
traffic. (2) Jordan would be offered a free port at Haifa,
transit rights across Israel. (3) Israel would consider establishing communications across the Negev desert between Egypt
and Jordan. (4) Arab planes could fly across Israel. (5) Israel
would compensate Arab refugees for property left behind in
Israel. (6) Israel would join in unified development of the
Jordan and Yarmuk valleys. (7) Israel would accept minor
frontier adjustments.

Israel's resources were further strained during this period
because of border tensions with Syria, which had signed a
mutual defense pact with Egypt in Damascus Oct. 20, 1955
and had set up a joint military command with Egypt Nov. 29.
Syrian shore batteries fired Dec. 10 on an Israeli police boat
in the Sea of Galilee (Lake Tiberias, or Lake Kinneret). Israel
responded Dec. 11 by raiding Syrian fortifications northeast
of the Sea of Galilee, killing 56 Syrians and capturing 30 while
losing 6 dead and suffering 12 wounded. Syrian delegate
Ahmad el-Shukhairy urged the UN Security Council Dec. 16
to impose economic sanctions against Israel for the Israeli attack on Syria. Israeli delegate Abba Eban replied that Israel
had raided Syria after a year of "persistent" Syrian attacks on
Israeli fishing boats on the Sea of Galilee, which "lies within
Israeli territory" and where Syria "has no political or geographical status." Eban quoted an Israeli communiqué of
Dec. 11 that said the Israeli raid was made "to silence the batteries responsible" for an attack on Israeli fishing boats Dec.
10 "and to insure the security of Israeli citizens engaged in
their lawful occupations." Eban said: "Either peaceful activity on the lake would have to be stopped in deference to
Syrian guns, or Syrian guns would become silent in order that
the conditions for work and development might be restored."

10 of the 11 Security Council members (Brazil was scheduled to speak later) criticized Israel Dec. 16 for the raid. U.S.
Amb.-to-UN Henry Cabot Lodge expressed the "shock" of the

U.S. government, which opposed "such acts of military violence." Regardless of whether or not there were provocations, he said, "the United Nations have undertaken not to resort to the use of force in the settlement of their disputes. Israel has specifically undertaken not to resort to force." Soviet delegate Arkady A. Sobolev criticized Israel in harsher terms. He said the Council should take steps to forestall recurrences. The Council deferred action pending a report from the UN truce chief in Palestine, Gen. E. L. M. Burns.

In his report Dec. 21, Burns called the Israeli raid "a deliberate violation" of the Syrian-Israeli armistice agreement of 1949. "Such actions may well produce a violent reaction by the . . . attacked country, and what had been conceived as a limited raid develops into full-scale hostilities," Burns warned. Burns said that the Syrian firing on Dec. 10 was directed at a patrol boat and that no fishing vessels were fired upon since the fishing season had begun in November.

Nasser Dec. 15 sent a letter warning UN Secy. Gen. Hammarskjöld Dec. 15 that further Israeli attacks on Arab countries would force Egypt "to take matters into her own hands." Egypt would "not hesitate to use her land, sea and air forces to insure her security and maintain peace in the area, as the Security Council has shown itself incompetent to prevent repeated occurrences of such incidents," Nasser said. He listed 6 incidents starting with the Israeli attack on Gaza Feb. 28. Nasser accused Israel of a "barbarous attack" on civilians as well as military positions Dec. 11. He said that future attacks on Syria or Egypt would bring "immediate retaliation" which would be "joint, not individual."

Egypt announced Dec. 26 that Saudi Arabia had agreed Dec. 24 to bring its armed forces into the joint Egyptian-Syrian command. Maj. Gen. Abdel Hakim Amer, Egyptian war minister, was commander of the joint forces. Nasser and Saudi Arabian Crown Prince Emir Faisal reportedly had agreed on a joint defense pact in Cairo Oct. 25.

The UN Security Council Jan. 19, 1956 unanimously

adopted the Western-sponsored resolution condemning the Israeli raid on Syria Dec. 11, 1955. The measure adopted by the Council charged Israel with "a flagrant violation" of the Council's 1948 Palestine cease-fire resolution, the 1949 Syrian-Israeli armistice agreement and "Israel's obligations under the United Nations Charter." It called on Israel "to comply with its obligations . . . in the future, in default of which the Council will have to consider what further measures under the Charter are required to maintain or restore the peace. . . ." It asked for further efforts through UN truce chief Burns to pacify the Sea of Galilee area where the Israeli raid occurred. Soviet delegate Arkady A. Sobolev voted for the U.S.-British-French resolution after a Council majority voted it priority over the harsher Soviet resolution.

The Israeli Foreign Ministry said Jan. 20 that the UN resolution was unrealistic in view of the situation in which Israel had found itself since its inception.

Big Powers & UN Seek Peace Formula

Soviet professions of neutrality in the Arab-Israeli dispute were reported by British Laborite MP Harold Wilson, ex-president of the British Board of Trade, in an article in the *N.Y. Tribune* Jan. 22, 1956. Wilson quoted Soviet Communist Party First Secy. Nikita S. Krushchev as having told him in Moscow Jan. 12 that Soviet policy "cannot be pro-Arab or anti-Israel. Ours is a policy which is sympathetic to all peoples." Krushchev had said he had spoken "against Israel" previously, Wilson reported, because Israel was playing "an unpleasant role" in the Middle East.

British Prime Min. Sir Anthony Eden warned at a Conservative Party rally in Bradford, England, Jan. 18 that a world war could be started in a critical area such as the Middle East. "Governments should beware lest in trying to undermine long-established friendships between others they embroil themselves in graver perils," he said.

In a House of Commons debate on surplus-arms exports

Jan. 24, British Foreign Secy. Selwyn Lloyd said that "it is unlikely that we can get the Israelis and Arabs together around a table in the immediate future," so Britain was trying to bring them "to a discussion in some other way." Lloyd did not explain what he had in mind. Lloyd was replying to a statement by Labor Party Leader Hugh Gaitskell that the "time has come formally and openly to ask the Russians whether they will join the discussions to safeguard the peace between Israel and the Arab states." Lloyd said that Western officials had approached the USSR "at more than one level" since the Soviet bloc had offered arms to the Arab states in Sept. 1955. The Russians had made clear that "they were not prepared to stop tilting the balance" in the Middle East, Lloyd told Gaitskell.

A British White Paper entitled "Export of Surplus War Material," issued Jan. 19, 1956, had reported that 50 to 100 old Sherman tanks reclaimed from scrap had been reconditioned and had been shipped to Israel from France in the past year in violation of British regulations. 151 "old Valentine self-propelled mountings" without breech blocks were illegally exported from Britain to Egypt through Belgium in a similar way, the White Paper added. Britain said the illegally exported weapons were "obsolete, ineffective and unreliable for war" and in "no way disturbed the balance" between Israel and Egypt. The French Foreign ministry Jan. 20 denied the White Paper's statement that tanks sold to France for scrap had been reconditioned and re-exported, despite French assurances to Britain that this would not be done. "The importation in France of the material concerned was, indeed, perfectly regular and was realized in conditions which could not leave any doubts as to the final destination of the material concerned," a French communiqué said. The British Foreign Office repeated Jan. 20 its statement that French assurances on re-export had been given.

Canadian External Affairs Min. Lester B. Pearson, defending arms sales to Israel and Egypt, told the Canadian House of

Commons Jan. 24 that his government sought to avoid the creation of a preponderance of power by either Israel or the Arab states or a Mideastern power vacuum to be filled by the USSR. He said Canada, in the past 2 years, had sold $2,067,685 worth of arms to Israel, $771,121 worth (mostly accounted for by 15 Harvard training planes) to Egypt. He observed that current Israeli boundaries were armistice demarcation lines that could be adjusted without "one-sided concessions of territory" or crippling of Israel.

Pres. Eisenhower and British Prime Min. Eden, meeting in Washington in early Feb. 1956, exchanged views on how to ease Middle East tensions. The talks ended with a statement in which the 2 leaders said:

We discussed the tensions which prejudice the stability of the area and carry a potential threat to world peace. It was agreed that every effort should be made to decrease sources of misunderstanding between this area and the Western world. We are eager to contribute wherever possible to the settlement of difficulties between states in the region. We wish to help peoples of this part of the world to achieve their aspirations.

A settlement between Israel and her Arab neighbors is the most urgent need. This will be possible only if both sides are willing to reconcile the positions which they have hitherto taken. Our 2 governments have declared their readiness to contribute to such a settlement by assisting financially in regard to the refugee problem and by guaranteeing agreed frontiers.

In the meantime we are concerned at the state of tension in the area and have considered what steps can be taken to reduce it. The Tripartite Declaration of May 25, 1950 provides for action both inside and outside the United Nations in the event of the use of force or threat of force, or of preparations to violate the frontier or armistice lines. We are bound to recognize that there is now increased danger of these contingencies arising. Accordingly, we have made arrangements for joint discussions as to the nature of the action which we should take in such an event. The French government is being invited to participate in these discussions.

We believe that the security of states in this area cannot rest upon arms alone but rather upon the international rule of law and upon the establishment of friendly relations among neighbors. The action of the Soviet bloc in regard to arms supplies to Middle East countries has added to the tensions in the area and increased the risk of war. Our purpose is to mitigate that risk.

We express our full support for the efforts of Gen. Burns, head of the UN Truce Supervisory Organization, to maintain peace on the borders. We would favorably consider recommendations for any necessary enlargement of his organization and improvement of its capabilities. . . .

We discussed the work of the Baghdad Pact and agreed upon its importance for the security of the Middle East. We noted that this association, in addition to its defense aspects, has an important part to play in the economic and political development of member countries. We believe that it serves the interests of the area as a whole and provides no reason for impairing the good relations we wish to maintain with non-member countries.

The U.S. government will continue to give solid support to the purposes and aims of the Pact, and its observers will play a constructive part in the work of its committees. . . .

The Anglo-U.S. statement provoked vigorous Soviet criticism, and the Soviets indicated a determination to take a strong stand against the Baghdad Pact and American influence in the Arab world. The Soviet Foreign Ministry said Feb. 13:

The Washington statement alleges that its participants desire the settlement of the dispute between Israel and her Arab neighbors. This would be a good thing, were it true. But in that case why have these decisions been adopted without the participation of the countries concerned, and behind their backs? The known facts show that there is a clear discrepancy between such statements and certain actions of the Western powers in relation to the countries of the Near and Middle East. Moreover, there have been frequent reports of late that certain states intend to move their armed forces into the above-mentioned areas. These reports have not been denied. . . . The movement of troops into the countries of the Near and Middle East would represent an act contrary to the interest of strengthening peace, would create dangerous friction and tension in the area, and would make even more difficult the possibility of settling disputed issues between the countries of this area. . . .

Any action leading to complications in the Near and Middle East, and to increased tension in that area, is bound to be the subject of legitimate concern on the part of the Soviet government. Such an act as the despatch of foreign troops to the countries of the Near and Middle East, without the consent of the interested states and without the sanction of the UN Security Council, would be a gross violation of the UN Charter and of the sovereignty of a number of countries. . . .

Certain joint measures are envisaged in the statement of Pres. Eisenhower and the British prime minister. . . . [They] affirm that the measures they have proposed with regard to the countries of the Near and Middle East are caused by the state of tension in the relations between

Israel and her Arab neighbors. At the same time they try to present the case in such a way as if the Tripartite Declaration of the U.S.A., Britain, and France of May 25, 1950, enabled them to undertake independent action outside the framework of the United Nations. . . .

It is not the first time that efforts have been made to impose on countries of the Near and Middle East the will of certain foreign circles whose interests are alien to the national aspirations of the peoples of that area. Not without reason, the peoples of these countries connect these actions of the Western powers with the aspirations of the oil monopolies to use the oil wealth of this area in the interests of their own enrichment, disregarding the interests of the peoples of those states. . . .

The U.S. State Department denounced the Soviet counterstatement as "propaganda." The British Foreign Office declared: "The Washington communiqué dealt with action which might have to be taken under the Tripartite Declaration of 1950. This declaration was designed to assist in the maintenance of peace and security in the area by making it clear that we should oppose the use of force to alter the frontiers or armistice lines resulting from the cease-fire of 1949. We said that we should take action both inside and outside the UN in the light of the increased tension caused primarily by Soviet action. The 3 powers decided in Washington that they had a duty to make it plain that the Tripartite Declaration means what it says. There has been no question of sending forces to Middle East countries without their consent. On the contrary, the purpose of the Washington statement . . . has been to show the countries concerned that, if they become the victims of an attack, there will be friends within reach and ready to act in their support."

Tripartite discussions on the Mideast were held by Britain, France and the United States at the ambassadorial level in February and March but arrived at no official resolution.

Pres. Eisenhower, at his news conference Mar. 21, offered US mediation to help effect "a decent solution" in the Middle East. The President warned that "any outbreak of hostilities. . .would be a catastrophe to the world." He noted that Europe had increasingly turned to Middle Eastern oil as a source of energy and said that the area "is of extraordinary importance to the free world." In a letter Mar. 24, Pres. Eisenhower told Israeli Pres. Izhak Ben-Zvi that the U.S. would do all in its power to settle the Middle East problem.

U.S. State Department officials revealed Mar. 22 that France had proposed informally a U.S.-British-French foreign ministers' meeting on the Middle East problem. The State Department reported Mar. 23 that no word had been received on the existence of a British "standby" plan for military action should war occur in the Middle East. French Premier Guy Mollet told a group of visiting U.S. editors in Paris Mar. 24 that "some kind of arms embargo" should be established in the Middle East, "probably through the UN." British Foreign Secy. Selwyn Lloyd told the House of Commons in London Mar. 26 that no joint plans for preventing an Arab-Israeli conflict had been agreed on by Britain, the U.S. and France. Lloyd said that "standby" war plans would remain secret.

The British Foreign Office had reported Mar. 23 that it had received word that 200 Egyptian army officers and men were training at a Soviet military base near Gdynia (Danzig), Poland in radar and antiaircraft defense. Egyptian pilots were said to be in training under Czechoslovak instructors near Alexandria, learning to use 30 Ilyushin bombers and 30 to 50 MiG fighters shipped under the Egyptian-Czechoslovak arms pact signed Sept. 27, 1955. Cairo sources Mar. 23 refused to confirm or deny the Gdynia reports. Press dispatches from London Mar. 23 said British officials were considering the sale of arms to Israel to counter growing Egyptian power. (6 Russian technical experts were reported in Cairo Mar. 26 for talks on Soviet aid to Egypt.)

The British Foreign Office Mar. 25 contradicted statements by Egyptian Premier Nasser (reported in British newspapers Mar. 22) that Nasser did not oppose British interests in the Middle East. It said that Egypt had conducted propaganda against Britain and its Baghdad (METO) Pact allies and that "such conduct has extended to areas where Egypt has no direct interests, for example, East Africa." Nasser had said that Egypt was determined to oppose any extension of the METO pact and the attendant isolation of Egypt, the British statement said. U.S. diplomats were reported Mar. 27 to have objected to British criticism of Nasser's statements.

The British embassy in Cairo Mar. 27 denied having protested "hostile" broadcasts by the Egyptian state radio. Egypt had reported the protest and denied the charge Mar. 26.

Pres. Eisenhower said at his press conference Apr. 4 that he would "never be guilty" of sending U.S. troops "into anything that can be interpreted as war, until Congress directs it." The President, referring to reports that British Prime Min. Eden had been urging a firmer U.S. Middle East policy, said that "they haven't pressed me" and that his constant communication with Eden had not brought him any urgent appeals for Middle Eastern action. (Israeli Forgn. Min. Moshe Sharett summoned U.S. Amb.-to-Israel Edward B. Lawson Apr. 4 in Tel Aviv and reportedly expressed Israeli dismay over U.S. refusal to release $63 million worth of defensive arms requested by Israel. Social Welfare Min. Moshe Shapiro had said Apr. 3 that "a country which we had regarded as a friend has deceived us.")

A statement issued by White House Press Secy. James C. Hagerty Apr. 9, with "the full approval of the President," said that the U.S. would "observe its [UN Charter] commitments within constitutional means to oppose any aggression in the [Middle East] area." The statement added that Eisenhower and State Secy. Dulles viewed the Arab-Israeli crisis "with the utmost seriousness" and that the U.S. was "determined to support and assist any nation which might be subjected to such aggression." Hagerty said in Augusta, Ga. Apr. 12 that Eisenhower had sent personal messages to both Premier Ben-Gurion of Israel and Nasser of Egypt urging restraint and outlining the current

U.S. policy of aid for either side should it be the victim of aggression. (Sir Winston Churchill said in London Apr. 12 that should Israel be attacked by Egypt, it would become "a measure of honor to make sure that they are not the losers.")

The Soviet government Apr. 17 offered its support for "UN measures directed toward. . . strengthening peace in the area of Palestine and the implementation of the corresponding decisions of the Security Council." The Soviet statement, issued in Moscow by Foreign Min. Vyacheslav M. Molotov, blamed "military alignments which serve the aims of colonialism" for generating friction in the Middle East. But the statement called on both Israel and the Arab countries to "refrain from any kind of action" that might increase tension. Questioned at a Moscow reception Apr. 17 on whether the Soviet statement could serve as a basis for forthcoming talks in London of British leaders with Soviet Premier Nikolai A. Bulganin and Communist Party First Secy. Nikita S. Khrushchev, Molotov replied: "Yes, it could lead to that." Moscow dispatches Apr. 17 said that the Russian statement overtly avoided criticism of Israel and noted "appreciation" of the role played by Britain and France in the Mideast.

Reports from London said Apr. 17 that the Eden government would bring the subject of the Middle East into talks with the Russian leaders and would urge that the USSR halt shipments of Czechoslovak arms to Egypt. U.S. State Secy. John Foster Dulles said in Washington Apr. 17 that he welcomed any "truly genuine" Russian support for UN Middle East peace moves.

A White House statement Apr. 18 said that "the Administration is of course still studying the [Apr. 17] Soviet statement, but if it demonstrates a real desire . . . on the part of the Soviet Union to back the UN effort, the president welcomes this support."

Reports from Cairo Apr. 21 said that the initially warm

Egyptian reception of the Soviet statement had cooled with the announcement that British and Soviet leaders were discussing the Middle East in London. The Cairo weekly *Akhbar al-Yaum* said Apr. 21 that "Middle East problems are for Middle East peoples to solve. . . .We want no guardians. . . We are not defendants being tried *in absentia.*" Moscow newspapers renewed attacks on the Baghdad Pact Apr. 19 and expressed sympathy "with Arab aspirations."

Dispatches from Jerusalem Apr. 23 said that an initially hopeful Israeli reaction to the Soviet statement of support for UN peace moves had been tempered by Foreign Min. Sharett, who told the Knesset Apr. 23 he "doubted that the authors of this declaration had given the necessary attention" to the "contradiction" between the sale of Soviet-bloc arms to Egypt and Soviet protestations of peace.

The UN Security Council convened Mar. 26 to discuss a U.S. resolution that UN Secy. Gen. Dag Hammarskjöld visit Israel and the Arab states, confer with Gen. Burns, head of the UN Truce Supervisory Organization, and report back to the UN within a month. The U.S. resolution was adopted Apr. 4, and Hammarskjöld left for the Mideast Apr. 8.

Hammarskjöld conducted negotiations in Cairo Apr. 10–14 in an effort to win firm cease-fire pledges from both the Israeli and Egyptian governments. Hammarskjöld opened talks with Egyptian Premier Nasser Apr. 11, reportedly presented a concrete UN cease-fire plan, and then met with Egyptian Foreign Min. Mahmoud Fawzi. The secretary general Apr. 12 released through the UN Security Council the texts of correspondence with Israeli and Arab leaders in which each side pledged to observe the 1949 Israeli-Egypt armistice agreement but reserved the right to armed defense.

A letter from Israeli Premier Ben-Gurion to Hammarskjöld, made public at UN headquarters in New York Apr. 12, charged Egypt with further *fedayin* raids despite Nasser's assurances that they had been halted.

Reports from Cairo Apr. 13 said that Egypt had "virtually accepted" an 8-point UN peace plan and that Hammarskjöld had answered Israel's Apr. 12 charges and requested Israeli assurances against Gaza Strip attacks. Hammarskjöld, accompanied by Gen. Burns, left Cairo Apr. 14 for a tour of the Gaza zone, stopped briefly at Lydda, Israel and continued on to his peace mission headquarters in Beirut.

Gaza zone dispatches said that attacks by Egyptian *fedayin* had continued sporadically Apr. 11-16 throughout the Gaza-Beersheba-Tel Aviv area. (An Israeli rabbi and 3 children were reported killed in an attack Apr. 11 near Tel Aviv.) The Israeli air force reported that a British-built Vampire jet of the Egyptian air force had been shot down over the central Negev Apr. 12 after a 4-plane Egyptian formation was intercepted by Israeli jets. The Egyptian air force claimed to have downed a French-made Israeli Ouragan jet in the same clash.

UN sources said Apr. 16 that Hammarskjöld had rejected Israeli requests for consideration of the Egyptian ban on Israeli use of the Suez Canal, citing the Apr. 4 Security Council resolution delineating his peace mission powers. Hammarskjöld said in Jerusalem Apr. 19 that Israel and Egypt had agreed to the enforcement of a Gaza Strip cease-fire effective at 6 p.m. Apr. 18. Hammarskjöld said that Israeli Premier Ben-Gurion and Foreign Min. Moshe Sharett had agreed in talks Apr. 17-19 to greater freedom for UN Truce Supervisory Organization observers and the construction of fixed UN posts on the Israeli side of the Gaza frontier. An Egyptian cease-fire pledge had been won in the Cairo talks Apr. 11-14.

Under the cease-fire agreement, Israel and Egypt pledged to observe Article 2, paragraph 2 of the 1949 Egyptian-Israeli armistice agreement forbidding any shooting or passing across the truce line by either side's forces. Israel also agreed Apr. 20 to restrict its patrol boats along the Sea of Galilee border with Syria and to give Syrian farmers access to water. Hammarskjöld said that, despite Israeli threats to renew work on the disputed Jordan River irrigation plan in the demilitarized Syrian border zone, he was "sure we are on the right road," and "personally I don't see any reason why we should lose it."

Dispatches from Cairo Apr. 19 said that cease-fire orders had been given to Egyptian forces and that charges had been filed listing 12 minor Israeli violations of the truce.

(Washington sources said Apr. 19 that U.S. officials were "optimistic" over Hammarskjöld's chances for winning a stabilized Palestine truce, but they observed that he had yet to win a rollback of Arab and Israeli armies from the Gaza Strip border.)

Hammarskjöld ended talks with Israeli leaders Apr. 20 and flew to Beirut, where Lebanese Foreign Min. Salim Lahoud reportedly rejected a UN request Apr. 21 to reopen talks on political aspects of the Palestine question. The secretary general flew to Damascus Apr. 23 for talks with Syrian Premier Said Ghazzi, who agreed Apr. 24 to observe the terms of the UN cease-fire plan for Galilee.

Premier Ben-Gurion told the Israeli Knesset Apr. 22 that Pres. Eisenhower's Apr. 9 statement on U.S. Middle Eastern policy and the 1950 British-French-U.S. Tripartite Declaration on Israeli-Arab frontiers were not a "substantial guaranty of Israel's security, or any deterrent to the aggressors who are planning war against us." The "only thing that might deter war against Israel is the supply . . . of sufficient defensive arms," Ben-Gurion said. Referring to Hammarskjöld's peace mission, Ben-Gurion said Apr. 22 that the new cease-fire "does not reduce in the slightest" the danger of war in the area. He said that when Arab armies attacked Israel in 1948, no UN member "could be found willing to lift a finger in Israel's defense."

Ben-Gurion said at an emergency session of the 24th World Zionist Congress in Jerusalem Apr. 24 that the U.S. and Britain had imposed an embargo on Israel and must bear a "terrible responsibility" for what might happen. Co-chairman Nahum Goldmann of the Jewish Agency Executive said Apr. 24 that the U.S. State Department had used "transparent subterfuge" in urging U.S. allies to arm Israel.

Israeli reports Apr. 23 had said that Syrian guns had fired on 15 Israeli fishing boats on the Sea of Galilee, and it was reported Apr. 24 that 4 Israeli surveyors had been killed in the Negev, apparently by *fedayin* infiltrators from Jordan. Israeli Foreign Min. Sharett Apr. 24 protested the killings in a telegram to Hammarskjöld in Damascus.

Egyptian reporter Ibrahim Izzat, 23, who spent 12 days touring Israel "as a guest of the Israeli government" Apr. 26–May 6, wrote in the Cairo magazine *Ruz-al-Youssuf* May 28 that Israeli Foreign Min. Sharett had told him that Israel "was ready to accept a limited number" of Arab refugees—"those who have families in Israel"—and was "also ready to pay indemnities to the rest of the [refugee] Arabs . . . in case they settle in the Arab states." Izzat had revealed his Israeli tour in Cairo May 19 and had reported an interview with Israeli Premier Ben-Gurion in which he was told that "when you go to Egypt and if you meet Nasser, tell him I am ready to meet him any time, any place he chooses, to discuss any problem . . . he wants—refugees, borders, political, economic or military questions . . . I am ready to meet him even in Cairo." Izzat, who posed in Israel as a Brazilian journalist, had reported to Nasser on his return to Cairo.

Dag Hammarskjöld returned to UN headquarters in New York May 6 and reported that Egypt, Israel, Jordan, Syria and Lebanon had reaffirmed their acceptance of the 1948 armistice. He said that Egypt and Israel had agreed to allow Gen. Burns to set up UN observation posts along the Gaza Strip border line. Reporting to the UN Security Council May 9, Hammarskjöld criticized Israel for its "reprisal actions" against Arab countries from which *fedayin* had struck against Israel.

Ben-Gurion, in a Knesset session Oct. 15, rejected Hammarskjöld's criticism. "Even if the UN Charter had not specifically guaranteed the right of self-defense to every nation," Ben-Gurion declared, "this right exists on its own. The apparatus of the UN has demonstrated its incapacity— I do not say its unwillingness—to prevent the continued and systematic murder of citizens of Israel. As far as I know, this is the only country where the lives of its inhabitants are endangered by bands of murderers sent in by the rulers of the neighboring states. I cannot imagine any other country reconciling herself to a situation in which her citizens were at the mercy of assassins organized by neighboring governments. The UN truce observers and the UN Secretary General well know that these bands act on behalf of their governments, and that Egypt is the prime and central mover in their organization, equipment and training, and in the planning of their operations. Members of the *fedayin* who have been captured by us have admitted this at their trials; and the Egyptian Wakfs minister, Ahmed Hassan al-Bakoury, said in a broadcast on 11 April this year over the 'Voice of Cairo' ['Sa'ut al Arab'], which is subordinate to the Egyptian dictator: 'There is no reason why the *fedayin* who hate their enemies should not penetrate deep into Israel and turn the lives of her people into a living hell.' The government of Israel will not allow the country to be turned into a living hell, and the assassins and their masters will not go unpunished."

UN proposals for the extension of Israeli-Jordanian truce violation meetings had been reported still unenforced May 24, 1956. Burns censured Jordan May 24 for firing on an Israeli policy patrol in the Jerusalem area May 23. The Israeli-Jordanian Mixed Armistice Commission under U.S. Navy Cmdr. Elmer Terrill had condemned Jordan May 19 for the ambush of 2 Israelis May 15 near Armageddon. Arab-Israeli border incidents had increased May 17-25, with an Israeli soldier killed May 23, an Israeli civilian killed May 25 and reports of rail sabotage and airspace violations made by both sides.

The Security Council reportedly had delayed any further consideration of the Palestine problem to give Burns time to win Israeli-Egyptian agreement [completed May 24] on the establishment of UN truce observer posts on the Gaza Strip border. Israel May 28 had dropped demands for a prior approval of the UN posts in the disputed El Auja-Nitsana demilitarized zone by the Israeli-Egyptian Mixed Armistice Commission.

British Delegate-to-UN Sir Pierson Dixon May 29 asked his counterparts at the first UN Security Council meeting, after Hammarskjöld had reported on his Middle East peace mission, for their approval of a resolution urging that Hammarskjöld "continue his good offices" toward the enforcement of Arab-Israeli armistice agreements. The flexible UN mandate that Dixon proposed avoided any definition of the basic Arab-Israeli points of conflict and asked for a settlement on a "mutually acceptable basis."

The British resolution, made public May 28 in advance of its formal introduction, noted that compliance with the armistice agreements "has been neither completely agreed upon [n]or put into effect." It requested that both sides "speedily" enforce "practical proposals" agreed on with Hammarskjöld and Gen. Burns. Israel was reported to favor the resolution. Arab delegates were said to be divided on it, with Lebanon, Jordan and Egypt prepared to support it and Syria opposed. The Arab delegates were said to be critical of a clause in the resolution mentioning "unconditional" cease-fire pledges. Dixon removed the clause May 29.

Among the Arab-Israeli incidents reported June 3–17: an Israeli civilian was killed by Arab Legion fire near Jerusalem June 3; 2 Israelis were wounded by Jordanian gunfire near Jerusalem June 5, and 2 Israeli jet planes were charged with violating the Egyptian frontier in the Gaza area; Egypt was charged June 6 with halting the Greek ship *Panagia*, bound for Eilat, at Port Said May 25; an Israeli Arab was killed by infiltrators June 15 in Bab el-Armasha, near Syria; Israel complained June 17 of Arab raids from Lebanon into Upper Galilee.

Moshe Sharett was replaced by Labor Min. Golda Myerson [later Meir] as Israeli foreign minister June 17, reportedly because Prime Min. Ben-Gurion felt Sharett was too cautious in his policies toward the Arab states. Ben-Gurion told the Knesset June 19, in debate following the change in foreign ministers, that Israel would reject any settlement of its dispute with the Arabs "imposed" by other states and would insist on the recognition of its current borders. He warned, however, that any Israeli move to launch "a preventive war would be madness."

Dag Hammarskjöld, on his 2d mission to the Middle East in 4 months, landed in Jerusalem July 19 and conferred with Ben-Gurion. A communique' July 20 said that their "full and fruitful" talks, joined July 20 by Israeli Foreign Min. Golda Myerson, had taken up "ways and means" to establish compliance with the Arab-Israeli armistice agreements negotiated by Hammarskjöld in April. Dispatches from Jerusalem July 21 said that Hammarskjöld's new visit had been prompted by UN observers' anxiety over a possible Israeli retaliation for Arab raids.

Gen. Burns had reiterated July 11 that Ben-Gurion June 28 had threatened retaliation for further Jordanian attacks, despite denials of this by Israeli Amb.-to-U.S. Abba Eban. Ben-Gurion reportedly assured Hammarskjöld July 20 that Israel would not launch large-scale reprisals. Israeli sources said July 20 that Ben-Gurion also had told Hammarskjöld that the Middle Eastern peace had deteriorated since April. Ben-Gurion reportedly cited accelerated Arab war preparations, propaganda and arms imports, the training of *fedayin* raiders by Egypt and Jordan and the continued Egyptian blockade of the Suez Canal to Israeli and Israel-bound shipping.

Hammarskjöld and Burns flew to Amman July 21 to confer briefly with Jordanian Premier Ibrahim Hashim, Foreign Min. Awni Abdul Hadi and Jordan's army chief, Maj. Gen. Ali Abu Nuwar. The UN officials then continued to Cairo, where Hammarskjöld told reporters July 21 that "this time there is nothing special to negotiate about," "the atmosphere is different." Hammarskjöld met with Foreign Min. Mahmoud Fawzi July 21 and Nasser July 22 to brief them on his Israeli and Jordanian talks. (Nasser had been elected president unopposed June 23.)

Hammarskjöld said July 23 that he had received assurances from both sides that no action would be taken within the next 3 months that would upset the relative calm along the Arab-Israeli frontiers. Hammarskjöld said that his brief "check-up" visit to the Middle East had convinced him that the armistice agreements were still working and effective.

Israel July 23 protested the boobytrapping of a vineyard July 22 and the bombing of the children's house in an Israeli settlement July 23—both incidents taking place near the Jordanian frontier—and demanded that Hammarskjöld account for "Jordan's policy with regard to implementation of the cease fire." The protest said that "Israel will consider further its policy toward Jordan in the light of whatever assurances" Hammarskjöld had obtained from Jordan.

2 Canadian UN truce observers, Maj. Marcel Breault and Maj. George A. Flint, and a Jordanian Mixed Armistice Commission member, Lt. Muhammad Daoud, were wounded July 24 in the detonation of an Israeli land mine while investigating an Israeli-Jordanian clash in the Mt. Scopus area of Jerusalem. Gen. Burns warned Israel and Jordan July 24 against any attempt to seize or enlarge the Israeli enclave in Jordanian territory and said that it was his "firm intention" to maintain UN authority over the zone.

Col. Salah Mustafa, military attache at the Egyptian embassy in Amman, had died in Jordan July 21 of wounds suffered a week earlier in the explosion of a bomb mailed to the embassy from Jerusalem. The death of another Egyptian, Col. Mustafa Hafez, under similar circumstances in Gaza July 11 was reported July 21.

Israeli-Egyptian Arms Race

By early 1956, news dispatches contained frequent reference to the arms shipments to Mideast countries. Arms-producing nations such as the USSR, Czechoslovakia, the U.S., Britain, France and Canada were shipping large quantities of weapons—often surplus—to both Egypt and Israel and arms in smaller amounts to Jordan, Syria and Saudi Arabia. Britain, the U.S. and Canada provided both sides in the Arab-Israeli dispute with arms often, apparently, for merely commercial motives. The USSR, Communist China and Czechoslovakia aided primarily Egypt, whereas France provided aircraft only to Israel.

The Soviet bloc appeared to be in the middle of an aggressive arms sales campaign. A Czechoslovak delegation arrived in Khartoum Mar. 22 to discuss the sale of arms to the Sudan. Dispatches from Cairo Mar. 28 said that the USSR had offered Egypt uranium and the aid required to build an atomic reactor and was training Egyptian scientists in Moscow under an agreement concluded in Feb. 1956 for the construction of an Egyptian nuclear laboratory.

Rep. Emanuel Celler (D., N.Y.) said Apr. 15 that under the terms of the Czechoslovak-Egyptian arms pact Egypt would get 6 Russian submarines that would soon be in the Mediterranean "manned by Communist technicians."

(Egyptian Commerce Min. Abu Noseir had opened a Communist Chinese trade fair in Cairo Apr. 1. The Chinese government was reported Apr. 2 to have bought $17½ million worth of Egyptian cotton since Aug. 1955, shipping Egypt iron and oils in exchange. Reports from Hong Kong Apr. 16 said that an additional $11.2 million cotton-machinery trade agreement had been signed by Egypt and China.)

Egypt soon appeared to be sharing arms and weaponry with its Arab-bloc allies. Reports from Cairo Apr. 24 said that Egypt had given the Sudanese Republic $1½ million worth of arms after talks with visiting Sudanese Premier Ismail el-Azhari. Azhari had disclosed Apr. 15 that arms talks were still under way in Khartoum with the Czechoslovak military delegation and that the Sudan had accepted a Soviet technical assistance offer. (According to reports from Hong Kong Apr. 14, a Chinese Communist trade delegation also had completed talks in Khartoum.) Saudi Arabian sources in Jidda had said Apr. 4 that the first of "several" squadrons of Egyptian jets sold to Saudi Arabia had been delivered in March. (A shipment of 18 U.S. light tanks was reported to have been unloaded Mar. 28 at Dammam, Saudi Arabia.)

Few Arab countries stayed out of the arms race. The Libyan parliament Mar. 30 had approved a rejection by the Libyan government of a Soviet aid offer. The Libyan government said Apr. 7 that U.S. aid had been increased from $7 million in fiscal 1955 to $9 million for the 1956 fiscal year and would total $11 million in fiscal 1957. Other reports said that the U.S. would provide equipment to raise Libyan army strength to 2,600 men and would increase grain relief to Libya.

A United Press (UP) survey report indicated Apr. 15 that Soviet-bloc aid pledged to underdeveloped countries in 1946 had totalled $506 million. The UP said, according to U.S. government statistics, Egypt received more of the Soviet-bloc aid than any other single country: $165 million. (Other shares listed in the survey: Afghanistan $115 million, Iran $3 million, Lebanon $2 million, Syria $8 million and Turkey $4 million.) Soviet Trade Min. Ivan G. Kabanov told the UN Economic Commission for Europe in Geneva Apr. 9 that current Soviet aid credits to Communist and non-Communist countries totalled $5 billion. Kabanov said that the USSR was ready to trade heavily with Europe when "extraordinary" U.S. expenditures there ceased.

Israeli sources in Apr. 1956 gave this estimate of arms deliveries to Israel and Egypt before the Czechoslovak-Soviet-Egyptian arms deal: *Egypt*—40 British Centurion tanks, 150 U.S. Sherman tanks, 200 British Valentine tanks (obsolete); 100 British Vampire and Meteor jet fighters; 7 frigates and 2 corvettes. *Israel*—A "somewhat smaller" number of Sherman tanks, no Centurion or Valentine tanks; a "far smaller number" of Vampire and Meteor jets; 3 frigates & 2 frigate-corvettes. (A British White Paper Jan. 19 said that 1955 arms deliveries included 50-100 old Sherman tanks to Israel, 151 Valentines without breech blocks to Egypt—all shipped illegally.)

Deliveries after the Czechoslovak-Soviet-Egyptian arms deal included: *Egypt*—100 Stalin III heavy tanks, 200 Czech T-34 tanks, 100 field pieces; 150 of 200 promised MiG-15 jet fighters, 45 of 60 promised Ilyushin-28 jet bombers; 2 British destroyers, 2 Soviet *Skoryi*-class destroyers (5.1-inch guns) and reports of promised Soviet-bloc submarines. *Israel*—"Some" French light tanks and British half-tracks; 24 French Mystere jet fighters, some French Ouragan jets (shipment of 12 had been reported), a "small" number of Metoer jets and night fighters, some obsolete World War II RAF Mosquito bombers (the Israeli air force had no jet bombers); 2 British destroyers (4.5-inch guns, built in 1944, ordered in 1954, delivered June 20 and renamed *Yaffo* and *Eilat*); some light naval antiaircraft guns.

Egypt, its Arab-bloc allies and Jordan and neutralist Lebanon moved in the spring of 1956 toward a mutual military operations accommodation. Egyptian Premier Nasser, Saudi Arabian King Saud and Imam Ahmed of Yemen Apr. 21 signed a 5-year pact in Jidda, the Saudi diplomatic capital, linking the 3 armies under the command of Egyptian War Min. Abdel Hakim Amer.

Reports from Syria that Jordan's new Arab Legion commander, Maj. Gen. Enab Radi, and the Syrian army staff chief, Brig. Gen. Shawkat Shukayr, had reached agreement

Mar. 24 on plans for common defense of the 2 nation's borders with Israel were denied by Jordanian officials Mar. 25. A communiqué said that the 2 commanders had met on the Syrian–Jordanian frontier only "for an exchange of opinion on matters of common interest to both the Arab armies."

British foreign office estimates published in London Mar. 22 had included the news that Britain planned a 1956–7 grant-in-aid for Jordan of £9,158,000 ($25,642,000), mainly for the Arab Legion (*Jaish al-Arab*) and Jordanian Home Guard. Another £2½ million represented a loan to balance the Jordanian budget, made despite the dismissal Mar. 2 of Lt. Gen. Sir John Bagot Glubb (Glubb Pasha) as Legion commander. All remaining British military officers in Jordan, save those on technical posts, were ordered home Mar. 24.

But a joint Syrian-Jordanian communiqué issued in Amman Apr. 11 had said that the 2 countries had agreed to unify their defenses and coordinate their military power against the "vigorous Israeli threat." The British War Office said Apr. 17 that 32 British officers still training Jordan's Arab Legion would remain until Arab officers became available. A communiqué issued in Cairo May 6 said that the Jordanian Arab Legion's commander, Maj. Gen. Radi Innab, and the Egyptian army staff chief, Maj. Gen. Muhammad Ibrahim, had agreed during talks held Apr. 25-May 6 on plans to coordinate and unify the 2 countries' armies. Innab and Arab Legion Lt. Col. Ali Abu Nuwar took part in Jordanian-Lebanese talks in Beirut May 17-21, when agreement was reached on plans for the unification of the Jordanian and Lebanese armies in the event of war.

Maj. Amin Shaker, once spokesman for the Revolutionary Command Council, wrote May 27 in the Cairo newspaper *Al Gomhouria* that Egypt could evade a UN embargo on Middle Eastern arms by buying from Communist China. The paper said May 27 that Egyptian Premier Nasser had decided to recognize Red China after learning of a rumored agreement between British Prime Min. Sir Anthony Eden and

Soviet leaders on ending the arms race. Nasser had said May 19 that Egypt was "free to buy arms from any place we like." (Eden had told the British House of Commons May 10 that Britain was ready to discuss international controls on Middle Eastern arms in the UN, but that the 1950 British-French-U.S. agreement to guarantee Arab-Israeli frontiers "would present considerable difficulties" to an embargo.

Nasser May 24 accepted an invitation to visit Communist China. He reciprocated with an invitation for Communist Chinese Premier Chou En-lai to visit Egypt. The Egyptian commander-in-chief, Gen. Abdel Hakim Amer, announced May 24 that an Egyptian military mission would go to Peking at the invitation of the Chinese defense minister, Marshal Peng Teh-huai, ex-commander of Chinese troops in Korea. The Nationalist Chinese government had broken relations with Cairo May 17 and had recalled Amb.-to-Egypt Ho Feng-shan.

Reports of arms deals in May created the appearance of a rush on the market. Cairo Radio May 20 announced an Egyptian-Polish arms agreement but following Polish diplomats' denials of the deal, withdrew the statement some hours later as "a mistake." The Egyptian radio said May 20 that Nasser had raised the Egyptian flag May 19 over torpedo boats and minesweepers received from Czechoslovakia. U.S. reports May 21 set total Egyptian contracts with Czechoslovakia at $250 million. A report from Vienna Apr. 3 said that Czechoslovakia was training Egyptian officers in rocket warfare. (Czechoslovak Premier Viliam Siroky told newsmen in Prague May 24 that his government was negotiating a general trade agreement with Syria and that "naturally Syria is interested in arms." London papers May 3 had reported the sale of 100 Czechoslovak tanks and 25 MiG jets to Syria, but sources in Beirut and Damascus May 3 were said to be skeptical of the British reports.)

The U.S. Defense Department confirmed May 16 that a shipment of ammunition and military supplies for Saudi

Arabia valued at under $1 million had been assembled at Sunny Point, N.C. under an agreement for $7 million worth of arms signed in 1955. A State Department spokesman said May 16 that the consignment was part of the same order under which the U.S. had shipped 18 M-41 tanks to Saudi Arabia in February. The new shipment reportedly left for Saudi Arabia aboard the freighter *Monterey* May 16.

Reports from Paris Apr. 16 said the Israeli government had applied to buy 12 more Mystère IV jet fighters. The French government was said to have previously sold Israel 12 Mystères and 12 Ouragan jets. Canadian External Affairs Min. Pearson said in Ottawa Apr. 17 that Israel had asked for permission to buy "between 20 and 36 F-86 jets" from Canada and that the U.S. had stated that it had no objection to the sale.

The U.S. State Department revealed May 18 that a shipment of 21 surplus Army half-tracks to Israel under an export license covering half-track spare parts had been halted in New York by the Customs Bureau May 10 after the discovery that the vehicles were fully assembled. The Israeli embassy in Washington said May 19 that the vehicles would be returned to the dealer who had sold them to the Israeli Purchasing Commission and would be replaced by $150,000 worth of spare parts permitted under the export license.

U.S. & Britain Refuse to Aid Aswan Dam

Pres. Gamal Abdel Nasser's most tangible proposal of economic improvements for the Egyptian people was a high dam to be built at Aswan in Upper Egypt. It was anticipated that the dam would make 2 million more acres of land arable, generate sufficient electricity for all the nation's needs, make possible the industrialization of Upper Egypt and bring considerable relief of a critical population pressure in Lower Egypt. The estimated cost of the 15-year project was $1.3 billion, almost all of which Egypt would have to borrow.

An international crisis developed in mid-July 1956 after the U.S. and Britain withdrew their offer to Egypt of a $70 million grant to start the dam project.

Egyptian Finance Min. Abdel Moneim el-Kaissouni had opened talks in Washington Nov. 21, 1955 with representatives of the World Bank to seek financing of the dam. Egyptian officials said that the construction of the dam (which would store 4 times as much water as Hoover Dam) was a "matter of economic life or death for Egypt," which would go ahead with the project "one way or another."

The U.S. and Britain had informed Egypt Dec. 17, 1955 that they would finance the start of the Project. The U.S. and Britain would, "subject to legislative authority," consider granting "further support toward financing the later stages to supplement World Bank financing," the State Department said. First-phase details had been drawn up in Washington Dec. 16 by the U.S. State Undersecy. Herbert Hoover Jr., British Amb.-to-U.S. Sir Roger Makins, World Bank Pres. Eugene R. Black and Egyptian Finance Min. Kaissouni.

The U.S. and Britain reportedly offered Egypt an initial $70 million grant, of which the U.S. was to contribute $56 million and Britain $14 million in blocked sterling balances (money Britain had owed Egypt for goods and services during and since World War II). This would be used to build 3 coffer dams and the foundations of the main dam and to bore 7 tunnels, each more than a mile long. The completion of the coffer dams alone would enable the controlled irrigation of 700,000 acres currently watered only when the Nile overflowed and of 500,000 acres currently receiving no water at all. The World Bank had not yet made a firm commitment on the project.

Soviet Amb.-to-Egypt Daniel S. Solod said in Cairo Dec. 18 that the USSR intended to help in the project "unless there is something in Egypt's agreement with the West which specifically excludes us." (Solod disclosed Dec. 17 that he was returning to Moscow to head the Middle Eastern desk in the foreign ministry.)   U.S. State Secy. John Foster Dulles said at his news conference Dec. 20 that "this dam is something which goes back 2 years and more and is not attributable at all to the Soviet proposal."

An agreement to coordinate Western policies to meet any Soviet penetration in the Middle East had been reached in Paris Dec. 15, 1955 by Dulles, British Foreign Secy. Harold Macmillan and French Foreign Min. Antoine Pinay, who were attending the semiannual North Atlantic Council meeting.

U.S. Senatorial opposition to foreign aid spending was stiff, however.   Sen. Walter George (D., Ga.), reiterating his opposition to long-term foreign aid commitments, came out specifically Apr. 27 and 29, 1956 against U.S. financial support for the Aswan project.   He called it "ill-advised" and "wholly inconsistant" for the U.S. to embark on such a project in the situation currently existing between Israel and the Arab states, among whom Egypt was "at the spearhead." George said Apr. 27 that the dam would make 2 million acres available for cotton growing and thereby cut into U.S. cotton exports.   He opposed seeking an Egyptian stipulation that the land would not be used for cotton because this would be "tying strings" to aid and therefore wrong in principle. George Apr. 29 expressed doubt that a large Middle East aid expenditure would help settle Arab-Israeli disputes.

The recognition of Communist China May 16, 1956 by the Nasser government gave the U.S. another cause for hesitation.   State Secy. Dulles May 22 called Egypt's move "an action that we regret."   Dulles told the press that, should Egypt accept Soviet aid for the Aswan project, "it would be unlikely . . . that we would find it practical" to join in financing it.   Dulles' comments followed reports from Washington May 17 that U.S. officials expected Syria, Saudi Arabia and Lebanon to establish relations soon with Peking.

Soviet Foreign Min. Dmitri T. Shepilov, who arrived in

Egypt June 16 on the first leg of a Mideastern tour, told Egyptian farm workers and government officials in the Nile Valley village of Bernesht June 18 that "the Arab countries may rely on the Soviet Union as their unselfish, faithful and reliable friend." Shepilov, who attacked the "aggressive Baghdad [Pact] military bloc," said in his June 18 speech that the USSR wanted "to improve relations and establish friendship [with] the U.S., France, Britain, Greece, Turkey, with all our neighbors," but it "cannot go on at the expense of our good relations with the Arab countries, with our friends in the East." Shepilov, invited to Cairo to attend celebrations centering on the British evacuation of the Suez Canal Zone, conferred with Egyptian Premier Nasser, Foreign Min. Mahmoud Fawzi, War Min. Abdel Hakim Amer and Soviet Amb.-to-Egypt Yevgeni D. Kiselev June 16 and reportedly presented Egyptian Trade & Commerce Min. Abu Nosseir June 17 with a list of industrial goods that the USSR was ready to trade for Egyptian cotton.

Soviet embassy spokesmen in Cairo confirmed June 18 that Shepilov and Nasser June 17 had discussed Soviet-Egyptian trade and Russian aid for Egyptian atomic plans and the Aswan project. Egyptian sources said June 18 that the USSR had offered £E400 million ($1.112 billion) for the Aswan project under the terms of a 20-year agreement with repayment at 2%.

World Bank Pres. Eugene R. Black arrived in Cairo June 19 after a 3-day visit with King Saud of Saudi Arabia. Egypt was reported June 19 to be continuing negotiations with the Bank, the U.S. and Britain on Western financing for the Aswan project. Reports from Cairo said June 19 that the U.S.-British offer was based on an initial gift of $70 million and later loans of $80–$150 million. Nasser reportedly asked Black in Cairo June 21 to urge rapid U.S. action on the offer—needed before the World Bank could grant a $200 million Aswan Dam loan request.

Soviet Foreign Min. Shepilov left Cairo June 22 after

talks there with Nasser June 16–22. A Soviet-Egyptian communiqué issued June 22 said that both sides had reached "complete agreement on the questions discussed." It stressed the increasing cordiality of "Soviet-Egyptian relations in all the fields of political, economical and cultural cooperation" but did not mention any Soviet commitment on the Arab dispute with Israel. (Shepilov arrived in Damascus, Syria June 22 for talks with Foreign Min. Salah el-Bitar and Pres. Shukri al-Kuwatly, then flew to Beirut, Lebanon, June 25 for meetings with Pres. Camille Chamoun, Premier Abdullah Yaffi and Foreign Min. Salim Lahoud June 26-28. Reports from Damascus June 23 and Beirut June 28 said that Shepilov had failed to issue a "clear statement" on Palestine demanded by Lebanese leaders.)

Israeli sources had said June 17 1956 that no reply had been received to an invitation to Shepilov to visit Israel. The invitation had been extended by Israeli Foreign Ministry Director Walter Eytan. Soviet Premier Nikolai A. Bulganin told Israeli Amb.-to-USSR Joseph Avidar June 18 at a French embassy reception in Moscow that "we believe that you want peace."

André Philip, member of a French Socialist delegation to Moscow in May, had said in Paris June 5 that Soviet Party First Secy. Nikita S. Khrushchev had denied the existence of anti-Semitic feelings among Soviet officials and had told the group that "there is still a cold war between us and Israel, but we expect to get it over quickly."

Khrushchev, in an interview published by the Cairo newspaper *Al-Ahram* July 1, said that "war between Israel and the Arab states would mean World War III." *Al-Ahram* quoted Khrushchev as saying that Israel, "an imperialist creation," was "launching aggressive attacks" against its Arab neighbors yet that "all the results will be in their [the Arabs'] favor."

Dispatches from Washington July 6-8 said that the State Department was "reexamining" U.S. policy toward Egypt but that an Anglo-U.S. aid offer for the Aswan project remained open despite the current allocation of the Aswan funds to other foreign aid projects.

The U.S. Senate Appropriations Committee's report on the annual foreign aid appropriation, published July 16, disclosed that the committee had adopted a "directive" to State Secy. Dulles that no Mutual Security Agency funds be spent on the Aswan project without the committee's "prior approval." Sen. Spessard L. Holland (D., Fla.) and other Southern Democratic members of the committee were said to have insisted on the directive even though Dulles had given assurances that he did not intend to use foreign aid funds for the project. The committee attached to the aid bill riders, sponsored by Sens. William F. Knowland (R., Calif.) and Styles Bridges (R., N.H.), declaring U.S. official "opposition to the seating in the UN of the Communist China regime" and calling on the President to consult with Congress on "implications . . . upon the foreign policy of the U.S." if Communist China did obtain a UN seat.

The U.S. government July 19, 1956 withdrew an offer of a $56 million grant for the Aswan Dam. The State Department explained that the grant had been contingent on an "Egyptian willingness and ability to concentrate its economic resources" on the project but that "developments have not been favorable" and the "U.S. government has concluded that it is not feasible in the present circumstances to participate" in the project.

Egyptian Amb.-to-U.S. Ahmed Hussein was informed of the aid withdrawal when he called on State Secy. Dulles July 19 to discuss the Aswan program. Hussein had returned from Cairo July 17, reportedly under orders from Pres. Nasser to "reach agreement as soon as possible" on the Dec. 16, 1955 U.S. and British offers on Aswan.

State Department officers July 19 stressed the economic factors behind the U.S. reversal and said that a heavy "mortgage" had been imposed on future Egyptian cotton crops by

Egyptian-Soviet bloc arms and industrial pacts. U.S. Congressional opinion was said in Washington reports July 16 to have been turned against the aid program by Nasser's increasingly anti-Western policies and the adverse effects that the Aswan grant might have among U.S. allies in the Middle East and Asia. The State Department July 19 also cited Egypt's failure to reach agreement with the Sudan on a division of the Nile's waters.

The cancellation of a proposed $14 million British grant for the Aswan Dam was announced July 20 by a British Foreign office spokesman who said that the decision had been made after "continuous consultation" with Washington. The Foreign Office said that the withdrawal had been made for substantially the reasons given by the U.S. and had not been affected by the July 19 meeting between Hussein and Dulles because "nothing new was revealed in the Dulles-Hussein talks."

World Bank officials in Washington said July 23 that the bank's $200 million loan offer to aid the Aswan project had been contingent on the U.S. and British grants and had "automatically expired" when they were withdrawn. The bank denied Egyptian Finance Ministry claims July 23 that Bank Pres. Eugene R. Black had termed Egypt's economy sound in a July 9 letter to Finance Min. Abdel Moneim el-Kaissouni.

Nasser made a bitter attack on the U.S. as part of an address just outside Cairo July 24 at the opening of a new oil refinery and pipeline to Suez. He ridiculed the argument that Egypt's economic prospects were the U.S.' and Britain's real motive for withdrawing the aid offers: "If rumor in Washington tries to represent that the Egyptian economy is not strong enough to warrant American aid, then I say: 'Choke on your fury, but you will never succeed in ordering us about or in wielding your tyranny over us, because we know our path—that of freedom, honor and dignity. . . . We shall yield neither to force nor to the dollar.'"

Soviet Foreign Min. Dmitri Shepilov had told reporters at the Belgian embassy during the Belgian National Day reception in Moscow July 21 that he did not consider Soviet aid for the Aswan dam "a live question." Shepilov said that "there are now more vitally important problems for the Egyptian economy," particularly "industrialization," although he did "not minimize the importance of the Aswan Dam." Shepilov said that "if the Egyptian government considers Soviet help" necessary, the USSR would "consider favorably any Egyptian requests." A *N.Y. Times* dispatch said July 22 that Western observers in Cairo had long believed that Egypt was using "inflated reports of Soviet aid offers to obtain more liberal Western terms" for the Aswan project. The *Times* reported July 20 that a "gasp of surprise and anger" had swept Cairo at news of the Western withdrawals but that officials had refused comment despite violent press attacks on the reversal.

Soviet Amb.-to-Egypt Yevgeni D. Kiselev told reporters in Cairo July 24 that the Western press had "exaggerated" Shepilov's remarks on Aswan Dam aid and said that "we are ready to finance the Aswan High Dam if Egypt asked for it." A Reuters dispatch said that the Soviet embassy in Cairo July 24 denied that Kiselev had made the offer. The embassy then said July 27 that Kiselev's offer was not official.

A report by the U.S. Senate Foreign Relations Committee's subcommittee on technical assistance July 22 estimated foreign aid credits currently offered by the USSR at more than $1 billion. The subcommittee's report quoted Egyptian National Production Min. Hassan Ibrahim as having said that the USSR had offered a $300 million 26-year loan to finance the Aswan Dam. Egyptian Amb.-to-U.S. Ahmed Hussein was quoted as having reported the Soviet offer at $200 million for 30 years, repayable in rice and cotton. The study listed these other Egyptian-Soviet-bloc trade negotiations and agreements": *Bulgaria*—negotiating to build oil-

processing and food plants since March. *Czechoslovakia—*
offered rubber and shoe plants in June 1955 and a pact to
aid a ceramic factory in Dec. 1955, and agreed in Mar. 1956
to build a cement plant. *Communist China—*a 3-year Egyptian trade-and-barter pact signed in July 1955. *East Germany—*negotiating since Feb. 1956 to build an Alexandria
shipyard, chemical, auto and sugar plants and a power station. *Hungary—*a pact to build 7 bridges reportedly made in
June 1955 and an agreement to aid power station construction in Dec. 1955. *Poland—*contracted to aid and equip an
enamelware plant.

SUEZ CRISIS (1956) & AFTERMATH

Britain Evacuates Canal

The 74-year British occupation of the Suez Canal Zone ended June 14, 1956 when Brigadier John H. S. Lacey in Port Said handed the keys of the Navy House to Egyptian Lt. Col. Abdullah Azouni and joined his rear guard of 11 British officers and 80 men aboard a Cyprus-bound British LST (landing ship-tank). Lacey left behind 800 British civilians manning Suez Zone repair, supply and Royal Air Force transit installations under the Oct. 1954 agreement for Egyptian control of the area.

Egyptian Premier Gamal Abdel Nasser, attending Evacuation Day celebrations in Port Said June 18, was hailed by cheering crowds as he toured the city in an open car. Nasser formally raised the Egyptian flag over the Suez Zone and said that Egypt had kept a "rendezvous with destiny when it saw the remnants of the foreign invader sneak out, back to where they came from."

British Foreign Secy. Selwyn Lloyd said in a letter to the Cairo newspaper *El Akhbar* June 18 that he regretted that the Suez agreement had failed to bring a "new era of friendship" between Britain and Egypt. Under the pact, Britain retained nearly 50% of the stock of the Compagnie Universelle du Canal Maritime de Suez (the Suez Canal Co.), which controlled the canal under a lease expiring in 1968. (2 warships described by observers as Russian "heavy destroyers" were displayed in Alexandria harbor June 18, Suez Evacuation Day. The vessels, renamed the *Victorious* and *Nasser*, had been delivered to Egypt June 11. British dispatches had reported June 6 that 2 destroyers flying the Polish flag had passed through the English Channel, possibly headed toward Egypt.)

Nasser June 20 reviewed the newly equipped Egyptian army units during Cairo celebrations marking the withdrawal of British troops from the Suez Canal Zone. Western observers said that the display, also attended by Soviet Foreign Min. Dmitri T. Shepilov and British Gen. Sir Brian Robertson, included such arms as: Stalin, Centurion and Czechoslovak T-34 tanks; MiG-15, Ilyushin-28, Meteor and Vampire jets; Soviet ABC (atomic, biological and chemical warfare) troop carriers and artillery and Soviet trailer-borne torpedoes. The paraders, estimated at 11,000 men, included units of the Jordanian Arab Legion, Saudi Arabian, Lebanese, Libyan and Yemeni armies and troops of the newly formed Palestine Army recruited by Egypt from among Gaza Strip refugee camps.

The Suez Canal Co.'s annual report Apr. 1, 1956 disclosed an increase of 11% in traffic for 1955, with 14,666 vessels carrying 107½ million tons through the canal. 65% of the tonnage traffic reported was in oil products carried by 7,878 tankers. The 48 nations using the canal were led by Britain, which accounted for 28.3% of the tonnage traffic, followed by Norway with 13½%, Liberia 12.1%, France 8%. U.S. flag tonnage ranked 9th, but shipments in U.S.-controlled vessels under Liberian, Panamanian and Honduran registry made the actual American share of Suez traffic 2d only to Britain's.

Nasser Elected President

Nasser was chosen Egypt's first elected president June 22, 1956, 4 days after the Cairo celebrations.

Nasser Jan. 16, 1956 had proclaimed a new Egyptian constitution designed to end rule by the Revolutionary Command Council, which had suspended the old constitution Jan. 16, 1953. The new constitution was approved in the national plebiscite June 22, and the first president was declared elected to a 6-year term July 7.

Nasser's formal presidential nomination had been made by the new unicameral National Assembly. Candidates to the Assembly had been nominated by a National Union pending the formation of new political parties. The current suspension of all political parties was to continue in force until the Assembly had approved a law regulating the formation of new parties.

The new constitution proclaimed Egypt an Islamic republic with a democratic form of government and Arabic as the official language. It provided for basic freedom of worship, press, assembly, speech and private ownership.

Nasser had already moved to curtail the military junta's rule in Egypt June 19 with proclamations that ended martial law and press censorship in effect since 1952. He said at a Cairo rally June 19 that "we must strengthen ourselves to liberate all Arabs . . . so that the Palestine tragedy may not be repeated and we may be able to restore to the people of Palestine their rights to freedom and [national] existence."

Nasser had also said June 19 that all 2,000 to 2,900 political prisoners previously held by the government had been freed. He promised that the Revolutionary Command Council would be dissolved following his election to the presidency—and it was dissolved June 24. He said he hoped the next meeting of Arab nations would include members of a "free" Algeria. Egypt "must strive to liberate all Arab countries, from Morocco to Baghdad," Nasser declared.

Egypt reported June 25 that 99.9% (5,496,965) of 5,508,291 Egyptians voting in the June 22 national plebiscite had approved Nasser as Egypt's first 6-year elected president and that 99.8% (5,488,225) had voted their acceptance of the new constitution. The plebiscite, in which voting was optional for women but compulsory for all males over 18, was to be followed by elections to the single-party National Assembly. The new constitution granted Nasser the power to promulgate laws until the National Assembly was convened. The Egyptian government announced June 25 that the Interior Ministry would retain for 10 years powers to place suspected revolutionists and grafters under administrative arrest.

The new Egyptian cabinet, as announced June 30:

President—Gamal Abdel Nasser; *Foreign Minister*—Mahmoud Fawzi; *Deputy Foreign Minister*—Abdel Fattah Hassan; *Interior*—Zakaria Mohieddin; *War*—Maj. Gen. Abdel Hakim Amer; *National Guidance*—Fathy Radwan; *Justice*—Ahmed Housni; *Industry*—Aziz Sidky; *Commerce*—Muhammad Abu Nosseir; *Works*—Ahmed Abdouel-Sharabassy; *Supply*—Kamal Ramzy Stino; *Finance*—Abdel Moneim el-Kaissouny; *Communications*—Mustaka Khalil Kamel; *Municipalities & Rural Affairs, State Minister for Planning*—Abdel Latif el-Boghdadi; *Education*—Kamal el-Din Hussein; *Health*—Dr. Nurreddin Tarraf; *Social Affairs & Labor*—Hussein Shafei; *Agriculture*—Abdel Razzak Sidky; *State Minister for Agriculture Reform*—Sayed Marei; *Wakfs* (Moslem charities)—Sheikh Ahmed Hassan al-Bakoury.

The Egyptian cabinet July 4 announced a £E280½ million general budget and £E47½ million nation-production budget for fiscal 1956–7. The general budget, up £E42.2 million over 1955–6, earmarked £E93,427,000 for internal and external defense and £E125,636,000 for public welfare.

Nasser Visits Yugoslavia

Nasser visited Pres. Tito of Yugoslavia in Belgrade July 12–14, 1956 and, after a trip to Bosnia, Croatia and Slovenia, rejoined Tito on the Adriatic Island of Brioni. A joint Yugoslav-Egyptian communiqué was issued July 18. The communiqué affirmed the principles of the Bandung Conference (at which Yugoslavia was not represented), especially insofar as they applied to the Mideast, and called for economic and cultural exchanges between the 2 countries.

Tito and Nasser were joined on Brioni July 18–19 by Premier Jawaharlal Nehru of India. Their tripartite talks concluded with a statement, initialled by the 3 leaders July 19, declaring:

... The 3 heads of government reviewed developments in the international sphere since they met each other separately 12 months ago. They noted with satisfaction that the policies pursued by their countries have contributed to some extent to the lessening of international tension and to the development of relations between nations based on equality.

The latest developments and contacts between the leaders of various countries following different policies have contributed to a better understanding of each other's viewpoints and to a growing recognition of the principles of peaceful and active coexistence. The 3 heads of government consider that these contacts and exchanges of opinions should continue and be encouraged.

The Bandung Conference . . . laid down certain principles which should govern international relations. The 3 heads of government reaffirm these 10 principles, which they have always supported. They realize that conflicts and tension in the world today have led to fears and apprehensions in the present and for the future. As long as these fears and apprehensions dominate the world, no firm base for peace can be established. At the same time it is difficult to remove such fears and apprehensions rapidly, and progressive steps will have to be taken towards their removal. . . .

The division of the world today into powerful blocs of nations tends to perpetuate these fears. Peace has to be sought not through division but by aiming at collective security on a world basis, and by enlarging the sphere of freedom and ending the domination of one country over another.

Progress towards disarmament is essential in order to lessen the fear of conflict. This progress should be made primarily within the framework of the UN and should include both nuclear and thermonuclear weapons and conventional armaments, as well as adequate supervision of the implementation of the agreements made. Explosions of weapons of mass destruction, even for experimental purposes, should be suspended as they involve a possible danger to humanity by pollution of the atmosphere, affecting other countries regardless of frontiers, and as they are a violation of international morality. Fissionable material should be used only for peaceful purposes, and its use for warlike purposes should be prohibited. The 3 heads of government are deeply interested in full and equal cooperation among nations in the field of the peaceful uses of atomic energy. Such cooperation should be organized within the framework of the UN and the proposed International Agency should be representative of all countries.

The intensification of efforts to quicken the development of underdeveloped areas of the world constitutes one of the principal tasks in the creation of permanent and stable peace among nations. In this connexion the 3 heads of government recognize the importance of international economic and financial cooperation and believe that it is necessary and desirable that the proposed Special UN Fund for Economic Development be constituted. . . .

... The 3 heads of government emphasized the great importance of removing embargoes and obstacles to the normal flow and expansion of international trade.

The 3 principal areas of tension and possible conflict are Central Europe, the Far East and the Middle East region. The problems of the Far East cannot adequately be solved without the full cooperation of the People's Republic of China. The 3 heads of government express their belief that the People's Republic of China should be represented in the United Nations. They also consider that those countries which have applied for membership in accordance with the Charter should be admitted to the UN.

The problems of Central Europe are intimately connected with that of Germany. This important question should be solved in conformity with the wishes of the German people by peaceful negotiated settlement.

In the Middle East the conflicting interests of the great powers have added to the difficulties of the situation. These problems should be considered on their merits, safeguarding legitimate economic interests but basing the solution on the freedom of the peoples concerned. The freedom and goodwill of the peoples of those areas are essential not only for peace but also to safeguard legitimate economic interests. The situation in Palestine particularly is one of danger to world peace. The heads of government support the resolution of the Bandung Conference in this respect. . . .

Nasser Nationalizes the Canal

Nasser left Yugoslavia July 19, 1956—the same day that the U.S. State Department informed Egypt through its Washington ambassador that the U.S. was withdrawing its offer of financial aid for the initiation of the Aswan High Dam project. Nasser's first publicized reaction was his assertion July 24 that the U.S. had lied about the true state of Egypt's economy in using his country's underdevelopment as a pretext for withdrawing the offer. The Egyptian president, pointing to a 34½% growth in his country's national income since 1952, pledged that "imperialists" would never rule Egypt again by either "dollar or force."

Nasser announced in a 3-hour speech in Alexandria July 26 that the Egyptian government had nationalized the Suez Canal Co. and would use its revenues (in 1955 amounting in net to $46.39 million) to build the Aswan High Dam. Nasser also said that Egypt had "frozen" all Canal Co. funds in Egypt and would pay off the company's shareholders at the final closing prices of the company's stock on the Paris Bourse (stock exchange), where it had been listed for daily sale for at least 85 years. He spoke in a colloquial Arabic dialect of Egypt—a tradition-shattering precedent—and his words were broadcast nationwide. Among other things, he told his countrymen that "120,000 Egyptians died building" the Canal and it "belongs to us."

Egyptian Commerce & Industry Min. Abu Nosseir July 27 issued a statement accusing the Suez Canal Co. of having "failed to comply with its obligations" to maintain the Canal properly—*e.g.*, to provide a suitable harbor at Ismailia for the largest ships and to furnish the adequate equipment for transit trade at Port Said. Nosseir announced in the statement that Egypt would not recognize the right of either the UN Security Council or the International Court of Justice to intervene in the matter. The Canal had been Egyptian since its inception, and only Egyptian courts had jurisdiction over it, Nosseir asserted.

Ceylonese Prime Min. S. W. R. D. Bandaranaike was reported July 28 to have prepared himself to call a mid-August meeting of the Colombo Powers (Ceylon, India, Pakistan, Burma & Indonesia)—all heavily dependent on the Canal—to study the Suez problem. Just south of Egypt, Sudanese Premier Abdullah Khalil said July 29 that the nationalization was "a daring step, and I wish Egypt success."

Nasser July 31 issued a statement reassuring the world's maritime states of freedom of navigation through the Canal. The statement read:

On July 26 the Suez Canal Co. was nationalized. This exercise by the Egyptian government of its right has, however, given rise to some opposition from a few governments, particularly those of France and Britain. Such opposition is devoid of all foundation. The Suez Canal Co. has always been an Egyptian company and, like all other Egyptian companies, liable to be nationalized. This nationalization does not in any way or to any extent affect Egypt's international commitments.

We are determined as ever to honor all our international obligations, and both the Convention of 1888 and the assurance concerning it given in the Anglo-Egyptian Agreement of 1954 will be fully maintained. Freedom of navigation on the Suez Canal is neither affected nor involved in any manner or to any degree. No one could be more interested than Egypt in the freedom of passage through the canal. We are certain that traffic through the canal will in the coming years justify all our hopes and those of the whole world. Egypt is confident of the righteousness of her stand. She will not be deflected from the course she has charted for herself but will proceed in the service of her own interests and those of the world community of nations.

The British government July 27 had protested Egypt's move as an "arbitrary action which constitutes a serious threat to the freedom of navigation on a waterway of vital international importance" and "the responsibility for the consequences" of which "must rest entirely on the Egyptian government." But Egypt rejected the protest. Britain July 28 froze Suez Canal Co. assets still in British hands and all Egyptian sterling accounts as well, including about $308 million left from balances deposited for safekeeping in Britain during World War II. Prime Min. Sir Anthony Eden July 30 banned all exports of war materiel to Egypt, including 2 warships of 1,700 tons each that had been bought by Egypt but still had not left British ports. Within the next 2 days Britain sent 3 aircraft carriers to the Mediterranean and a number of Canberra jet bomber squadrons to Malta and alerted an infantry battalion and a marine commando unit to prepare to move to an undisclosed destination.

France had also protested against the Egyptian move. The French government July 29 froze $1.285 billion worth of Egyptian assets in France. In doing this, France was said to have ignored the existence of larger French accounts in Egypt. Premier Guy Mollet in a press statement July 30 described Nasser as an "apprentice dictator" whose style was "the policy of blackmail alternating with flagrant violations of international agreements." France Aug. 2 ordered its Mediterranean fleet to sail from Toulon and maintain close cooperation with the British Navy. Britain and France advised all British and French nationals lacking "compelling reasons" for staying to leave Egypt at once.

Soviet Communist Party leader Nikita S. Khrushchev in Moscow July 31 had urged the international community to react calmly to Nasser's takeover of the Canal. He asserted that Egypt's nationalization action was "in the spirit of the times" and "an action that the Egyptian government, as a sovereign government, is entitled to take." He added: "We think that the policy of putting pressure on Egypt is a mistaken one. Rashness and haste in this matter can bring only undesirable consequences for the cause of peace and can only damage the interests of the Western powers themselves in that area. The Suez Canal's nationalization does not affect the interests of the peoples of Britain, France, the U.S. and other countries. Only the former Suez Canal Co., which received high profits from the canal's exploitation, is now being deprived of the possibility of self-enrichment at Egypt's expense. The Soviet Union, directly interested in the maintenance of the freedom of shipping through the Suez Canal and noting the Egyptian government's statement to the effect that the Suez Canal will remain free for all, considers that there are no grounds for alarm and concern over this matter. We are confident that the situation in the Suez Canal will not become aggravated if it is not artificially aggravated from outside." Khrushchev expressed confidence that the diplomatic "common-sense, experience and political sobriety" of Britain and France would enable those 2 countries to understand "this historic act" and to ignore the counsels of "unreasonable voices." For its part, Khrushchev said, the Soviet Union supported all countries striving to "free themselves from colonial enslavement."

Wing Cmndr. Ali Sabry, an aide to Nasser, told reporters July 31 that "freedom of navigation in the Suez Canal" was not "involved in any manner" in the nationalization proceedings. Sabry cited Nasser's assurances that Egypt would honor the Constantinople Convention of 1888 and the

Anglo-Egyptian agreement of 1954. He said that Egypt had received no formal notice of British and French proposals for an international Suez Canal board to replace the private company's directors but that Egypt would "study those proposals when we receive them officially and answer them in due time."

Sabry acknowledged that London and Paris banks were refusing checks drawn in or to the name of Egypt's new Suez Canal Authority. (Vice Chairman Mahmoud Yunis of the new Canal authority July 28 had ordered all Canal tolls paid to the Egyptian government through designated banks in London, Paris and Egypt. Commerce Min. Nosseir had said the same day that all ships refusing payment to the new administration would be barred from the Canal. Deputy Foreign Min. Abdel Hassan said July 29 that all shipping was proceeding normally through the Canal.) But the seized Suez Canal Co. notified shippers Aug. 1 that it could not be responsible for the safe operation of the Canal and warned that tolls paid to the Egyptian government would not be credited to the company's accounts with the shippers.

The Canal Co. July 27 had urged banks holding the firm's assets to refuse to honor the Egyptian decree. The company told its employes—among them 350 French, 135 British and 2 American personnel—to accept instructions only from the company and to "execute only the tasks strictly necessary to the functioning of traffic."

The company Aug. 6 gave its employes until Aug. 15 to choose between loyalty to their contracts and collaboration with "the *de facto* authority that has taken over" the Canal. The company was reported Aug. 8 to have offered all European employes in Egypt indefinite leaves with full pay if they would leave their posts. 27 foreign pilots did not return from their summer vacations, and Egypt was forced to curtail service to one Canal convoy each way per day after mid-August.

Suez Canal Co. Director-Gen. Jacques Georges-Picot had

said Aug. 9 that the Egyptian use of force in seizing the Canal justified Western force use in reasserting international control. Georges-Picot asserted Aug. 14 that the Canal Co. could close the Canal in 24 hours by withdrawing its technicians. The company Aug. 13 denied charges made by Nasser Aug. 12 that Georges-Picot had sought U.S. support for an extension of the Canal concession beyond 1968, its expiration date.

British Prime Min. Sir Anthony Eden said in a radio-TV address Aug. 8 that "our quarrel is not with Egypt, still less with the Arab world; it is with Col. Nasser." Eden said that when Nasser came to power "we felt no hostility toward him"; "we hoped he wanted to improve the conditions of life of his people and to be friends with this country." However, Eden declared, Nasser "has shown he is not a man who can be trusted to keep an agreement."

Eden said: The industry of Britain and Western Europe "could not be kept going" without Suez-shipped oil. "This is a matter of life and death to us all" and, should Nasser's action succeed, "each one of us would be at the mercy of one man for the supplies on which we live." "We could never accept that. With dictators you always have to pay a higher price later on—for their appetite grows with feeding." A London conference of Canal users had been called to avoid "a solution by force" and to "produce a workable scheme for the future of the canal" under "the broadest possible international agreement." Eden warned, however, that "we have too much at risk not to take precautions." "We must make sure," he said, "that the lives of the great trading nations of the world cannot in the future be strangled at any moment by some interruption of the free passage of the Canal."

Paris and London banking circles were reported Aug. 11 to believe that Egypt could pay full compensation for the $233 million Suez Canal Co. by using current Egyptian sterling balances of £110 million ($308 million).

Indian Prime Min. Jawaharlal Nehru told the Indian

House of the People (lower house of parliament) in New
Delhi Aug. 8 that India, after discussion with both Britain
and Egypt, would attend the conference in London Aug. 16.
Nehru said that assurances had been received that "participation in the conference will not injure the interests or sovereign rights and dignity of Egypt." He said he was "well aware
that this conference can reach no final decisions, for that
requires the agreement of Egypt." Nehru backed "the sovereignty of Egypt" as "beyond question" in the dispute and
said that the Canal seizure had resulted from the withdrawal of Aswan dam aid in a way that "hurt Egypt's pride
and self respect." Nehru denounced Anglo-French military
moves in the Middle East as having "aggravated the situation" and said that "in Asia as a whole, with its colonial
memories, great resentment has been aroused."

Reports from New Delhi and Cairo Aug. 8 said that
Indian sources had indicated that India, which had strong
interests in keeping the Canal open under any auspices, would
speak on Egypt's behalf and attempt a mediating role at the
London conference. V. K. Krishna Menon, chief Indian
delegate to the London meeting, stopped in Cairo Aug. 12
while en route to London for talks with Foreign Min.
Mahmoud Fawzi and Nasser.

The British Labor Party formally dissociated itself Aug.
13 from the Conservative government policy in the Suez
dispute and demanded assurances that the British military
moves were "solely intended for defense against possible
aggression and not preparations for armed intervention . . .
inconsistent with" the UN Charter. The Laborite statement,
made after a 2-hour meeting of party leaders, urged that
any resolutions produced by the prospective London conference of Canal users be submitted to a special session of the
UN General Assembly.

The Labor Party leadership's demand was not met. Instead, British Foreign Secy. Selwyn Lloyd said in a radio
address Aug. 14 that Egypt's nationalization of the Canal

was more serious than either the 1948 Berlin blockade or the 1950 invasion of Korea. Lloyd asserted that "with Britain, force is always a last resort" but that a new Suez agreement "must include some form of international control."

French Premier Guy Mollet's cabinet Aug. 14 approved a plan for international control of the Canal to be presented at the London conference by Foreign Min. Christian Pineau. The cabinet also supported Mollet's intention to "impose" London conference decisions on Egypt by force, if necessary, though Paris dispatches said Aug. 14 that likelihood of an armed resolution of the Suez dispute had decreased since Western moves to convene the London talks.

The *N.Y. Times* had reported Aug. 11 that Pineau, in a National Assembly speech June 1 on reported Egyptian aid to the Algerian rebels, had rejected the idea that Nasser was a new Hitler and had asked what action France should take against Egypt. He implied that economic sanctions would not work because "France has 450 billion francs invested in Egypt, which has nothing invested in France." "Do you want the French fleet to bombard Alexandria?" he continued. "There can be no question of it. There is no worse humbug than to make threats that will not be carried out. Let us not brandish a saber when it is a wooden saber."

The official U.S. reaction to Egypt's move was disapproving but not condemnatory, unlike the official attitudes of France and Britain. The State Department July 27 issued this 3-sentence statement: "The announcement by the Egyptian government with respect to the seizure of the installations of the Suez Canal Co. carries far-reaching implications. It affects the nations whose economies depend upon the products which move through this international waterway, as well as the owners of the company itself. The United States is consulting urgently with other governments concerned." Lincoln White, the State Department's chief spokesman, said July 27 that the U.S. was then consulting with Britain and France and that the 3 countries would soon broaden the circle involved in the talks to include other countries affected because of goods transit via the canal.

The U.S. Treasury July 31 issued under the Foreign Assets Control Statute an order to and through the Federal Reserve banks temporarily "freezing" all Egyptian government and Suez Canal Co. assets in the U.S. "pending determination of their ownership and the existing situation." Private Egyptian funds in the U.S. were not affected by the order. The Treasury Aug. 3 gave U.S. shippers permission to pay Canal tolls to Egypt's new Suez Canal Authority provided payment was accompanied by a statement that it had been made "under protest and without prejudice to all rights of recovery." The Aug. 3 Treasury order lifted undisclosed provisions of the July 31 Egyptian assets freeze, which banned all business dealings with the Egyptian government.

U.S. Administration leaders, however, were personally critical of Egypt. State Secy. Dulles returned to Washington July 29 from a visit to Peru and said that the Egyptian government, by its action, had "struck a grievous blow at international confidence." Pres. Eisenhower, who had conferred on the matter July 27 with his cabinet and Acting State Secy. Herbert Hoover, said at his press conference Aug. 1: "We are manifestly faced with a grave issue, important to every country that has a seacoast." Freedom of navigation in the Canal was "vital" to the U.S.' own economy and future welfare.

Deputy State Undersecy. Robert Murphy had gone to London July 29 for the opening of talks on the Suez crisis with French Foreign Min. Christian Pineau and British Foreign Secy. Selwyn Lloyd. Murphy had a separate meeting July 30 with British Prime Min. Eden. Eisenhower sent Dulles to London July 31 to conclude the talks. The tripartite discussions ended Aug. 2, and the 3 countries agreed to take part in the conference of 24 Suez Canal-using countries scheduled to begin in London Aug. 16 on freedom and security of navigation in the Canal. The U.S., Britain and

France issued a joint communiqué that said:

The governments of France, the United Kingdom, and the United States join in the following statement:

(1) They have taken note of the recent action of the government of Egypt whereby it attempts to nationalize and take over the assets and the responsibilities of the Universal Suez Canal Co. This company was organized in Egypt in 1856 under a franchise to build the Suez Canal and operate it until 1968. The Universal Suez Canal Co. has always had an international character in terms of its shareholders, directors and operating personnel and in terms of its responsibility to assure the efficient functioning as an international waterway of the Suez Canal.

In 1888 all the great powers then principally concerned with the international character of the Canal and its free, open and secure use without discrimination joined in the Treaty and Convention of Constantinople. This provided for the benefit of all the world that the international character of the Canal would be perpetuated for all time, irrespective of the expiration of the concession of the Universal Suez Canal Co.

Egypt as recently as Oct. 1954 recognized that the Suez Canal is a waterway economically, commercially and strategically of international importance and renewed its determination to uphold the Convention of 1888.

(2) They do not question the right of Egypt to enjoy and exercise all the powers of a fully sovereign and independent nation, including the generally recognized right, under appropriate conditions, to nationalize assets, not impressed with an international interest, which are subject to its political authority.

But the present action involves far more than a simple act of nationalization. It involves the arbitrary and unilateral seizure by one nation of an international agency which has the responsibility to maintain and to operate the Suez Canal so that all the signatories to, and beneficiaries of, the Treaty of 1888 can effectively enjoy the use of an international waterway upon which the economy, commerce and security of much of the world depends.

This situation is the more serious in its implications because it avowedly was made for the purpose of enabling the government of Egypt to make the Canal serve the purely national purposes of the Egyptian government rather than the international purpose established by the Convention of 1888.

Furthermore, they deplore the fact that, as an incident to its seizure, the Egyptian government has had recourse to what amounts to a denial of fundamental human rights by compelling employees of the Suez Canal Co. to continue to work under threat of imprisonment.

(3) They consider that the action taken by the government of Egypt, having regard to all the attendant circumstances, threatens the

freedom and security of the Canal as guaranteed by the Convention of 1888. This makes it necessary that steps be taken to assure that the parties to that convention and all other nations entitled to enjoy its benefits shall in fact be assured of such benefits.

(4) They consider that steps should be taken to establish operating arrangements under an international system designed to assure the continuity of operation of the Canal, as guaranteed by the Convention of Oct. 29, 1888, consistently with legitimate Egyptian interests.

(5) To this end they propose that a conference should promptly be held of parties to the convention and other nations largely concerned with the use of the Canal. The invitations to such a conference, to be held in London on Aug. 16, 1956, will be extended by the government of the United Kingdom to the governments named in the annex to this statement. The governments of France and the United States are ready to take part in the conference.

Parties to the Convention of 1888—Egypt, France, Italy, Netherlands, Spain, Turkey, the United Kingdom, the USSR. [The signatories of the 1888 Convention were Great Britain, France, Germany, Austria-Hungary, Spain, Italy, the Netherlands, Russia and Turkey.]

Other nations largely concerned in the use of the Canal, either through ownership of tonnage or pattern of trade—Australia, Ceylon, Denmark, Ethiopia, the German Federal Republic [West Germany], Greece, India, Indonesia, Japan, New Zealand, Norway, Pakistan, Persia, Portugal, Sweden, the United States.

Dulles, who had returned at once to Washington, told Americans over radio and TV Aug. 3:

This trouble about the Suez Canal started when Pres. Nasser announced that he was going to take over the operation of the Canal. He tried to seize the monies, property and personnel of the Universal Suez Canal Co., which is the operating company of that Canal. This act by Pres. Nasser goes far beyond a mere attempt by a government to nationalize companies and properties within its territory which are not international in character, because the Suez Canal and the operating company are international in character.

The Suez Canal is an international waterway which was built by the Universal Suez Canal Co. with international funds. . . . In 1888 all the great powers principally concerned with the Canal made a treaty providing that the Suez Canal shall be open at all times, in war as well as in peace, to the shipping of all nations on free and equal terms. Egypt is a party to that treaty and has repeatedly recognized it. Indeed, only a couple of years ago Pres. Nasser himself reaffirmed the allegiance of Egypt to that treaty. In all the world there is no international waterway as fully internationalized as is the Suez Canal.

The Universal Suez Canal Co. . . . has been the means of assuring that the canal would in fact be operated as a free and open international waterway as pledged by the 1888 treaty. That company itself is of an international character. Registered in Egypt, it operates under a franchise given it by the government of Egypt. Shareholders are of many nationalities, the board of directors is international, and the Canal work—the building of the Canal and the keeping of it in good repair—is supervised by an international body of engineers. . . .

In 1955, 14,666 ships passed through the Canal. They had a tonnage of over 115 million, flew the flags of more than 40 nations, and carried the products of all the world. There are 187 pilots from 13 nations—56 French, 52 British, 32 Egyptian, 14 Dutch, 11 Norwegian, and so on. 2 of the pilots are Americans. It is by far the world's greatest highway. It has nearly 3 times the traffic that goes through the Panama Canal.

Now, why did Pres. Nasser suddenly decide to take over the operation of the Suez Canal? He has told us about that in a long speech he made. In that speech he did not for a moment suggest that Egypt would be able to operate the Canal better than it was being operated. . . . The basic reason he gave was that if he took over this Canal, it would enhance the prestige of Egypt. He said that Egypt was determined to score one triumph after another, in order to enhance what he called the 'grandeur of Egypt.' And he coupled his action with statements about his ambition to extend his influence from the Atlantic to the Persian Gulf. He also said that by seizing the Suez Canal he would strike a blow at what he called 'Western imperialism.' And he thought also that he could exploit the Canal so as to produce bigger revenues for Egypt and so retaliate for the failure of the U.S. and Britain to give Egypt the money to enable it to get started on the $1 billion-plus Aswan high dam.

Pres. Nasser's speech made it absolutely clear that his seizure of the Canal Co. was an angry act of retaliation against fancied grievances. No one reading that speech can doubt for a moment that the Canal, under Egyptian operation, would be used, not to carry out the 1888 treaty better, but to promote the political and economic ambitions of Egypt. . . .

Of course, the government of a free and independent country . . . should seek to promote by all proper means the welfare of its people. . . . But it is inadmissible that a waterway internationalized by treaty, which is required for the livelihood of a score or more of nations, should be exploited by one country for purely selfish purposes, and that the operating agency which has done so well in handling the Suez Canal in accordance with the 1888 treaty should be struck down by a national act of vengefulness. To permit this to go unchallenged would be to encourage a breakdown of the international fabric upon which the security and the well-being of all peoples depend.

The question is not whether something should be done about this Egyptian act, but what should be done about it. There were some people who counselled immediate forcible action by the governments which felt themselves most directly affected. This, however, would have been contrary to the principles of the UN Charter and would undoubtedly have led to widespread violence endangering the peace of the world. At London we decided upon a different approach. We decided to call together in conference the nations most directly involved, with a view to seeing whether agreement could not be reached upon an adequate and dependable international administration of the Canal on terms which would respect, and generously respect, all the legitimate rights of Egypt. . . .

We believe that out of this conference will come a plan for the international operation of the Canal which will give assurance that the objectives of the 1888 treaty will in fact be realized, and that the Canal will continue to be operated by those who feel that it is their duty to serve the international community and not the special interests of any one nation. This plan should give both security to the nations principally concerned with the Canal, and also fully protect the legitimate interests of Egypt. Egypt, we believe, should be adequately represented on this operating authority and be assured, also, of a fair and reasonable income for the use of the property, because the Canal, although it is internationalized, is on Egyptian territory.

There is every desire that Egypt shall be treated with the utmost fairness. And also, the owners and the employes of the now dispossessed Universal Canal Co. should also be fairly treated. . . .

I have been asked: 'What will we do if the conference fails?' My answer to that is that we are not thinking in terms of the conference's failing. But I can say this: We have given no commitments at any time as to what the United States would do in that unhappy contingency. We assume that the conference will not fail but will succeed. And I believe that by the conference we will invoke moral forces which are bound to prevail. . . . I am confident that out of this conference there will come a judgment of such moral force that we can be confident that the Suez Canal will go on as it has for the last 100 years, to serve in peace the interest of mankind.

It was reported from Paris Aug. 4 that Dulles' TV report had underlined differences in the U.S. and Franco-British policies on Suez, particularly on the use of military force should Egypt refuse to accept international control of the Canal. The Paris newspaper *Paris-Presse* said Aug. 4: "We cannot count on the solidarity of Washington in the defense of our Mediterranean positions."

(It had been reported from Paris May 6 that Dulles had urged that the North Atlantic Council [composed of the foreign ministers of the 15 NATO countries] create a permanent high-level NATO cabinet to coordinate political planning among NATO nations, reportedly on problems such as Cyprus, North Africa and the Middle East. Several NATO members were said May 7 to be reluctant to place their international problems in the hands of a NATO cabinet, but the Committee of 3 Wise Men [Canadian External Affairs Secy. Lester B. Pearson, Italian Foreign Min. Gaetano Martino and Norwegian Foreign Min. Halvard M. Lange] was said to be studying the plan.

(French Foreign Min. Christian Pineau had said May 6 that he, Dulles and Lloyd had agreed that the U.S.-British-French Tripartite Declaration of 1950, guaranteeing Israeli-Arab frontiers, could be used no longer as a basis for action in case of Middle East aggression. Pineau said that action could be taken only through the UN Security Council.).

Dulles conferred with Pres. Eisenhower on the Suez dispute Aug. 6, and informed Washington sources reported that he had told the President that Western use of force against Egypt would entail a possible war with the entire Arab world. Saudi Arabian Amb.-to-U.S. Abdullah al-Khayyal met with Dulles Aug. 6 and told reporters that Saudi Arabia "backs" Egypt but believed force could be averted. Syrian Amb.-to-U.S. Victor A. Khouri also saw Dulles Aug. 6 and predicted that Lebanon would "follow the general line of the Arab states."

Dulles Aug. 7 briefed 20 Latin-American ambassadors on the Suez dispute in a closed session reportedly called to insure Latin support for the West should Egypt bring the Suez issue before the UN. Dulles was said to have agreed that Egypt's seizure of the Canal might have violated Article 51 of the UN Charter, but he was represented as implying that the U.S. government did not feel this would justify the use of force at Suez. Dulles reportedly urged economic sanctions against Egypt if the Aug. 16 London party failed. U.S. Defense Secy. Charles E. Wilson told reporters Aug. 7 that the

Suez crisis was "a relatively small thing" when compared with the total U.S. military program. "We should seek honorable means of reaching a peaceful settlement rather than wave the big stick and threaten people," Wilson said.

The Soviet government Aug. 9 announced its acceptance of the Western Big-3 foreign ministers' invitation to the mid-August conference of Suez Canal users in London and the substance of 2 counter-proposals—(1) that the east European countries, the Arab states and China and other countries (22 more, in all) also should have been invited, and (b) that the conference should have been put off until the end of the month to allow time for better arrangements. The Kremlin also posed 2 preconditions: (a) that the Soviet government did not consider the conference as an international conclave authorized to make any decisions about the Canal, and (b) that Soviet participation in the conference would not *per se* commit it to undertake any of the "obligations" foreseen by the Western Big 3 or signify the adoption of any position challenging Egypt's right to nationalize the Suez Canal. The Soviet note, made public Aug. 9 by Tass, said that Egypt's nationalization move in no way affected freedom of transit through the Canal, since Egypt had pledged again to respect the 1888 Convention of Constantinople and to guarantee freedom of navigation and shipping. The Kremlin said it saw "no reason to express any concern in that regard, the more so as Egypt . . . can ensure normal navigation on the Canal in a manner not inferior to any private company." The note also said:

> The nationalization of the property of enterprises situated in the territory of any country is, according to accepted principles of international law, an internal business of the state concerned. . . . The UN General Assembly, in Dec. 1952, passed a special resolution on the rights of peoples to dispose freely of their natural wealth and resources . . . In view of this, the Soviet government considers the decision of the Egyptian government to nationalize the Suez Canal Co. as a fully legal act stemming from the sovereign rights enjoyed by Egypt. . . .
> The fact that the Suez Canal has for decades remained in hands

other than Egyptian—in the hands of a company in which British and French capital predominated and which used the Canal for its enrichment and interference in the internal affairs of Egypt—cannot serve as a foundation for the preservation of such an abnormal situation in the future. One must take account of the fact that relations created in the past through conquest and occupation . . . do not conform to the principles of cooperation between sovereign and equal states, that is, to the principles and aims of the United Nations. Since the governments of Britain and France, as well as of the United States, recognize the high principles of the UN and state that they welcome the changes which have taken place in their relations with countries which were formerly in a state of colonial dependence, the governments of these powers should not hinder the realization by these states of their sovereign rights. . . .

. . . The choice of countries invited to the conference has been tendentiously made, with a view of securing a majority of its participants to support the proposals prepared by Britain and France. . . .

Among the signatories of the 1888 Convention were Austria-Hungary and Germany. Austria, Hungary, Czechoslovakia and Yugoslavia are the legal heirs of Austria-Hungary; none of these countries has been invited to the conference. From Germany, only one part of the country has been invited—the German Federal Republic—but not the other part, the German Democratic Republic. . . . There have not been invited to the conference the Arab states whose territories are directly adjacent to the Canal and which are vitally interested in the settlement of this question—namely, Syria, Lebanon, Saudi Arabia, Jordan, Sudan, Libya, Yemen, Iraq, Tunisia and Morocco. The majority of the Arab states are the successors of the former Ottoman Empire, which was a party to the 1888 Convention. Nor have there been invited to the conference such maritime powers making extensive use of the Canal as the Chinese People's Republic [Communist China], Poland, Bulgaria, Rumania, Burma and Finland.

Thus the projected London conference is a conference of a group of countries which are shareholders of the Suez Canal Co., with another group arbitrarily chosen by these shareholders. The conference has been called in a manner bypassing the United Nations. . . . Without the agreement of the parties to the 1888 Convention, London has been chosen as the venue of the conference, although, if one adheres to the spirit of the 1888 Convention, the discussion of all issues linked with the operation of the Canal should take place in Cairo. . . .

The Soviet government regards it as most appropriate to discuss the problems connected with freedom of navigation on canals and straits of international importance within the framework of the United Nations. There are a number of canals and straits which are of international importance. As the tripartite statement raised the problem of the Suez Canal, the question logically arises: Why is the Suez Canal singled out from a number of no less important straits and canals?

In this matter the Soviet government proceeds from the principle that any solution of the problem of canals and straits possessing international importance must be based on the necessity of respecting the sovereign rights of the states through whose territory these sea-lanes pass.

The Kremlin suggested also that the following countries be invited to the London conference: Austria, Albania, Bulgaria, Burma, Czechoslovakia, Finland, the German Democratic Republic (East Germany), Hungary, Iraq, Jordan, Lebanon, Morocco, Poland, Rumania, Saudi Arabia, Sudan, Syria, Tunisia, and Yugoslavia. The Soviet note said it was also "essential that such a great power as the Chinese People's Republic should take part in the conference."

Nasser Aug. 9 proclaimed the formation of a National Liberation Army integrating the National Guard, Youth League and women's units under the unified command of Maj. Kamal el-Din Hussein, Egypt's education minister. Egypt's armed strength Aug. 9 was estimated at 100,000 regular army troops and 50,000 National Guardsmen. The government Aug. 10 ordered around-the-clock production in all small arms plants and the late-August mobilization of the Egyptian Red Crescent Society, an organization similar to the Red Cross. The Egyptian destroyer *Ibrahim* interrupted its refitting in Malta Aug. 11 and sailed for Egypt.

Arab sources in London reported Aug. 10 that a clandestine radio transmitting anti-Nasser, anti-British and anti-Israeli propaganda was being operated by members of the outlawed Moslem Brotherhood. British listening posts had monitored a broadcast in which the overthrow of "the mad tyrant Nasser" had been advocated.

Nasser called a news conference Aug. 12 and announced at it that Egypt would not attend the projected London conference of Canal users. Nasser proposed instead the holding of a conference under the sponsorship of Egypt and all other signatories of the 1888 Constantinople Convention; participants at Nasser's conference, he said, would draft a new agreement reaffirming international freedom of navigation in

the Canal and have such a new agreement registered in the
UN, where it could receive universal ratification.

Nasser denounced the Western plan for international control of the Canal as "collective colonialism." Egypt would
use all money received from tolls for improving the Canal
and whatever profits might accrue for building the Aswan
High Dam, he said. He also said that his government had
rejected an offer from World Bank Pres. Eugene Black for
a $1 billion loan to improve the Canal or build a new one.

Nasser, speaking in Cairo, insisted that the Suez Canal
Co. was an Egyptian company subject to government seizure.
He denied that Egypt had violated any international agreement. Nasser scored Britain and France's economic and military threats and termed those countries' freezing of Egyptian
assets a violation of both the UN Charter and Egypt's agreements with the 2 countries. Nasser said that he regarded
Britain and France's moves as a threat to world peace but
also that Egypt was not considering recourse to the UN Security Council over the matter. He said that his government
was preparing Egyptians for a possible attack by those 2
countries but had not declared a state of emergency.

The 9-country Arab League Council, meeting in Cairo
Aug. 13, declared "solidarity with Egypt in her determination to preserve her sovereignty" and said that the League
would consider "aggression against . . . any Arab state to be
an act of hostility directed against all Arab states." The
Federation of Arab Trade Unions' executive committee
called on oil workers in all Arab countries Aug. 13 to destroy
installations and halt oil shipments to the West in the event
of Anglo-French action against Egypt. Syrian government
spokesmen said Aug. 13 that Syria might not be able to halt
the sabotage of Western pipelines should Western countries
attack.

First London Conference (Aug. 16-23, 1956)

The first London Conference on the Suez Canal opened
Aug. 16 at Lancaster House in London as scheduled. Egypt

refused to attend the conference, and Pres. Nasser also declined to negotiate any settlement under the threat of force from Britain and France, both of whom were concentrating troops in the eastern Mediterranean. Greece also declined to attend the conference, since it was at odds with Britain over Cyprus. A Greek government spokesman in Athens said that his country would have preferred to attend a later-scheduled conference of wider membership somewhere other than in London. The spokesman also took the position that Egypt, "the main interested power," had not been consulted before the conference was called and that the conference was being held under circumstances of "war tension and pressure."

The heads of the 22 delegations attending the London conference were: Australia—Prime Min. Robert Gordon Menzies (accompanied by External Affairs Secy. Richard G. Casey); Britain—Foreign Secy. Selwyn Lloyd; Ceylon—Sir Claude Corea, high commissioner in London; Denmark—Premier Hans Christian Hansen (also Denmark's foreign minister); Ethiopia—Foreign Min. Tsehafe Tezaz Aklilu Habte-Wold; (West) Germany—Foreign Min. Heinrich von Bretano: France—Foreign Min. Christian Pineau; India—V. K. Krishna Menon, minister-without-portfolio; Iran—Foreign Min. Ali Gholi Ardalan; Italy—Foreign Min. Gaetano Martino; Japan—Foreign Min. Mamoru Shigemitsu; Netherlands—Co-Foreign Min. Joseph M. A. H. Luns; New Zealand—External Affairs Secy. Thomas L. MacDonald; Norway—Foreign Min. Halvard M. Lange; Pakistan—Foreign Min. Hamidul Huq Choudhury; Portugal—Foreign Min. Paulo Cunha; Soviet Union—Foreign Min. Dmitri Shepilov; Spain—Foreign Min. Alberto Martin Artajo; Sweden—Foreign Min. Osten Unden; Turkey—Foreign Ministry Gen. Secy. Nuri Birgi; U.S.—State Secy. John Foster Dulles.

The delegates appointed Selwyn Lloyd as chairman for the duration of the conference.

The first London Conference on the Suez Canal produced rival plans for operating the Canal—a U.S. plan for international operation and a Soviet-backed Indian plan for Egyptian operation with international advice.

State Secy. Dulles had opened the conference with a speech outlining the principles under which he thought the Canal should henceforth be run. Dulles said that Nasser, by his own admission July 26, had seized the Canal for the "grandeur of Egypt." But "the grandeur of a nation is not rightly measured by its ability to hurt or threaten others," Dulles declared, adding that interdependence was as much a characteristic of the modern world as was independence. He said:

> In the Suez Canal, the interdependence of nations achieves perhaps its highest point. The economic life of many nations has been shaped by reliance on the Canal system, which has treaty sanction. To shake and perhaps shatter that system, or to seek gains from threatening to do so, is not a triumph, neither does it augment grandeur. . . .
>
> Pres. Nasser . . . says that Egypt will accord freedom of transit through the Canal, that operations will be efficient and that tolls will continue to be reasonable. But we are bound to compare those words with other words which have perhaps a more authentic ring. We are also bound to note the difference between what the Treaty of 1888 called 'a definite system destined to guarantee at all times and for all powers the free use of the Suez Canal' and an Egyptian national operation which puts other nations in the role of petitioners.
>
> One thing is certain. Whatever may be the present intentions of the Egyptian government, the trading nations of the world know that Pres. Nasser's action means that their use of the Canal is now at Egypt's sufferance. Egypt can in many ways slow down, burden and make unprofitable the passage thorugh the Canal of the ships and cargoes of those against whom Egypt might desire, for national political reasons, to discriminate. Thus Egypt seizes hold of a sword with which it could cut into the economic vitals of many nations. . . .
>
> What is required is a permanent operation of the Canal under an international system which will, in fact, give confidence to those who wish to use it. Confidence is what we seek, and for this it is indispensable that there should be an administration which is non-political in character. The Canal should not be allowed to become the instrument of the policy of any nation or group of nations, whether of Europe, Asia or Africa.
>
> The United States does not believe that the Egyptian government had the right to wipe out the convention establishing the rights of the Suez Canal Co. until 1968. That arrangement had the status of an in-

ternational compact. Many nations relied on it. The operating rights and assets of the company were impressed with an international interest. . . .

Dulles, asserting that he was convinced that "a fair and equitable plan can be devised which will recognize the legitimate interests of all," enunciated 4 principles for such a plan: (a) that the Canal should be run efficiently in accordance with the stipulations of the Constantinople Convention of 1888 as a free and guaranteed international waterway; (b) that its operation should be kept separate from the influence of national politics of any kind; (c) that the Suez Canal Co. should receive fair compensation for the Canal, and (d) that all legitimate Egyptian interests and rights in the Canal, including an equitable and fair return from its operation, should be recognized and satisfied.

Dulles then proposed this 4-point plan, which, he said, would not infringe on Egypt's sovereignty but would help Egypt avoid confusion in its resolve to continue to recognize the binding force of the Constantinople Convention: (1) Operation of the Canal would become the responsibility of an international board set up by treaty and associated with the UN. Egypt would enjoy representation on such a board, but no one country would dominate it. It would be so composed as to assure the best possible operation and to preclude favoritism of prejudice. (2) The treaty would make adequate provision for the payment of fair compensation to the Suez Canal Co. (3) The treaty would entitle Egypt to an equitable return from the Canal's operation and take into account Egyptian sovereignty over and all legitimate Egyptian rights in the Canal. (4) The International Court of Justice at The Hague would be empowered to appoint a commission of arbitration having jurisdiction over all disputes arising from these last 2 points.

Dulles said in conclusion: "We recognize that at this stage any proposal should be flexible, within the limits of such basic principles as we have outlined. Egypt's views should be ascertained. But we believe that the principles set forth, and a plan such as that outlined, contain the basic elements needed to restore confidence and to assure that the Suez Canal will be operated in accordance with the Treaty of 1888."

Dulles' plan received the support of these 18 countries at the London conference: Australia, Britain, Denmark, Ethiopia, (West) Germany, France, Iran, Italy, Japan, the Netherlands, New Zealand, Norway, Pakistan, Portugal, Spain, Sweden, Turkey and the U.S. Ethiopia, Iran, Pakistan and Turkey sought some amendments in the plan's features pertaining to international control of the canal.

Soviet Foreign Min. Dmitri Shepilov said Aug. 17 that the "establishment of an international authority for the operation of the Suez Canal would actually mean the restoration of the former Suez Canal Co., but under a new signboard." Shepilov warned that the Anglo-French "threat to use force with regard to Egypt" could "flame up into a large conflict which could cover the area of the Near and Middle East" and spread beyond those areas. Shepilov charged Aug. 21 that the amended U.S. proposal for international control of the Canal was "based on the principle of denying to Egypt her sovereign rights, of establishing under the guise of a concession a colonialist regime" through "foreign operation of the Suez Canal." "Clearly," Shepilov said, "some powers have not yet reconciled themselves to the fact that Egypt has become an independent state."

V. K. Krishna Menon of India Aug. 20 presented an alternative plan calling for the Canal's operation by Egypt assisted by an international advisory group representing the Canal's users. Menon's plan gained the support of the Soviet Union, Indonesia and Ceylon. Menon, in presenting the Indian draft proposal, said Aug. 20 that the Suez Canal Co. was "a concessionaire from the Egyptian government" whose status was "derived from the concession granted by Egypt." Although seizure of the firm "was quite within the competence of the

Egyptian government," "it is necessary to state that this waterway has an international character," Menon asserted. He said that 3 primary problems had been raised by the seizure of the Canal company: freedom of navigation, "which the Egyptian government has to" guarantee under "international law"; security of the Canal and of its shipping which "can only be dealt with . . . by the authority of the Egyptian state"; Canal tolls and charges, which must remain competitive "if the Egyptian government . . . wants to make a profit." Speaking of the Egyptian blockade of Israeli shipping through Suez, Menon said that the "right procedure is for the aggrieved party to go to the World Court," and "if the World Court verdict were against the Egyptian government then they ought to abide by it." On differences between the functions of the Suez Canal Co. and the 1888 Convention, Menon said: The company "did not guarantee freedom of navigation. In fact, when the Suez Canal Co. was in ownership, and what is more, when the British troops were in occupation of the Suez Canal, it was at that time that freedom of navigation was obstructed [against Israel]."

Menon Aug. 21 called the amended U.S. proposal "entirely impracticable" and said Egypt would not negotiate on it.

The U.S., France, Britain and the 15 other countries supporting Dulles' plan agreed Aug. 23 to appoint a 5-member committee that would "approach on their behalf the government of Egypt" to ask whether it would negotiate a Suez settlement on the basis of the U.S. proposal. The majority, under a statement of intent proposed by New Zealand, named Australian Prime Min. Robert G. Menzies as chairman of the committee. (Other delegates named to the Menzies committee by Aug. 28: U.S. Assistant State Undersecy. Loy W. Henderson, Iranian Foreign Min. Ali Gholi Ardalan, Swedish Foreign Min. Osten Unden, Ethiopian Foreign Min. Aklilu Habte-Wold.)

British Foreign Secy. Selwyn Lloyd had said Aug. 22

that, as conference chairman, he would submit full transcripts of the London meetings to the Egyptian government—the records to include opposing views on internationalization of the Canal and both Indian and U.S. proposals made to the conference.

Soviet Foreign Min. Shepilov Aug. 23 submitted a draft communiqué calling for the negotiation of a Suez settlement "solely by peaceful means" through a committee including the U.S., Britain, France, India and the USSR. The proposal reportedly would have barred the use of force by Britain and France in the event that negotiations failed. The draft was blocked by French Foreign Min. Christian Pineau on the ground that the USSR had joined in refusing conference voting procedures and thus had prevented the issuance of a final communiqué.

Shepilov told London newsmen Aug. 24 that the U.S. proposal was "based on an unacceptable colonialist position." He charged that the plan was "closely connected with those influential classes" holding interests in the Suez Canal Co. The Menzies committee, Shepilov said, was "outside the conference" and lacked status to negotiate. But, he said, the conference had resulted in a "moral and political defeat" for the "forces" seeking to reimpose imperialism on Egypt.

(Soviet Communist Party First Secy. Nikita Khrushchev had said Aug. 23 that in the event of a Western attack on Egypt, "there would be volunteers" and the Arabs "would not stand alone." The Soviet newspaper *Izvestia* Aug. 25 called the London conference a "fiasco" and said that the "policy of strength" against Egypt had failed.)

Anglo-French Troops Transferred to Cyprus

During Aug. 1956 large numbers of British and French troops and great quantities of military material were transferred to the British base on the island of Cyprus in the Eastern Mediterranean, ostensibly to put pressure on Nasser.

Britain Aug. 12 launched an airlift of 5,000 troops to the Middle East after a 48-hour delay reportedly due to Libyan protests against the reinforcement of Britain's 10th Armored division there. 2 troopships and 2 cargo vessels were reported moving troops to the Mediterranean and shuttling vehicles detached from British NATO units in Germany. French Admirals Henri Nomy, naval staff chief, and Pierre Barjot, Mediterranean Squadron commander, had arrived in London Aug. 8 for Anglo-French General Staff talks on joint action against Egypt. Britain also was reported to have informed the West German government of its intentions to withdraw troops and equipment from NATO contingents in Germany. Dispatches said that the withdrawals of communications and engineer specialists were being made on an individual basis to avoid provisions of the Western European Union Forces Agreement.

It was reported from Cairo Aug. 25 that the Egyptian government had begun canvassing UN officials on the possibility of a special Security Council session to take up British and French military moves in the Mediterranean. Egyptian leaders were reported still wary of an appeal to the UN for fear it would constitute an admission that the Suez dispute was international.

Britain Aug. 29 agreed to the temporary stationing of "a contingent of French troops" on Cyprus. The British Foreign Office said Aug. 29 that France had asked permission to base forces on the island to insure "the protection of French nationals and their interests in the Eastern Mediterranean." Advance elements of the French Army's 10th Parachute and 7th Mechanized Divisions reportedly were withdrawn from Algerian service and arrived on Cyprus Aug. 21 aboard the freighter *Aulne*. The French cruiser *Georges Leyques*, the carrier *Arromanches* and several destroyers and transports were reported to have left the French naval base of Toulon. 2 more French vessels reportedly landed paratroopers and supplies in Famagusta, Cyprus, Sept. 1. The 30,000-

ton liner *Pasteur* was reported en route from Marseilles to Algiers Sept. 1 with 4,000 troops aboard and orders to load additional forces and equipment for transshipment to Cyprus.

Cyprus Gov. Sir John Harding Sept. 1 invited "visiting forces" of the U.S., France, Canada, Australia, South Africa, India, Pakistan and Ceylon to use British facilities on the island as a base for Mideastern operations. He extended to the foreign troops full privileges, including the use of communications, postal and logistic systems.

(Washington dispatches Aug. 29–Sept. 3 said that U.S. officials had indicated misgivings on the deployment of French forces to Cyprus and the continuing Anglo-French Mediterranean buildup. U.S. diplomatic sources were said Sept. 3, however, to feel that divergent U.S. and Anglo-French Suez moves could be part of an agreed policy to maneuver Egypt into agreement on control of the Canal.)

The NATO Permanent Council was asked Aug. 30 by Britain to "consider the Suez Canal question" at a meeting in Paris Sept. 5. Prime Min. Sir Anthony Eden met with his cabinet Sept. 4 to review a statement that Foreign Secy. Selwyn Lloyd was to present to NATO on Britain's military policy during the Suez crisis. West German dispatches said Sept. 1 that Britain had withdrawn 4,000 to 5,000 troops from NATO garrisons but that Bonn government officials had received no notice of additional reductions in force.

French Foreign Min. Christian Pineau Sept. 2 reiterated French determination to exert military pressure on Egypt for a Suez settlement. He charged that Soviet support had incited Nasser "to refuse to negotiate on the only possible basis." Pineau said France had "no right to practice a policy of surrender and to bow before the act of violence of the Egyptian dictator." He disputed the belief that French military moves could lead to war or meet with united Arab opposition.

The French Foreign Ministry Sept. 4 protested the complete mobilization reportedly ordered by Egyptian military leaders. Ministry spokesmen said that France "deeply regrets" the Egyptian moves as "exorbitant" and "out of proportion to the present situation." The French officials noted that France had not ordered mobilization. They referred to redeployment of French forces to Cyprus as "small."

(Egyptian War Min. Abdel Hakim Amer was quoted by the Cairo newspaper *Al Akhbar* Sept. 3 as saying that, with the completion of the callup of the National Guard and "all popular combat units," the "Egyptian army is ready to the last details" and "shall never be taken by surprise." He warned that "war against us will not be recreation, as is believed by those who dream of it.") (Nasser said Sept. 15, in a speech at Bilbeis, Egypt, that of "8 million Algerians, 10,000 are fighting a half million French soldiers." "We have arms sufficient to equip those who can fight," Nasser said.)

Hugh Gaitskell, the British Laborite (opposition) leader, had said in an interview in the *Manchester Guardian* Aug. 31 that the basing of French troops on Cyprus "may unfortunately give the impression" that "precautionary measures announced by the British government were, in fact, the prelude to imposing a solution on Egypt by force." The British Trades Union Congress' General Council Aug. 31 approved, 26-4, a resolution urging Britain not to use force against Egypt without UN consent. Laborite ex-War Min. John Strachey charged Sept. 2 that deployment of French forces to Cyprus was "the most dangerous" of "all the foolish and wicked things which the [Eden] government had done over Suez." He warned Sept. 2 that Britain risked involvement "in the hopeless attempt of the French to crush the Arab movement for independence in Algeria."

Nasser said at a news conference in Cairo Sept. 2 that Egypt would continue "watching and waiting" in the face of a "threat of war." "It is natural that if we are attacked we shall ask anyone to help us," Nasser said when asked whether

Egypt would seek Soviet assistance in the event of an armed attack. Nasser refused to place full reliance on the UN to halt the Anglo-French military menace. Egypt, he said, "would prefer to go before world public opinion than to face these 2 aggressive powers in the Security Council."

Nevertheless, strong indications were said to exist to support the inference that Egypt was anxious to negotiate with Britain and France—and that it hoped to enlist U.S. diplomatic offices in this aim. Nasser, at his news conference, denied all knowledge of "any compromise" but asserted that his country would "accept any solution that does not affect our sovereignty." Referring to U.S. Pres. Eisenhower's view of Aug. 31 that the Suez Canal was "Internationalized" in "the sense of usage of the Canal" but that the Constantinople Treaty "did not mean that . . . [the signatory] nations owned the Canal," Nasser declared that Eisenhower's explanation of U.S. Suez policy had "lifted the worry we had about the American stand on international justice." Nasser said that the Eisenhower view of an Egyptian-owned canal operating under international guarantees was the "same general point of view as that of Egypt."

2d & 3d London Conferences

In the next phase of the Suez nationalization crisis, there appeared to be a growing willingness on the part of Egypt to negotiate its way out under UN auspices and an increasing resolve on the part of Britain and France, the 2 most interested Western powers, to punish Nasser decisively and to nullify his act of nationalizing the Canal.

It was reported from Cairo Aug. 25 that the Egyptian government had begun canvassing UN officials on the possibility of a special Security Council session to take up British and French military moves in the Mediterranean. Egyptian leaders were reported still wary of an appeal to the UN for fear it would constitute an admission that the Suez dispute

was international.   Nasser agreed Aug. 28 to discuss the
settlement of the dispute.   Nasser said that he would meet
with a committee representing 18 of the 22 conference
nations.   Nasser's agreement to discuss the dispute reportedly
was drafted and dispatched from Cairo Aug. 26. It followed
an Egyptian cabinet session and talks Aug. 26 between
Nasser and his London conference observer, Ali Sabry. The
Egyptian note, delivered Aug. 28 to the committee chairman,
Australian Prime Min. Robert Menzies, said that Nasser had
agreed to the committee's desire "to place before me and
explain the views of the governments mentioned" in a message sent by the committee Aug. 24.

Spokesmen for Egyptian Amb.-to-Britain Sami Abdel
Foutouh denied Aug. 28 that any additional conditions had
accompanied the Egyptian acceptance, but Cairo sources
reiterated Aug. 28 that Egypt had made it clear that the
discussions would not bind Egypt to any form of international control over the Canal. Menzies reportedly proposed
to Nasser Aug. 28 that meetings begin in Cairo within a week.

Nasser had said Aug. 27, in an interview in the *N.Y.
Herald Tribune*, that he would be willing to hear the committee's views but did not see how "bright phrases" about
internationalization of the Canal could lead to any practical
settlement.   Nasser also denied Aug. 27 that Egypt had become economically or politically dependent on the USSR.
"What use to escape one domination to fall to another?"
Nasser asked.   "Until now," he said, "all Egyptian policy
decisions have been made here in this office, not in Moscow,
not in Washington."

U.S. State Secy. Dulles said at a press conference in Washington Aug. 28 that he believed Nasser "has sufficient influence and authority to accept a fair" solution on Suez.
Dulles said "the 18-nation plan, in its general outlines, is
fair."   As to whether the U.S. would accept "physical control" of the Canal by Egypt under international guarantees,

Dulles said that the question was not "primarily of U.S. concern but primarily of concern to the many countries—about 20—whose economies are vitally dependent on the Canal." Dulles said that "all but one of the countries at the London conference"—the USSR—had sought a genuine Suez settlement.   The USSR, he charged, had emitted "vicious propaganda" in Arabic broadcasts calling the conference a manifestation of "colonialism" and "imperialism" and had attacked the U.S. proposal on "the very morning I was . . . explaining" it to Shepilov.

Nasser began talks in Cairo Sept. 3 on the proposed negotiations for international control of the Canal. Nasser received the 18-nation committee and was presented with an amended U.S. proposal for direct operation of the waterway by an international Suez board.

Prime Min. Menzies, the Suez Committee chairman, said Sept. 3 that the initial meeting with Nasser had been "amicable." Menzies said that the Cairo discussions would remain secret until ended "because we are handling very important talks unassisted." The Menzies Committee, which had handed Nasser a statement urging talks "in an objective manner and not in a spirit of hostility," met Nasser Sept. 3 to explain the U.S. proposal in detail.

Nasser reportedly outlined Egypt's views on control of the Canal to the Menzies Committee Sept. 4. Egyptian sources said that Nasser had expressed firm opposition to the American proposal but had not categorically rejected negotiations on the waterway's future. Menzies said after the Sept. 4 meeting that the 2 opposing groups "haven't started attacking each other yet."

By Sept. 9 the negotiations had reached an impasse. An exchange of documents representing the 2 conflicting positions was published after the talks. The 2 principal documents were a letter from Menzies and a reply from Nasser. Menzies' letter, sent Sept. 7, reiterated the Western "majority plan" position:

From the outset, you will have observed that the 18 nations have not attempted to arrive at any joint opinion as to the validity or otherwise of Egypt's nationalization decree. The London Conference felt that a debate on this point would be fruitless, since the conference possessed no authority to make any judicial determination. It was therefore considered much more practical to work out constructive proposals which assumed that the act of nationalization had occurred; that the problem of the payment of compensation to the Suez Canal Co. would be properly dealt with, with provision for arbitration in the event of difference; and that what was needed was the establishment of principles and methods for the future . . . The proposals evolved in this atmosphere have been placed before you and have been much debated between us. We have, as you know, gone beyond the mere presentation of the proposals and have sought to explain and establish what we believe to be the large questions of principle involved.

It would be tedious and unnecessary to recapitulate all the discussions that have occurred on all the points of interpretation that have arisen. The simple truth is that we quite early realized on both sides of the table that there were certain central matters, without agreement upon which subsidiary matters could not usefully be determined. The 2 crucial proposals emerging from London were:

(1) That the operation of the Canal should be insulated from the influence of the politics of any nation; and

(2) That, to enable this to be done, there should be established, under an international convention to which Egypt would be a party, a body charged with the operation, maintenance, and development of the Canal. Such a body, we propose, should be constituted of people from various countries, including Egypt. The members would not be subject to political direction, and should be given in the convention, with the free consent of Egypt, wide powers of management and finance so that it could inspire confidence, deal with the future financial requirements of the Canal, and ensure a non-discriminatory and non-political management of Canal traffic. The proposed body would naturally have due regard for the laws and institutions of Egypt.

You have with complete frankness made it clear to us that the existence of such a body operating the Suez Canal would, in the view of Egypt, be a derogation from Egyptian sovereignty; that it would in substance represent a reversal of the policy announced by you on July 26.

We cannot agree with this view. Nowhere in our proposals is there any denial of Egypt's territorial sovereignty. On the contrary, the London proposals expressly recognized these rights in paragraph (2) of the resolution. The whole essence of what we have put forward is—to use a homely illustration—that Egypt's position as the landlord of the Canal being completely accepted, she should proceed by international agreement to install a tenant so constituted that the future of the Canal would be satisfactory both to its owners and to those many nations who use it.

We believe . . . that it cannot seriously be maintained that when a landlord grants a lease of premises, that lease derogates from his ownership. The fact is that the lease is an expression of and conditional upon his ownership. On this analogy our proposals would mean that the tenant of the Canal would pay to Egypt a substantial rental which must unquestionably grow as the traffic through the Canal increases, and that in the meantime the tenant would, in the exercise of his managerial and financial powers, be constantly improving the value of Egypt's asset. Indeed, as the 'tenant' in this analogy would be a body which includes Egypt herself, the position of Egypt would be even stronger. . . .

In short, what we have proposed is that, Egypt's sovereignty being fully recognized, the actual operation, maintenance and expansion of the Canal should be reposed in a body (established under international convention) which would include people from various nations—including, of course, Egypt—with extensive financial powers and responsibilities. . . .

There are in our proposals marked advantages for Egypt . . . which we now summarize as follows:

(1) Egypt's ownership of the Canal being recognized, it is to her great advantage to have the Canal maintained, improved, and made more profitable as the years go on.

(2) The future financial burdens involved in such maintenance and improvement would be carried and handled by the new body and, therefore, Egypt would in fact be relieved of them.

(3) Egypt alone would draw profit from the Canal.

(4) A just and fair method of compensating the shareholders of the Suez Canal Co. would have been agreed upon.

(5) The dangerous tension now existing internationally would be relaxed on terms satisfactory to the user-nations and entirely consistent with Egypt's proper dignity, independence, and ownership, and thus a world contribution would be made to the peaceful settlement of international problems.

It is the understanding of the committee that you have taken the position that you are unable to accept the basic proposals put before you. I would be grateful if your exellency would inform the committee whether or not this understanding is correct, supplementing your statement with such views as you may care to express.

If, unfortunately, the understanding of the committee is correct, the task entrusted to the committee by the 18 powers of presenting and explaining these proposals, and ascertaining the attitude of the Egyptian government with respect to them, would have been carried out. In such an event, there would appear to be no alternative other than for the committee to request your excellency to receive it at your early convenience so that it may be prepared, after a final conversation with you, to take its leave.

Nasser replied to Menzies' letter Sept. 9:

You have referred to the 18 countries as representing over 90% of the users of the Canal. Besides this being distinctly a statistical exaggeration, our understanding of 'users of the Canal' includes those countries which, even though they have no ships passing through the Canal, use the Canal for the passage of the bulk of their foreign trade. An illustration of this would be such countries as Australia, Siam, Indonesia, India, Pakistan, Persia, Iraq, Saudi Arabia, Ethiopia and the Sudan. Furthermore, the principle of sovereignty, the right of owner-ship, and the dignity of nations are all deeply involved in this problem.

At least in appearance, the starting-point of the present crisis was July 26, 1956, when, in the exercise of one of its prerogatives, the government of Egypt nationalized the 'Universal Maritime Company of the Suez Canal.' That the government of Egypt was fully entitled to nationalize that Egyptian company cannot be seriously contested. In nationalizing that company, the government of Egypt stated unequiv-ocally that it considers itself bound by the 1888 Convention guarantee-ing freedom of passage through the Suez Canal, and its readiness to give full and equitable compensation to the shareholders. Furthermore, on Aug. 12 the government of Egypt announced its willingness to sponsor, with the other governments' signatories to the Constantinople Convention of 1888, a conference—to which would be invited other governments whose ships pass through the Suez Canal—for the purpose of reviewing the Constantinople Convention and concluding an agree-ment between all these governments reaffirming and guaranteeing freedom of passage through the Suez Canal.

Nowhere and at no date can there be found any instance where the government of Egypt has violated any of its international obligations concerning the Suez Canal. For nearly 50 days, and in spite of the difficulties created by France and the United Kingdom, and by seg-ments of the former Suez Canal Co., the traffic through the Canal has been proceeding with regularity and efficency.

The crisis and the so-called 'grave situation' are, therefore, artificially created by the above-mentioned quarters, as witness among other things: (a) statements containing threats of force; (b) mobiliza-tion and movements of troops by France and the United Kingdom; (c) incitement to employes and pilots working in the Suez Canal to abandon their work, made by France and the United Kingdom and by some officials of the former Suez Canal Co.; and (d) hostile economic measures taken against Egypt.

With all this going on we have repeatedly been made to listen to references to a 'peaceful solution' and to 'free negotiations' to achieve such a solution. Need one emphasize the contradiction between the reality and the professed aim? If there is anything which flagrantly violates and disdains the letter and spirit of the UN Charter, it is such acts of attempted intimidation, economic pressure, and incitement to sabotage.

In contrast to this, the government of Egypt has announced its full readiness to negotiate a peaceful solution in conformity with the purposes and principles of the UN Charter. This remains the policy and intent of the Egyptian government. We have studied most carefully all the proposals submitted in and outside the London conference with regard to this problem, including the proposals of the 18 countries which the committee represents. We find ourselves in agreement with the 18 countries when they state that the solution must: (a) respect the sovereign rights of Egypt; (b) safeguard freedom of passage through the Suez Canal in accordance with the Convention of 1888; (c) respect Egypt's right of ownership; (d) ensure the efficient and dependable operation, maintenance, and development of the Canal.

When, however, we come to consider the ways and means proposed by the committee to attain these objectives, we find that they are self-defeating and that they lead to opposite results from those aimed at. The 'definite system' as proposed by the committee would, in fact, mean 'taking over the operation of the Canal'. . . .

The system proposed is bound to be considered by the people of Egypt as a hostile infringement of their rights and sovereignty, all of which precludes real cooperation. It can, moreover, be asked whether it was the Suez Canal Co. which guaranteed freedom of passage through the Canal? Was it not indeed the government of Egypt which safe-guarded, and still safeguards, that freedom of passage? Would that freedom be, or could its actual practice be, safeguarded by the pro-posed Suez Canal Board? Is it not to be expected that this board would be not a source of comfort and help, but of misunderstanding and trouble?

In all this we keep constantly in our mind the vital importance of genuine international cooperation as distinct from domination by any country—be it single domination, as the one which Egypt has just got rid of, or collective domination, as the system proposed by the Com-mittee would inevitably be considered. Any attempt to impose such a system would indeed be the signal for incalculable strife and would plunge the Suez Canal into the turmoil of politics, instead of insulating it from politics as seems to be the professed desire of the committee.

Whatever the system of operation of the Canal, it will depend on the close, full, and willing cooperation of the people of Egypt, through whose country the Canal runs. It is obvious that such indispensable cooperation cannot be obtained if the people consider the operating body as hostile and as derogating from their sovereignty, rights and dignity.

Strangely enough, those who pose as protagonists of 'insulating' the Suez Canal from politics have been the authors of many acts which diametrically contradict this announced purpose. What is the 'internationalization' of the Suez Canal, the convening of the London Conference, with for the most part tactically-selected invitees, the delegating of the 5-member committee, the threats, the deployment of armed forces, the economic measures—what are all these, if not politics? . . .

It should be abundantly clear by now that Egypt, by the very nature of things, is vitally interested in the maintenance of peace and security, not only around the Suez Canal but also throughout the area in which it exists and all over the world. It should be equally clear that, if only from sheer self-interest, Egypt is devoted to freedom of passage through the Canal and is equally devoted to the concept of an efficient, enlightened, and progressive operation of the Canal without any discrimination or exploitation whatsoever. In this last connection I mentioned to the committee that the government of Egypt is ready to enter into a binding arrangement concerning the establishment of just and equitable tolls and charges.

As for the future development of the Suez Canal, to which you referred, I wish to reiterate that the government of Egypt is determined to do everything possible in this respect. It has already announced its intention to carry out the development program which was planned by the former Canal company, and other programs of much wider scope and longer range. . . . We have also announced our intention to earmark an adequate percentage of the revenues of the Canal to its future development and to divert none of the revenues needed for such development to other channels.

Both for the development and for the operation of the Canal the government of Egypt does, and will always be ready to, benefit by the knowledge and experience of experts from all over the world. The crux of the present situation is, in our opinion, that the proposed system . . . aims at securing for a group of users of the Canal control of it by taking over its operation; of taking the Suez Canal out of the hands of Egypt and putting it into other hands. It is difficult to imagine anything more provocative to the people of Egypt than this. Such an act is both self-defeating and of a nature to generate friction, misunderstanding, and continous strife. It would be, in other words, not the end but the beginning of trouble.

I would like, on the other hand, to reaffirm that the policy of my government remains:

(1) Freedom of passage through the Suez Canal and its secure use without discrimination.

(2) The development of the Canal to meet the future requirements of navigation.

(3) The establishment of just and equitable tolls and charges.

(4) Technical efficiency of the Suez Canal.

We trust that the Suez Canal will thus be insulated from politics and, instead of being a source of conflict, will again become a link of cooperation, mutual benefit, and better understanding between the nations of the earth . . .

On his return to London Sept. 10, Menzies said at a press conference at London Airport: "The answer to our proposals, after long detailed arguments to and fro, is that Egypt will have nothing to do with any peaceful solution of the Canal issue which does not leave Eygpt the absolute and undisputed master of the whole of the operations of the Canal, subject only to the 1888 [Constantinople] Convention, which, in a broad way, guarantees freedom of traffic—a freedom, of course, which could be set on one side with the greatest of ease by political management, which we sought to avoid by having a guaranteed non-political management."

Reporting to the Australian House of Representatives Sept. 25, Menzies said that "if the UN, once more frustrated by Soviet action, proves ineffective [and] . . . cannot impose economic sanctions," the "user nations" must "be ready to impose sanctions ourselves." He said the right to use force could "not be completely abandoned or made subject to impossible conditions." He charged that the USSR had been "in constant and persuasive touch with Nasser during the recent negotiations" and "is willing to stir up and foment trouble."

Egyptian spokesmen Sept. 25 labelled the Menzies statements "surprising" in view of an imminent UN debate and said that Menzies was urging "force against Egypt, thus exposing himself before world public opinion as an imperialist."

After the negotiations between Nasser and Menzies had ended in failure in Cairo Sept. 9, the British and French governments had moved to coordinate military, economic and diplomatic pressure against Egypt to force the acceptance of international operation of the Canal. French Premier Guy Mollet and Foreign Min. Christian Pineau visited London Sept. 10–11 for talks with British Prime Min. Eden and

Foreign Min. Selwyn Lloyd about Nasser's refusal to consider
the proposals of the Menzies committee. After the discussions they issued a joint communiqué that said:

> ... The general purpose of this [Anglo-French] meeting was to
> consider the situation arising from the refusal of Pres. Nasser to agree to
> negotiations on the basis of the proposals of the 18 powers for the
> future regulation of the Suez Canal. ...
>
> The ministers recalled that from the outset their governments
> acted in full conformity with the purposes and principles of the United
> Nations. Their immediate reaction to the unilateral act of Pres. Nasser
> was to join with the U.S. government in summoning a meeting of those
> mainly interested in the Canal, including Egypt, in order to discuss this
> evident threat to the well-being of a very large proportion of the
> inhabitants of the globe. Though Egypt unfortunately refused to
> attend, this conference succeeded in producing a plan, approved by
> states representing over 90% of the user-interests in the Canal, which
> was eminently fair to all concerned and took full account of Egypt's
> sovereignty and interests.
>
> The ministers agreed that the refusal of Pres. Nasser to negotiate on
> this basis created a very grave situation. They discussed the further
> measures to be taken and reached full agreement upon them.
>
> The ministers were glad to note that present events had clearly
> demonstrated the identity of French and British will to uphold the
> rule of law in international affairs. They expressed their determination
> to develop their cooperation and to resist, by all appropriate means,
> any arbitrary interference with rights established under international
> agreements and any action incompatible with 'justice and respect for
> the obligations arising from treaties and other sources of international
> law.' [The quotation was taken from the Preamble to the UN Charter.]

The U.S., Britain and France Sept. 12 proposed the
creation of an international Suez Canal Users' Association
(SCUA, or SUA) to supervise pilotage through the canal. The
Western powers called Sept. 14 for a new London conference
despite its immediate rejection by Egypt. British Prime Min.
Eden said at an emergency session of Parliament Sept. 12
that: (a) The SCUA would "employ pilots" and "undertake
responsibility for coordination of traffic through" Suez.
(b) "Transit dues" would "be paid to the users' association
and not to the Egyptian authorities," but Egypt would
"receive appropriate payment" for the "facilities provided
by her." (c) "The government of Egypt" would "have an

important bearing on the capacity of the association to fulfill its functions" and would "be requested to cooperate in maintaining" traffic. (d) Britain was dependent on Middle Eastern oil, and to boycott the canal "would be very expensive." "There are not the tankers to maintain the supplies we need" though more could be built at "enormous" capital cost. (d) The formation of the SCUA did not "exclude" taking the dispute to the UN. Britain and France had addressed a letter to the president of the Security Council, "informing him of the situation that has arisen."

The U.S. State Department said Sept. 12 that the U.S. would join in the SCUA if it were advanced by Britain or other states and "organized by the 18 nations which sponsored the London proposals" for international control of the Canal. The State Department emphasized that backers of the SCUA would "seek such cooperation with Egypt as would achieve" guarantees contained in the 1888 Constantinople Convention.

State Secy. Dulles said at a news conference Sept. 13 that "we do not intend to shoot our way through" the Canal. "If physical force should be used to prevent passage" of SCUA shipping, he declared, "the alternative . . . would be to send our vessels around the Cape [of Good Hope]." Dulles denied that the U.S. had joined in planning a boycott if the Canal were closed. Under those conditions, he said, "each country would have to decide for itself what it wanted its vessels to do." Dispatches from Washington Sept. 12 had attributed the basic SCUA plan to Dulles, who reportedly had formulated the proposal in an effort to avert military action against Egypt and delay action before the UN. He was described Sept. 12 as irritated at Eden's representation of the SCUA scheme as "gunboat diplomacy." Dulles said of the users' association plan Sept. 13: (a) "The idea that this is a program which is designed to impose some regime upon Egypt is fantastic." "It is normal for users" to "work in association when rights which they possess jointly are in jeopardy."

(b) An SCUA test vessel could approach the Canal with an experienced Suez pilot aboard and "hope" to be let through the Canal. Should a test vessel be attacked in the Canal "if it had any means to defend itself, it would be entitled to use those means." (c) "The question of oil" had been studied and "the loaning capacity of the Export-Import Bank" "could be made available" for SCUA purchases of Western Hemisphere oil. (d) Shipping via the Cape of Good Hope had been considered and would not "be catastrophic or beyond the capacity to deal with it." Some tankers of the Maritime Administration and Military Sea Transport Reserve fleets would "be taken out of mothballs." (e) The SCUA "should be developed by the group" of 18 nations that backed international control for the Canal at the London conference, but if some refused "then we would go along on a 3-party basis."

(It was reported in Washington Sept. 16 that the U.S. planned to offer $500 million in credits for oil purchases, that 35 to 40 tankers had been ordered reactivated and reconditioned at a cost of $350,000 each and that 14 U.S. oil firms had agreed to supply 450,000 barrels of the 2½ million barrels of oil needed daily by Europe. Dulles Sept. 17 denied any knowledge of the $500 million credit but said that the U.S. Export-Import Bank was ready to offer loans.)

The USSR charged Sept. 15 that the Western SCUA plan was "a great provocation against Egypt" and that attempts to impose it by force "would lead to immense destruction in the Suez Canal and in the oil fields" of the Middle East. A lengthy Soviet statement broadcast by Moscow Radio said that the Anglo-French military build-up on Cyprus was "an act of aggression" against Egypt, and that the withdrawal of non-Egyptian Suez pilots "aimed at disruption of normal work in the Canal." The statement said that "the USSR, as a great power, cannot stand aside from the Suez problem" and "consider that the UN cannot but react to the existing situation." The Soviet government warned that "in the age" of the "atomic and hydrogen weapon, one cannot threaten and rattle the saber." It said the USSR considered "any violation of peace in the Near and Middle East" to be linked to "the security of the Soviet state." The statement criticized Eisenhower for not protesting British and French military policy at his Sept. 11 press conference. The Russians said that they would attend an Egyptian-sponsored Suez conference.

It was reported that the Egyptian government had already showed signs of the strain of withstanding international pressure. It called Sept. 10 for the formation of a new "negotiating body" "representative of the different views held among the states using the Suez Canal." A note, sent to all nations having diplomatic relations with Egypt, urged immediate talks on "the freedom and safety of navigation of the Canal," "development of the Canal" and "establishment of just and equitable tolls and charges." A new conference, Egypt said, could be "entrusted the task of reviewing the Constantinople Convention of 1888." The Egyptian note protested "displays of force" against Egypt and "inducements from certain quarters to cause defection of technical personnel with the intention of hampering the navigation in the Suez Canal." Egypt "wishes now to declare that it believes . . . solutions can be found," the note said.

The British Foreign Office said Sept. 10 that the Egyptian offer did "not appear to suggest any basis for negotiations." British spokesmen charged Egypt with "unqualified refusal" of the proposals offered by the Menzies committee. Pres. Eisenhower said at a news conference Sept. 11 that he saw "no substantive point on which to base" a new Suez conference.

The Suez Canal Co. in Paris Sept. 11 issued a statement authorizing its non-Egyptian employes in Egypt to cease work and to arrange to be repatriated. (These workers included 121 European and North American pilots and 270 European administrative personnel.) The company thanked its non-Egyptian employes in Egypt for "the effort they have made for nearly 7 weeks in the service of the international waterway." The statement continued: "The board is aware of the very great difficulties these employes have had to face and the distressing moral atmosphere in which the company has asked them to work in response to the wishes of the British and French governments, who were anxious to facilitate, first, the work of the London Conference, and then the mission of the Committee of 5 presided over by Mr. Menzies. The mission now being completed, the further period of work called for by the company a fortnight ago is now coming to an end. Consequently, all non-Egyptian employes who, before Aug. 15, asked to be repatriated, thereby intimating that they did not accept any contract with the *de facto* Egyptian authority, are authorized to stop working on either Sept. 14 or 15, according to the particular requirements of the department in which they are employed. They should forthwith make arrangements for repatriation with the assistance, if required, of diplomatic and consular representatives."

The company had said Aug. 28 that all but a few of its non-Egyptian workers had registered with their consulates in Cairo Aug. 15 and had asked to be repatriated. It added that it could not rightfully ask these employes to remain longer than "a time limit agreed to in consideration of the mission with which . . . Menzies was entrusted by the London Conference." The company said it would issue orders to its employes about further service on the completion of the Menzies mission's Cairo talks. (The company flew 500 of its non-Egyptian employes out of Cairo Sept. 15.)

Egypt in mid-August set about recruiting 300 new pilots through its embassies and legations in France, Greece, India, Italy, the Netherlands, the Scandinavian countries, the Soviet Union, the U.S., West Germany and Yugoslavia, among other countries. The Egyptian Suez Canal Authority reported later that it had signed up 15 pilots in Greece, 12 in India from the Hooghly River service and 10 in Yugoslavia. It was also reported—without confirmation—that the new authority had recruited 30 German pilots from the Kiel Canal. Egypt's embassy in Bonn said Aug. 30 that 300 pilots, mostly Germans, had inquired about Suez employment. It was reported from the Soviet Union Sept. 4 that several Soviet Baltic Sea pilots had volunteered for service with the new authority. Moscow Radio said Sept. 4 that a number of Soviet Black Sea pilots had agreed to join the Suez Canal force. Egypt had been permitted to place ads for pilots in Soviet newspapers Sept. 2. Egypt's embassy in Paris said Sept. 4 that it had received nearly 200 applications for Suez pilot posts—100 from the USSR, 50 from Spain, and 20 each from France and the Netherlands. Egyptian ads for Canal pilots had appeared in U.S. newspapers Aug. 30. Although U.S. maritime circles refused to indorse the recruiting, the Egyptian consulate in New York reported Aug. 31 that it had received "more than 25" applications, and more were reported by the Egyptian consulate in San Francisco and Egyptian embassy in Washington.

Egypt took over full operation of the Canal at midnight Sept. 14–15, reporting a complement of 70 pilots, including 12 foreigners, mostly Greeks. Egypt had already recruited 27 Egyptians to replace departing foreign pilots in August, and 39 Egyptian pilots had already been in service when the crisis began in July. The new authority's pilots received double-schedule assignments. (Egypt's delegate to the UN, Omar Loutfi, commenting Sept. 17 on the efficiency of the Egyptian Canal Authority, noted that an average of 42 ships per day had passed through the Canal since the Western pilots had left Sept. 14 and that a total of 2,216 vessels had passed through the Canal since July 26, compared with 2,103 for the same period of 1955.)

Nasser told an Egyptian Air Force College graduating class at Bilbeis Sept. 15 that the Suez Canal Users' Association scheme was "in truth one for declaring war" on Egypt.

Nasser reiterated that Egypt would not "discriminate between Canal users" and would defend the nationalized Canal.
Nasser said: "Those who attack Egypt will never leave alive";
"we shall fight a regular war, a total war, a guerrilla war";
"he who attacks Egypt, attacks the whole Arab world";
"they do not know how strong we really are." Nasser said
in an interview with the Press Trust of India Sept. 16 that
Egypt would "not allow the Western-proposed [Suez] Canal
Users' Association to function through the Canal." "We
Egyptians shall run the Canal smoothly and efficiently,"
Nasser declared, "and if, in spite of this, the Canal Users'
Association forces its way through the Suez Canal, then it
would mean aggression and would be treated as such."
(Col. Mahmoud Yunis, deputy director of Egypt's Suez
Canal Authority, warned Sept. 18 that if an SCUA vessel ap-
proached the canal, "regulations say they must ask us for a
pilot." Asked what would happen if an SCUA vessel tried
to pass without an Egyptian authority pilot, Yunis said,
"Let them try.")

Egyptian Commerce Min. Muhammad Abu Nosseir said
Sept. 18 that Egypt would "restrict or ban" imports from
"unfriendly" countries and reject their offers on Egyptian
development projects even if favorable. Nosseir said that
licenses had been granted for £E2.6 million ($7½ milion) in
imports from "friendly" (presumably pro-Soviet) countries
under a "new foreign trade policy." Members of the Egyptian National Production Council were said to have already
left for trade talks in Czechoslovakia.

The British government, meanwhile, had invited the U.S.,
France and 13 other nations Sept. 14 to discuss the creation
of the Suez Canal Users' Association at another conference in
London. Pres. Eisenhower ordered State Secy. Dulles Sept.
14 to attend the parley with the other representatives of the
18-nation majority of the Aug. 16–23 conference. Dispatches from London said Sept. 15 that a proposed conference agenda included in the invitations had slated discussions

on (a) action to be taken following Egypt's Sept. 9 rejection of negotiations on international control of the Canal, (b) Egypt's Sept. 10 counterproposal to renew negotiations with enlarged participation and (c) the establishment of the proposed Suez Canal Users' Association.

Representatives of the 18 nations held their 2d London conference Sept. 19–21. An agreement on basic SCUA aims was reached after much debate and substantial revision, but France at once rejected the revised scheme. The 2d conference had opened with the 18 invited countries openly divided on the SCUA plan, on measures envisaged against Egypt and on the possibility of UN action. A bloc of SCUA supporters, led by the U.S., Britain and France, included West Germany, Australia and New Zealand. Pakistan Sept. 19 refused membership in the SCUA. Spain urged new talks with Egypt. Norway, Sweden, Denmark and the Netherlands pressed for UN consideration of the dispute.* Japan, Ethiopia, Iran, Turkey and Portugal were said Sept. 19 to be uncommitted on the SCUA.

Dulles told the conferees Sept. 19 that the "great restraint" exercised by the West toward Egypt could not last indefinitely. He said that the Suez crisis, "a problem of great peril which could have been solved by force by nations sitting here," demanded the unity of the 18 conferring powers and a just solution in accord with international law. "If we emphasize just one side—trying to prevent the use of force—the effort will be doomed," Dulles said. Dulles suggested that the SCUA would: (a) "Continue our present association" and stand on "our joint statement of Aug. 23, 1956" as "a basis for the negotiation of a permanent solu-

---

*A resolution submitted at the conference Sept. 19 by Italian Foreign Min. Gaetano Martino with the support of the Netherlands, Denmark and Norway sought to limit SCUA functions to the negotiation of a new Canal convention with Egypt. The resolution called for bringing the Suez dispute before the UN and opening the SCUA to all nations using the waterway.

tion" of the Suez dispute. (b) Need "a small operating staff which would be ready to assist our ships" in "operating through the Canal" under an administrator acting "on behalf of the ships of the members." (c) Depend on the administrator to "make available experienced pilots," to "assist" SCUA "participation in the pattern of traffic through the canal" and to "help coordinate routes through or around the Canal." (d) Authorize the administrator to act as "agent of the owners" and to "collect and pay out" money for the "maintenance of and transit through the Canal." (e) Be controlled by a "small governing board" formed to "appoint the administrative agent and fix his authority" and to maintain liaison with planning affecting dependence on the Canal. (f) "Suggest a provisional solution which the UN might find it useful to invoke while the search for a permanent solution goes on."

"Membership" in the SCUA "would not involve the assumption by any member of any obligation," Dulles said, although he expressed the hope that "members . . . would voluntarily take such action with respect to their ships and the payment of canal dues as would facilitate the work of the association." Dulles told Japanese Amb.-to-Britain Haruhino Nishi that under the SCUA plan, Egypt would continue to operate the Canal and its installations and that cooperation with Egypt would permit SCUA members to bar Soviet pilots from their ships. Dulles stressed in his Sept. 19 statement that Egyptian cooperation would be necessary under any Canal plan. "Obviously," he said, "if Egypt makes it obligatory to use only pilots that are chosen and assigned [by] it, then I do not see that pilots of the association would practically have very much to do and that part of the [SCUA] plan would have collapsed." The SCUA could, in this event, constitute "a bargaining body" "*vis à vis* Egypt."

Britain and France, however, appeared to be taking a crucially different view of the SCUA's prime function—which, in their view, was to serve as a means of denying Canal dues to

Egypt. Prime Min. Eden had instructed Foreign Secy. Lloyd to make this view clear to Dulles and to have the SCUA chartered as the exclusive dues-collection agency of the members. This was not done.

Dulles, in a letter to London Conference Chairman Lloyd, said Sept. 21 that he would confer with U.S. Treasury officials and "owners of American-flag vessels" to assure U.S. alignment with SCUA "operating practices." Reports Sept. 21 said that much U.S. shipping, under Panamanian and Liberian registry, could not be compelled to stop paying Suez tolls to Egypt. But U.S. Treasury spokesmen said Sept. 25 that American trade and currency regulations applied to American-run vessels "irrespective of registry."

The SCUA scheme had undergone revision Sept. 20 in an effort to reach a formula acceptable to a majority of the 18 nations represented. Dispatches from Washington said Sept. 21 that the U.S. had abandoned the organization of a boycott of the Canal in the face of European opposition and continued Egyptian success with Canal operations. Other reports said Sept. 21 that Egypt, currently receiving little of the Canal's income, would not suffer from a boycott as much as European shippers, who, it was estimated would have to spend $500 million yearly for increased shipping costs via the Cape of Good Hope.

The 2d London Conference ended Sept. 21 with a joint Suez policy statement and declaration of SCUA aims. The statement noted "with regret" Egypt's rejection of the first London Conference's proposals for international control of the Canal and the Egyptian failure to "make any counter-proposals to the 5-nation committee" headed by Menzies. The statement rejected Egypt's Sept. 10 call for a new Suez conference as "too imprecise to afford a basis for discussion."

The Sept. 21 declaration said that the SCUA would aim to: "facilitate" a "final or provisional solution"; "promote safe . . . transit of the Canal" and "seek the cooperation of the competent Egyptian authorities"; "extend its facilities" to "non-member nations"; "receive, hold and disperse the revenues accruing from [Canal] dues" "pending a final settlement"; "consider and report to members" on "developments" affecting the Canal; "assist" with "problems arising from [any] failure of the Suez Canal" and study means "to reduce dependence on the Canal"; and "facilitate" any "provisional solution of the Suez problem that may be adopted by the UN."

The SCUA declaration provided for a council of all members, a council "executive group" to which the council might "delegate such powers as it deems appropriate," and an administrator to "make the necessary arrangements with shipping interests" and "serve under the direction of the council through the executive group."

The U.S., British and Italian governments formally accepted the SCUA declaration Sept. 21. French Foreign Min. Christian Pineau rejected the declaration on direct orders of Premier Guy Mollet and returned to Paris Sept. 21. The Mollet cabinet, weakened by the conference's failure to require toll payments to the SCUA, was reported split, with one faction demanding outright rejection of the SCUA scheme, another seeking the Mollet govenment's resignation. The cabinet met Sept. 22 and agreed to join the SCUA with the "express reservation" that "international operation of the Canal, defined by the first London Conference," remained subject to "no transaction." The cabinet said that "France intends to retain its freedom of action and refuses to collaborate in any measure which" may "be contrary to its essential interests." Mollet said Sept. 22 that, with regard to the SCUA, "the reservations of the English are the same as our own." He expressed "bitterness and anxiety" Sept. 23 that "the free peoples are not all aware as we are, of the danger" posed by Egyptian-led Pan-Arabism. Mollet stressed that the Western division lay between U.S. and Anglo-French views on how to counter Egypt.

British Foreign Secy. Lloyd Sept. 22 invited the 18 London Conference member-countries to meet in London Oct. 1 for a 3d conference on the ambassadorial level to organize the SCUA. The Suez Canal Users' Association was formally inaugurated Oct. 1 by Lloyd at the opening session of the 3d London Conference on the Suez dispute. The conference, attended by ambassadors of the 15 SCUA member states,* divided Oct. 1 into 3 committees—on organization, operations and finance—to begin drafting a formal SCUA constitution.

U.S. State Secy. Dulles had said at a news conference Sept. 26 that the U.S. would practice "patience and resourcefulness" to reach an "agreed settlement" with Egypt on the Suez problem. Dulles warned that Egypt would find that "foreign markets and foreign sources of credit" were "not readily available to a nation which rejects" "interdependence" with its neighbors. Dulles said that the U.S. "would expect to be in accord" with Britain and France in the presentation of the West's case to the UN Security Council. He said that under plans for the operation of the Suez Canal Users' Association:

● (a) It was "quite likely" that an SCUA-piloted vessel would attempt to use the Canal and, if refused entry, "we assume" it would bypass the Canal, although "we have no" "power to direct ships."

● (b) Use of either SCUA- or Egyptian-controlled pilots would be "primarily for the master of the ship to decide." "If he wanted to take the Egyptian pilot, he is entitled to do so."

---

*Nations that had indicated their acceptance of the SCUA plan before the opening of the 3d London Conference Oct. 1: Australia, Denmark, France, West Germany, Iran, Italy, Netherlands, New Zealand, Norway, Portugal, Spain, Sweden, Turkey, U.S., Britain. Denmark, Norway and the Netherlands were reported to have made membership conditional on ratification of the SCUA Charter by their parliaments. Iran was said to have insisted on an SCUA pledge against the group's resort to force. Pakistan, Ethiopia and Japan remained uncommitted to the SCUA and were represented at the 3d London Conference by observers.

- (c) There "is no obligation which results from joining the users association to act in unison." "Each vessel" and "each country" would "decide for itself"—we "cannot create" a "universal boycott of the Canal."
- (d) The U.S. "would not expect" that "U.S.-flag vessels" would continue to make Suez toll payments to Egypt, although "there is no authority to compel payments" to the SCUA, and "we do not have in mind" restrictions on non-U.S. flag vessels.
- (e) The "amount of money which Egypt gets out of the Suez Canal is not a major factor," and "the pressure which could be exerted by going around the Canal would be relatively little."
- (f) "Israel would not be eligible" for SCUA membership under requirements proposed in London, but "Israeli ships" "would have all the facilities of the association."

Pres. Eisenhower said at his press conference Sept. 27 that the "great hope" of the user nations would be their "unanimity in what they believe should be a proper" settlement. The President expressed the belief that "Egypt will see that her own best interests" would be served by such a settlement and that if user nations were successful in winning "a provisional method of operation," the Canal blockade of Israeli shipping could be "cured" simultaneously.

Egyptian Suez Canal Authority officials said Sept. 25 that Egypt had 89 pilots currently at work and 120 others (75 foreigners) under training. The Indian government had announced Sept. 22 that it would send Egypt 2 pilots. 7 Yugoslav pilots reportedly had arrived in Egypt Sept. 23, 11 Poles Sept. 24, a South African Sept. 25.

U.S. State Department press officer Lincoln White said Sept. 20 that 10 U.S. citizens who had applied for passports to enter the Suez pilot force would be interviewed by the State Department, and if "they still want to proceed, that is their business." The U.S. naval attaché in Egypt notified the Egyptian-Suez Canal Authority Sept. 25 that U.S. warships would refuse to accept Soviet pilots for passage through the Canal. Chief Suez Administrator Tewfik el-Dib said Sept. 25 that Egypt never intended to assign Soviet pilots to U.S. warships.

A joint statement by the Far Eastern Freight Conference, Japan Outward Freight and Philippines-European Conferences Sept. 25 cancelled a 15% rate increase (announced Sept. 15 for cargoes going through the Canal) because the "great majority of their vessels have continued to transit the Canal without material delay."

Egyptian Suez Canal Authority reports Oct. 2 listed 1,192 vessels cleared through the waterway during August, compared with 1,197 ships passed in Aug. 1955. 51 vessels were reported to have gone through the Canal Oct. 1 and 45 Oct. 2 despite delays caused by grounding of the British freighter *Hendrick* Oct. 2 30 miles south of Port Said. Egyptian Canal officials had said Oct. 1 that 100 new pilots were in training and that only 30 more men would be required to complete the new Suez pilot force. 5 U.S. pilots arrived in Egypt Sept. 26 and 4 Sept. 29. Egypt reported Oct. 2 that the first U.S. pilot had completed a training run through the canal aboard the Soviet tanker *Kaunas*, and that a Soviet pilot had for the first time taken a ship, the Italian tanker *Antonio Zotti*, through the Canal unaided.

The Institute of London Underwriters had announced Sept. 28 a 50% reduction in prior increases in war risk insurance for Egypt-bound cargoes. New rates were set at 4 shillings 6 pence (63¢) per £100 ($280) worth of cargo going through the Canal or transshipping in Egyptian ports.

Reports from Cairo Oct. 2 said that Helmi Bahgat Badawi, Egyptian Suez Canal Authority director, was flying to the U.S. with Egyptian proposals that a group of U.S. oil and shipping firms set up and run a $56 million Suez Canal maintenance and development program. Egyptian informants said that Badawi would urge the American companies to submit bids on the project, to be underwritten financially by

Egypt.   The plan, regarded in Cairo Oct. 2 as reflecting a
major shift in Egyptian policy, would call for direct supervision of the development program by the U.S. firms in an
effort to convince the West that the Canal would remain
open to world commerce.   Badawi told newsmen in The
Hague Oct. 1 that he would "talk to the customers" while
in the U.S. to "learn what they wish and how they expect
Canal traffic to develop."   Badawi reiterated that the Canal
was open to all nations except Israel, whose ships were
"stopped before they enter" and "are none of my business."

Badawi said Oct. 3 that under the proposed Canal development program, U.S. firms' participation in Canal operations would be limited to the control of actual construction projects.   Badawi Oct. 4 denied reports that the program
would require a $1½ billion investment for 15 years.   He
said the plan considered by Egypt would be far less costly.
He insisted Oct. 4 that Egypt would be unwilling to yield
Canal toll collection rights to a foreign consortium.   (Washington sources said Oct. 4 that the program was under
study and was similar to a plan discussed by private interests in 1955 as a possible basis for extension of the Suez
Canal Co. concession.)

U.S. State Secy. Dulles conceded at a press conference
Oct. 2 that there "has been some difference" with Britain
and France "in our approach to" the Suez problem.   In an
amended State Department transcript released Oct. 2, Dulles
commented that "this is not an area where we are bound
together by treaty."   He cited "other problems where our
approach is not identical," with one being "the so-called
problem of colonialism," toward which "the U.S. plays a
somewhat independent role" and tried to assure the country
that the "process moves forward" constructively.   (In a para-
phrase of Dulles' original remarks published Oct. 2, the *N.Y.
Times* reported: Dulles denied a "detectable change" in the
SCUA plan; he said that "there is talk that the teeth were
pulled out of it—there were no teeth in it"; he asserted that

differences with Britain and France over Suez policy were related "to some rather fundamental things." It was then that he had mentioned "the so-called problem of colonialism," on which the U.S. maintained an "independent role.")

British Prime Min. Eden was incensed by Dulles' statement, according to Foreign Affairs State Min. Anthony Nutting, who reported in *No End of a Lesson* (1967): "I was at . . . [Eden's official residence] when the news-flash of Dulles' press conference came across the tapes. Eden's private secretary brought it in at the very moment when I was pleading with the prime minister not to get too far out of step with the U.S. and not to despair of carrying them with us in the Security Council and subsequently. Eden read the Dulles statement quickly and then, with a contemptuous gesture, he flung the piece of paper at me across the table, hissing as he did so, 'And now what have you to say for your American friends?' "

The French leadership, too, was known to have been angered by Dulles' statements. Reports from Paris Oct. 2 said that French officials had been troubled by Dulles' dissociation of the U.S. from the major colonialist powers. French sources were said to believe that Dulles' statement had been intended to delineate long-term U.S. policy, rather than its policy on the Suez crisis and that it particularly applied to the French problem in Algeria.

UN Negotiations & Debate

By mid-Sept. 1956 pressures had mounted among Canal-using countries in the West and elsewhere for a UN solution to the nearly 2-month-old dispute. The foreign ministers of Norway, Sweden and Denmark, meeting in Stockholm Sept. 16, reportedly criticized the SCUA plan and recommended referral of the dispute to the UN. Pakistan was said Sept. 17 to be opposed to the users association scheme and to have accepted an invitation to the Egyptian-sponsored Suez con-

ference. Spanish Foreign Min. Alberto Martin Artajo reportedly urged Sept. 17 that other Western governments attend
the Egyptian-proposed conference. Italy indicated Sept. 17
that it was doubtful of the value of SCUA plan. West Germany was uncommitted and Australia divided on it. Indian
Prime Min. Jawaharlal Nehru conferred on the Suez dispute
Sept. 15 with envoys of the Colombo Powers (Pakistan, Indonesia, Burma, Ceylon) and ordered his political adviser, V. K.
Krishna Menon, to Cairo for talks with Nasser. Menon met
with Nasser Sept. 17 and Ali Sabry Sept. 18, reportedly in
an unsuccessful attempt to press Egypt into a public statement of terms for a Suez compromise. Indian reports had
said Sept. 14 that Egypt would be willing to agree to international control of Suez transit fees. Nasser continued talks
Sept. 19–20 with Menon, who was said to be attempting to
establish contact with U.S. diplomats for a joint mediation
effort between Egypt and the West. Menon flew to London
Sept. 22 and conferred with British Foreign Secy. Selwyn
Lloyd Sept. 24 on his Cairo talks.

 Nehru said in New Delhi Sept. 23 that India backed
Egypt's ownership of the Suez Canal, "but India would not
have followed the same procedure by which Egypt nationalized the Canal." He repeated warnings against a Western-
imposed settlement by force. Nehru flew to Dhahran, Saudi
Arabia Sept. 23–24, saying he was "a pilgrim in search of
peace and friendship," and conferred with King Saud in
Riyadh Sept. 25–28. On the conclusion of the talks, the
2 leaders said in a joint communiqué that there "can be no
settlement of the [Suez] dispute by methods of conflict or
by the denial of the sovereign rights of Egypt over the Suez
Canal." The communiqué urged a negotiated settlement and
expressed "the hope that there will be no recourse to political and economic pressure."

Nasser had conferred with King Saud and Syrian Pres.
Shukri al-Kuwatly Sept. 22–24 in Dammam and Riyadh. The
meetings were held amid reports that Saudi Arabia, dependent

on full operation of the Suez Canal for continued high oil royalties, had pressed for Egyptian moderation on the problem. (The historically antagonistic Hashemite King Feisal of Iraq and Saudi Arabian King Saud had met Sept. 18–20 in Saudi Arabia. The Suez crisis was believed to have been the central topic of their talks.) A joint communiqué issued by Nasser, Saud and Kuwatli in Cairo Sept. 24 supported Egypt "in every attitude she takes" on the Suez question. The 3 leaders pledged "unbreakable Arab solidarity" and backed "Egypt's declared readiness to reach a peaceful settlement that would safeguard Egypt's national interests and conform with the aims of the UN." They urged a settlement through "negotiations with Egypt, the owner of the Canal," "free from pressure" or intent "to impose any unilateral solution." (The communiqué also said that the 3 conferees had given "attention to consolidating Arab security, warding off the Israeli threat" and steps to "complete the Arab policy drawn up in Cairo" at the first meeting of the 3 rulers Mar. 7.)

Soviet Premier Nikolai A. Bulganin had said Sept. 19 that the USSR would be "prepared to take part in a meeting of the heads of government of Egypt, India, France, Britain, the U.S. and the Soviet Union" to seek a "just and peaceful solution of the Suez Canal issue." Bulganin, replying to questions submitted to him Sept. 13 by J. Kingsbury Smith, general manager of the International News Service, said that an "agreement on freedom of navigation in the Canal must in the end be reached" by a "wide international conference" and that the USSR "would have no objection to handing" any Suez agreement "to the UN" for ratification.

But Britain and France—the 2 most "aggrieved parties"— were still opposed to any direct UN role in the dispute. Delegates-to-UN Sir Pierson Dixon of Britain and Louis de Guiringaud of France had charged in a joint letter to UN Security Council Pres. Emilio Nuñez-Portuando Sept. 12 that the Egyptian refusal to negotiate a "just and equitable solution" to the Suez dispute had aggravated "the situation, which, if allowed to continue would" be a "danger to peace and security." But Nuñez said Sept. 12 that the letter had requested no action and that a Security Council meeting "is not considered necessary."

Egyptian Rep.-to-UN Omar Loutfi said in a letter to Secy. Gen. Dag Hammarskjöld Sept. 13 that "the former Suez Canal Co." had with British and French "indorsement," ordered Suez pilots to leave their posts and that this was "an act of intimidation." Loutfi wrote that Egypt wished "to assure the continuation of normal passage through the Canal" and that if navigation were hampered, "the responsibility" "would lie with those" who had attempted to obstruct "the so far unaffected" Canal traffic.

Sir Pierson Dixon, in a 2d note circulated to UN members Sept. 14, criticized "the inaccuracy of [the Egyptian] statements." Dixon reviewed British and French requests to pilots to stay at their posts and Egyptian threats to imprison those quitting. He quoted Prime Min. Eden as saying Sept. 12 that "if these pilots decide to leave Egypt, it will clearly, in our view, be the responsibility of" Egypt.

Loutfi transmitted a 2d Egyptian letter to the Security Council Sept. 17. It charged that the SCUA plan was "incompatible with the dignity and sovereign rights of Egypt" and in "flagrant violation" of the UN Charter and 1888 Constantinople Convention. The SCUA scheme, Egypt said, "would seek to establish in an unprecedented manner an organization within the territory of a sovereign state member of the UN without the consent of the state."

A Soviet note to the Security Council Sept. 17 said that the SCUA plan was a "provocation" and could only be enforced by "an act of aggression." A joint Syrian-Lebanese letter to the Security Council charged Sept. 17 that the dispatch of French troops to Cyprus was "a threat" to "peace and security" in "the immediate vicinity" of Syria and Lebanon.

The British and French governments, under increasing

U.S. pressure, finally asked UN Security Council Pres. Nuñez-Portuando Sept. 23 to call the Council into session Sept. 26 to consider the "situation created by the unilateral action" of Egypt in ending "the system of international operation of the Suez Canal" as "completed by the Suez Canal Convention of 1888."

Omar Loutfi countered Sept. 24 with the request that the Security Council be "urgently convened to consider" the "actions against Egypt" by "some powers," particularly Britain and France. Loutfi's letter to Dr. Nuñez charged that Anglo-French moves in the Mediterranean were "a danger to international peace and security" and were "serious violations of the charter of the UN." Loutfi was reported Sept. 24 to have agreed to prior action on the British-French request, with Egypt to be given a non-voting seat during the debate.

Britain and France Sept. 25 rejected Egypt's complaint to the Security Council. British Foreign Office spokesmen said that Britain would "not accept that any moves made by us could be described as a threat to peace." French Rep.-to-UN Bernard Cornut-Gentille said Sept. 25 that "we definitely cannot accept" Egypt's charges of UN Charter violations.

The Security Council voted unanimously Sept. 26 to debate (starting Oct. 5) the Anglo-French complaint against Egypt's nationalization of the Canal. The Council then agreed by 7–0 vote (U.S., Nationalist China, Cuba, Iran, Peru, Yugoslavia and the USSR in favor; Britain, France, Australia, Belgium abstaining) to consider Egyptian countercharges that the British-French military buildup in the Mediterranean was endangering peace and a violation of the UN Charter. The Council Sept. 26 rejected a Yugoslav motion for simultaneous debate on the 2 complaints. It agreed that the prior Anglo-French charge would be heard first. The Council adopted a British-French proposal that Egypt be invited for non-voting participation in the Suez debate. It approved an Australian resolution delaying action on Israeli requests for inclusion until the next Council session.

The Security Council, before adjournment Sept. 26,

heard Soviet delegate Arkady A. Sobolev attack Britain and France for having used "crude pressures" against Egypt. U.S. Amb.-to-UN Henry Cabot Lodge Jr., who cast the decisive vote on inclusion of the Egyptian complaint, told the Council that the U.S. did not agree with Egypt's charges but "generally" followed a "liberal policy" on UN agenda items.

It was reported from Washington Sept. 29 that the U.S., Britain and France were conferring on a possible joint resolution to be presented to the Security Council. U.S. officials reportedly advocated a text that would embody international control over the Canal but characterize it as international "participation" in the Canal's operation. British Foreign Secy. Lloyd, arriving in the U.S. for pre-UN session talks Oct. 2, reasserted that the interests of underdeveloped nations could not "be assured if the Canal" remained "under the control of one man or one government."

British Prime Min. Eden and Lloyd had conferred in Paris with French Premier Min. Pineau on the Suez dispute Sept. 26–27. Mollet and Eden, appearing together on TV Sept. 26, indicated that they had established Anglo-French solidarity on the issue. Pineau said Sept. 26 that his first talks with Eden had "very clearly shown" a "desire for common action." A joint communiqué issued Sept. 27 said that France and Britain had "defined their common position" on "the recent British decision to place the question" before the UN and on "the line to be followed by them in the forthcoming debate."

Paris sources reported Sept. 27 that Britain and France had agreed to maintain their Mediterranean force on standby alert, to consult closely on Middle Eastern policy and to discuss French objections to the Baghdad (METO) Pact linking Britain and Pakistan, Iran, Iraq and Turkey. The British carrier *Albion* arrived at Malta Sept. 27 with operational air units transferred from Britain. A fleet of French landing craft reportedly left Malta the same day for the

Eastern Mediterranean. British Foreign Office spokesmen
Sept. 26 had rejected an absolute prohibition on the use of
force against Egypt. A Foreign Office statement that day
indorsed Australian Prime Min. Robert G. Menzies' Sept. 25
defense of the user nations' right to "impose sanctions." The
London statement reiterated that "the use of force in settling
[the Suez dispute] would be a last resort." French Premier
Mollet said Sept. 30 that Britain and France had achieved
"unshakeable" unity on the Suez issue and that "the responsible men" of the U.S. were "profoundly in agreement with
us on the objectives to be reached."

The UN Security Council opened debate Oct. 5, 1956 on
a complaint of France and Britain against Egypt's nationalization of the Suez Canal. The session was convened by
French Foreign Min. Pineau, Council president for October,
after Western, Soviet and Egyptian diplomats had conferred
with other UN members and UN Secy. Gen. Dag
Hammarskjöld Oct. 3–4 on policies to be presented in the
Council's Suez debate. A joint Anglo-French draft resolution
on the Suez question was submitted to the Council Oct. 5 by
Pineau and British Foreign Secy. Lloyd. It charged Egypt
with subjecting "the operation of an international public
service" to "the Egyptian national interest and to exclusive
Egyptian control." Egypt, the resolution said, had seized the
waterway "contrary to the principles of respect for international obligations" and had endangered "international peace
and security."

The British-French draft called on the Security Council
to: (a) Reaffirm "the principle of the freedom of navigation"
through the waterway in "accordance with the Suez Canal
Convention of 1888." (b) Consider that the rights of "all
users of the Suez Canal" should "be safeguarded and the
necessary guarantees restored." (c) Indorse "the proposals
of the 18 states" at the first London Conference as "designed" to solve "the Suez Canal question." (d) Recommend
that "Egypt should cooperate by negotiation" of a "system

of operation to be applied to the Suez Canal." (e) Recommend that "Egypt should, pending the outcome of such negotiations, cooperate with the Suez Canal Users' Association."

U.S. State Secy. Dulles told the Security Council Oct. 5 that "the U.S. adheres" to "the 18-nation proposals" and "intends to vote for the [Anglo-French draft] resolution." Dulles was reported to have met with Lloyd and Pineau earlier Oct. 5 in an effort to soften the wording of the draft and to enable the U.S. to join in the sponsorship of the resolution.   UN informants said Oct. 5 that, pressed by Dulles, Lloyd and Pineau had agreed to direct negotiations with Egyptian Foreign Min. Mahmoud Fawzi before the Council vote on the draft resolution.

The Council seated Fawzi Oct. 5 as a non-voting participant in the Suez debate but indefinitely postponed action on similar permission for Israel and other Arab states.   Israeli Amb.-to-U.S. Abba Eban had promised Oct. 4 that Israel participation would, if granted, be limited to the Suez question. (Non-voting seats had been requested Oct. 4 by 7 Arab nations—Iran, Jordan, Lebanon, Libya, Saudi Arabia, Syria and Yemen.)

Fawzi charged in the Security Council Oct. 6 that Britain and France had attempted to ensure "that the Suez Canal be finally amputated and severed from Egypt." Fawzi said Britain and France had continued their threats of "military and economic measures" against Egypt despite "standing offers to negotiate a peaceful settlement." Egypt, he said, had refused the "ultimatum and insult" surrounding invitations to the London Conference and would continue to resist "dictation of a solution" for the Canal crisis. Fawzi told the Council that the Menzies committee talks in Cairo Sept. 3–9 had been conducted on a "take it or leave it" basis and that Menzies had confined the talks to the "presentation of the 18-power proposals." Fawzi charged that the "sudden withdrawal" of U.S. and British aid offers for the Aswan High Dam had been accompanied "by a vicious campaign against the Egyptian economy." He called for new Suez talks through "a negotiating body of reasonable size."

Egyptian Pres. Nasser told the Cairo newspaper *Al Massaa* Oct. 7 that Suez was "a decisive test case for the UN." Nasser warned that UN "submission" to "demands of the big imperialist countries" would bring the "collapse of the UN like the League of Nations before it." *Al Massaa* reported Oct. 8 that Nasser had told the Indonesian magazine *Gar* of plans for an economic organization to link the African and Asian Bandung powers. Nasser was said to have advanced the plan "to foil Western conspiracies against their economies" and to teach Africans and Asians to "depend on ourselves since it is useless to depend on Western help."

Fawzi informed the UN Security Council Oct. 8 of offers to compensate Suez Canal Co. shareholders on "the average value of the shares during the 5 years preceding nationalization" or to submit the case to international arbitration. Fawzi urged a Suez settlement based on: a "system of cooperation" between Egypt and the user nations; a toll system that "guarantees . . . fair treatment free from exploitation"; a "reasonable percentage of the revenues" for development of the Canal.

Soviet Foreign Min. Dmitri T. Shepilov told the Council Oct. 8 that efforts to internationalize the Canal were the work of "reactionary elements" attempting "to force Egypt to her knees" and to "serve a lesson to other peoples of the East." Shepilov charged that, according to press reports, "major oil and shipping companies" in the U.S. were planning a consortium aimed at "taking over the Suez Canal" and dislodging their "French and British rivals from the positions they now hold." Shepilov proposed that "an authoritative committee of the Security Council," including Egypt, Britain, France, the U.S., India and the USSR, "be set up for [Suez] negotiations." The committee should "be balanced in such a way as to forestall the prevalence of some one point of view" and could include other nations, Shepilov said. It "could also be instructed to draw up the draft of a new convention" and "be entrusted with the preparations for a broad international conference to be attended by all countries using the Suez Canal to consider and approve the new convention."

Dulles Oct. 9 rejected the Soviet call for a new negotiating body. He told the Council that the Shepilov plan was designed to "perpetuate controversy" by "establishing a committee which is so constituted that we can know in advance that it will never agree." "The U.S.," he repeated, "intends to vote for [the Anglo-French] resolution." Dulles stressed the need for insulation of the canal from politics and said that "if Egypt accepts that simple and rudimentary principle of justice, then I believe that the subsidiary problems can be resolved."

British Foreign Secy. Lloyd, French Foreign Min. Pineau and Egyptian Foreign Min. Fawzi met privately with UN Secy. Gen. Hammarskjöld Oct. 9 in an effort to reach a compromise settlement. The private talks followed a closed Security Council session earlier Oct. 9 at which Fawzi reportedly rejected the principle of international control over the Canal. Hammarskjöld refused to comment on the private talks Oct. 9 but said that he would continue talks with the 3 diplomats.

It was reported from the UN Oct. 9 that the Western powers were shifting toward acceptance of a proposed British solution similar to that advanced by India at the first London conference. Under the British plan, it was reported, an international commission would oversee canal operations and rule on alleged toll or priority discrimination against shippers. The commission could impose sanctions by forcing Egypt to give victimized vessels free canal passage and withholding Suez development funds. A U.S. version of the plan was said Oct. 9 to provide for appeal of violations directly to the UN.

(Reports said Oct. 9 that the British plan would permit Egypt to continue the Suez Canal blockade against Israeli

shipping and Israel-bound cargoes. The Israeli UN delegation
Oct. 8 had charged Egypt with blacklisting and blockading
103 vessels from 14 nations.   Israel said the Egyptian
blacklist had in Feb. 1956 included 45 British and 8 U.S.
ships plus smaller numbers from Sweden, Greece, Morocco,
Denmark, Italy, the Netherlands, Liberia, Costa Rica, Switzerland and the USSR.)

Egypt, Britain and France continued direct negotiations
toward the settlement of the dispute Oct. 10–12. Foreign
ministers of the 3 powers, meeting in private with Hammarskjöld, moved from the deadlock Oct. 10–11 to agreement Oct. 12 on 6 principles to govern future operation of
the canal.   The 6 principles, first presented by Lloyd at the
outset of the Security Council debate, were accepted as a
basis for further talks Oct. 12 by Mahmoud Fawzi, Lloyd
and Pineau.   The 6 principles, made public following their
presentation at a closed session of the UN Security Council
by Hammarskjöld Oct. 12, were: (1) "There shall be free
and open transit through the Canal without discrimination,
overt and covert."   (2) "Egypt's sovereignty shall be respected."   (3) "The operation of the Canal shall be insulated
from the politics of any country."   (4) "The manner of
fixing tolls and charges shall be decided by agreement between Egypt and the users."   (5) "A fair proportion of the
dues shall be allotted to development."   (6) "In case of
dispute, unresolved affairs between the Suez Canal Co. and
the Egyptian government shall be settled by arbitration. . . ."

The direct negotiations were recessed by Egypt, Britain
and France Oct. 12 amid reports that they had failed to agree
on enforcement of the 6 principles. According to Anthony
Nutting in *No End of a Lesson*, these reports were false and
the result of an announcement by Pineau to the press that
"no progress was being made in the talks and that there was
no basis for negotiation with Egypt."   Pineau acted in bad
faith in doing this, Nutting alleged, because Pineau was
attempting "to ensure that continuing state of deadlock

which France wanted in order to fulfill her plans with Israel" for military action against Egypt. Nutting recorded the following information, held in strict confidence until the publication of his book early in 1967:

• French Premier Guy Mollet telegraphed British Prime Min. Anthony Eden the morning of Oct. 13 to say that he was sending Labor Min. Albert Gazier (the acting foreign minister while Pineau was in New York) and Gen. Maurice Challe, deputy chief of staff of the French air force, to Eden's summer residence at Chequers Oct. 14 "with a message of the utmost importance."

• British Amb.-to-France Sir Gladwyn Jebb returned to London Oct. 13 with a report that "the French government had recently delivered to Israel no fewer than 75 of the latest French Mystère Fighter aircraft."

• Gazier and Challe met Eden, Eden's private secretary and Nutting at Chequers at 3 p.m. Sunday, Oct. 14. Gazier asked Eden whether Britain would intervene if Israel attacked Egypt. Nutting interposed that Britain was bound to do so under the Tripartite Agreement of May 25, 1950 with the U.S. and France. Gazier thereupon noted that Egypt "had recently contended that the Tripartite Declaration did not apply to Egypt."

• Eden's secretary, at Gazier's and Eden's insistence, stopped taking notes. Challe then outlined "a possible plan of action for Britain and France to gain physical control of the Suez Canal." The plan called for Israel to attack Egypt across the Sinai Peninsula and for Britain and France, "having given the Israeli forces enough time to seize all or most of Sinai," then to order "both sides" to withdraw their forces from the Suez Canal. (This would put Egypt back to the west of the Canal and Israel on its eastern bank.) An Anglo-French force would then intervene and occupy the Canal "on the pretext of saving it from damage by fighting."

In mid-October the Israeli armed forces were in secret collusion with the French armed forces. The Israeli government had become alarmed in previous months by several developments. The first of these was the possibility that the Egyptian government might be able to halt permanently all Israeli and Israel-bound shipping through the Suez Canal.

The British and French governments apparently believed that world public opinion was substantially behind them. They asked Egypt to comply with the "6 principles" but, under the assumption that Nasser would not do so, agreed Oct. 16, in secret talks in Paris attended by Prime Min. Eden, Foreign Secy. Selwyn Lloyd, Premier Mollet and Foreign Min. Pineau, to use military force to restore the Suez Canal to "international" status. The Israeli government was informed of these plans secretly by the Anglo-French allies, and the French also sent a military mission to Israel to train Israeli pilots to fly French-made jet aircraft.

Lloyd met Israeli Premier David Ben-Gurion secretly outside Paris Oct. 22 and learned from Ben-Gurion that Israel would not proceed without assurance that Britain and France "would 'take out' the Egyptian air force as soon as Israeli forces began their attack." Israel had no bombers and feared that Egypt would raid Tel Aviv and other Israeli cities with their Russian-made bombers. Eden received French Foreign Min. Pineau in London late Oct. 23 and held unrecorded talks with him. Lloyd, who had been present, conferred with Anthony Nutting the morning of Oct. 24, and Nutting gathered that Pineau had received Eden's assurance that Britain would give Israel the requested support. Lloyd told Nutting that Israel would attack the evening of Oct. 29, that Britain and France would issue their ultimatum early Oct. 30 and that, when Egypt refused it, the British and French would start bombing Egyptian airfields.

In the private talks during the first days of the UN Security Council's debate, Egyptian Foreign Min. Fawzi had offered (a) a system of cooperation between Egypt and the Canal's users that would recognize both Egypt's rights and the users' interests; (b) a fair program of tolls and charges; (c) the use of a rational amount of the Canal's revenues for the improvement and development of the Canal, and (d) an agreement to consider the question of user participation in the Canal's operation.

The UN Security Council met in open session Oct. 13 to consider a revised Anglo-French draft resolution on Suez. Lloyd told the Council that while "no basis for negotiation" had been found in talks with Fawzi, the "6 principles" could "provide a framework" for future negotiations. France and Britain, he said, while not abandoning the intent of their earlier draft Suez resolution, had submitted this softened version to attempt a settlement "by a different road." The revised Anglo-French resolution: (a) Urged "that any settlement of the Suez question" should meet conditions of the 6 principles agreed on by Britain, France and Egypt. (b) Considered "that the proposals of the 18 powers" were "designed to bring about a settlement" by "peaceful means in conformity with justice." (c) Noted that Egypt had accepted "the principle of organized collaboration" with the users but had not yet "formulated . . . precise proposals." (d) Urged continued "interchanges" and invited Egyptian "guarantees to the users" and cooperation with the Suez Canal Users' Association pending an agreement.

A final clause was added requiring cooperation with the SCUA until the resolution of the current dispute, but this clause was vetoed by the USSR. The 6 principles, minus the vetoed final SCUA clause, were unanimously approved Oct. 13 by the UN Security Council.

Following the vote, U.S. State Secy. Dulles urged UN Secy. Gen. Hammarskjöld to continue his talks with British, French and Egyptian envoys, "a procedure which has already yielded positive results." Hammarskjöld agreed Oct. 14 to "be of assistance" in obtaining an Egyptian counter-offer based on the 6 principles.

British Foreign Secy. Lloyd met with Dulles Oct. 14 and urged the U.S. to join in beginning SCUA operations. Lloyd asked the U.S. to back initial SCUA moves and to divert Suez Canal tolls from Egypt to the SCUA before the final agreement on the organization of the users' group. Dulles promised to answer the Lloyd request through "normal diplomatic channels." British UN sources said Oct. 14 that a U.S. agreement would be followed by a British attempt to force the opening of the Canal to SCUA vessels in the event that Egypt refused cooperation.

Soviet First Deputy Premier Anastas I. Mikoyan told newsmen in Moscow Oct. 15 that "absolutely all states should have equal rights in the Canal." Mikoyan, said to be the first Soviet official to acknowledge publicly the Suez blockade of Israel, conceded that "for a long time they [the Israelis] have not been able to use it and nothing has been said about it." Dispatches from Moscow said Oct. 15 that all mention of the blockade had been deleted from Soviet press accounts of the Suez crisis.

British Prime Min. Eden had taken his case before his own political party. Eden, at the Conservative Party's annual conference in Llandudno, Wales Oct. 13, cited as a "happy consequence" of the Suez problem a growing "sense of partnership" with Europe and unity with "our French allies." He conceded there had been "a little progress" toward solving the dispute in the UN. He credited it "to the firmness and resolution which we and those who think like us have been showing throughout the crisis." Eden repeated that no acceptable Suez settlement could "leave it [the Canal] in the unfettered control of a single power." He asserted that Britain had "always said that with us force is the last resort, but it cannot be excluded." "No responsible government could ever give such a pledge," he said. Eden said that

Britain would continue her military buildup in the Eastern Mediterranean because "to relax now before a settlement is reached would be fatal."

Dispatches from Paris Oct. 10–16 cited continued French bitterness against U.S. Suez policy and the repeated instances of calls in the press for firm action against Egypt. Foreign Min. Pineau, answering critics at the opening of a National Assembly debate on Suez Oct. 16, conceded that U.S. policy had been "very difficult for us to follow." Pineau, defending the effectiveness of NATO with respect to the Suez problem, said that France "often has the impression that the U.S. does not understand, as we do, the obligations of the Atlantic Alliance."

Egyptian Foreign Min. Fawzi, in a letter to the Security Council Oct. 15, had said that Eden's reference in his Llandudno remarks to a possible use of force over the Canal had been "extremely unfortunate" and "a matter of deep regret." Fawzi charged that France and Britain were "persevering in the military and economic measures which they initiated" after the Canal seizure July 26. "These statements," Fawzi said, did not insulate the Canal from politics but "throw this question into the turmoil of politics."

A joint Anglo-French communiqué said Oct. 17 that France and Britain were "ready to consider together" any new Egyptian proposals for a Suez settlement. The communiqué, issued following talks in Paris Oct. 16–17 among Mollet, Pineau, Eden and Lloyd, said that Britain and France were "resolved to adhere to the requirements" of the UN Security Council resolution on Suez but also would "stand by the 2d part of the resolution . . . vetoed by the Soviet Union." The communiqué said that Britain and France would continue to consider "the 18-power proposals, including the international operation of the Canal," as "the basis for settlement." Any acceptable Egyptian proposals would have to meet the requirements of the 18-power proposals and afford "equivalent guarantees to the users," the communiqué said.

Nasser, interviewed by Hanson W. Baldwin of the *N.Y. Times* for the *Times'* Oct. 18 editions, maintained that Egypt was ready for "any form of consultation or cooperation" with the Canal users toward a solution of the crisis but would not accept foreign "domination" of the Canal. (Nasser insisted to Baldwin that the "Russians are ready to give Egypt long-term loans" for the Aswan High Dam. He said that the loans had been offered by Soviet Amb.-to-Egypt Yevgeni D. Kiselev and that the final decision on the bid would be deferred until a planned visit to the USSR.)

The Suez Canal Users' Association Council, meeting in London Oct. 19, appointed Eyvind Bartels, Danish consul general in New York, as chief SCUA administrator. From Washington Oct. 19 came reports of Western disagreement on the payment of Suez tolls into SCUA accounts. Britain and France were said to feel that the funds should be blocked and that the SCUA should be used to coerce Egyptian cooperation in the absence of a firm Canal agreement. The U.S. was reported to be backing the distribution of a share of SCUA tolls to Egypt and the use of the SCUA as an instrument of cooperation with Egyptian Suez officials.

Nasser conferred on the Suez question Oct. 19–20 with V. K. Krishna Menon of India, who had arrived in Cairo from talks in London Oct. 19. Before leaving for New Delhi Oct. 20, Menon said he had "put various plans" before Nasser "for consideration." The Cairo newspaper *Al Goumhouria* reported Oct. 21 that Menon had proposed a new Suez plan under which Egypt would "recognize" the Suez Canal Users' Association, which would "function in an advisory capacity." The plan would provide for the UN appointment of chiefs for the 3 divisions of the Egyptian Suez Canal Authority during the first 3 years of the plan's operation. Egyptian spokesmen said Egypt expected to begin talks with Britain and France in Geneva.

After French Foreign Min. Pineau's meeting with British Prime Min. Eden in London Oct. 23, however, Pineau said that Britain and France had agreed that they could not consider "seriously" a new Egyptian offer of direct negotiations on a possible Suez settlement. The British and French leaders reportedly had been informed Oct. 23, through UN sources, of an Egyptian bid to discuss guarantees for unrestricted use of the Canal. UN Secy. Gen. Hammarskjöld had met with Egyptian Foreign Min. Fawzi and British UN delegation chief Sir Pierson Dixon at UN headquarters in New York Oct. 19 in an effort to renew direct 3-power Suez negotiations.

Anthony Nutting reported in *No End of a Lesson* that Eden and Lloyd sent "a senior Foreign Office official [to Paris Oct. 24] with further assurance for the French to pass on to the Israelis that we . . . would do all that the Israelis required in the way of air strikes against Egyptian airfields to forestall the bombing of their cities. These assurances turned the scale, and on Thursday, Oct. 25th, Eden learned that the Israelis had decided finally to play their part in the Sinai campaign. That afternoon the [British] cabinet came to its final . . . decision" to commit Britain to full cooperation in the Franco-Israeli plans.

In Israel, meanwhile, Premier Ben-Gurion Oct. 15 had opened a general debate in the Knesset (parliament) on Israeli defenses and foreign affairs by attacking British support for a plan to have Iraq, a Baghdad Pact partner, send a battalion of troops to Jordan in accordance with the Jordanian-Iraqi defense treaty. Israel would consider itself free to act in keeping with its own standards of self-defense if Iraqi troops entered Jordan, Ben-Gurion said. (Israeli infantry and Jordanian police, army and national guard contingents had fought in the Qalqilya area Oct. 4. Israel later admitted losing 18 soldiers in the battle, and UN observers put Jordanian losses at 45 servicemen and 3 civilians killed.)

Ben-Gurion denounced as "a disguised attack on the integrity of our borders" a proposal by Iraqi Premier Nuri as-Said that Israel settle its border disputes on the basis of the UN General Assembly's partition resolution of Nov. 29, 1947.

Ben-Gurion, replying in the Knesset Oct. 17 to right-wing and left-wing attacks on his position, refused to go any further than his statement of Oct. 15 in regard to the projected Iraqi troop movements. He said that "a number of favorable developments in the last few days" with respect to both the Iraqi threat and the Suez crisis had underscored to him the advantages of patience, but he cautioned against overoptimism and excessive reliance on "verbal promises." The greatest danger of all, he told the Knesset, rested with "the Egyptian dictator," who had repeatedly expressed an intention to destroy Israel. Ben-Gurion won from the Knesset a 76–13 vote of confidence Oct. 17.

U.S. State Secy. Dulles had warned at a press conference in Washington Oct. 16 that, "within constitutional means," the U.S. would carry out an Apr. 9, 1956 White House declaration and "assist" and "give aid to any victim of aggression" in the Middle East. Dulles attributed mass Israeli reprisal raids against Jordan to "deterioration of the situation" and "failure of the efforts" by UN Secy. Gen. Hammarskjöld. (48 Jordanians and 18 Israelis had been killed Oct. 11 in an Israeli reprisal raid on Qalqilya, Jordan.)

It is generally agreed that a low ebb in Anglo-U.S. relations was reached during and immediately after the Suez crisis. Dulles and Eden were at odds. According to Muhammad Heikal, a confidant of Nasser and the publisher of *Al-Ahram*, the Cairo daily, certain Americans informed Nasser of the plan for an armed attack against Egypt. In *Nasser: The Cairo Documents*, Heikal wrote: "In their efforts to persuade Egypt of the dangers of the situation and to agree to the 6 principles, the Americans had leaked to [Egyptian Amb.-to-U.S.] Ahmed Hussein the news that Gen. Keightley had been chosen to command an invasion of Egypt and . . . [was] training his men in Cyprus. This was one of a number of warnings about Britain and France's determination on military intervention."

Egypt Oct. 25 an agreement concluded in Amman, Jordan an agreement with Jordan and Syria establishing a joint Egyptian-Jordanian-Syrian military command under the leadership of Maj. Gen. Abdel Hakim Amer, the Egyptian army chief of staff, to operate in the event of war with Israel. Also signing were Maj. Gen. Ali Abu Nuwar, the Jordanian general staff chief, and the Syrian chief of staff, Maj. Gen. Tewfik Nizameddin. Also under this agreement, Iraqi forces would enter Jordan; this point had been proposed by the Jordanian government in the face of Iraqi-Egyptian antagonisms. Amer said Oct. 24 that the agreement would provide for Egyptian strategic leadership of the 3 armies in the event of war with Israel but would not place the Syrian or Jordanian forces under direct tactical command of Egypt. In case of conflict, Iraqi forces entering Jordan would remain under Jordanian command, Amer said. (Jordanian King Hussein denied Oct. 24 that the pact had aligned Jordan with the Egyptian-Saudi Arabian-Syrian "southern tier" alliance.)

The pact, however, did not operate. Instead, after Israel actually did invade Egypt Oct. 29, Iraq sent troops into Jordan (ostensibly at Jordanian King Hussein's request for protection against Israel), and Syria and Saudi Arabia did likewise. The Iraqi and Jordanian governments confirmed Nov. 3 that Iraqi and Syrian troops had entered Jordan Nov. 1–2. Jordanian sources reported Nov. 4 that $^2/_3$ of the 20,000-man Syrian army and a full Iraqi division had taken up positions on Jordanian territory. Egyptian spokesmen said Nov. 2 that both Syria and Jordan had asked for activation of the Egyptian-Jordanian-Syrian defense agreement and offered to place their armies under the Egypt's Gen. Amer.

The Israeli foreign ministry said Nov. 2 that Israel would

not take any action against the reported movement of troops into Jordan but would "strike back" if attacked.

Sinai & Suez Campaign

The Anglo-French effort to regain control of the Suez Canal culminated in a 9-day campaign—Operation Musketeer—that opened Oct. 29, 1956, when Israeli armed forces penetrated deep into Egypt's Sinai Peninsula and drove toward the Canal.

The Israeli forces crossed the Egyptian border from the Negev Oct. 29 on a front north of Eilat, the southern Israeli seaport near Aqaba. The drive began with the destruction of Egyptian bases near Ras el Naqb and Kuntilla on the southern Egyptian-Israeli frontier. The Israeli units, described in reports from Israel as being "too big for a reprisal and too small for a war," reportedly advanced more than 75 miles to a line within 25 miles of the Suez Canal. Israeli officials said Oct. 29 that the attackers had taken up positions west of Nakhl. Sinai was said to be "lightly defended" by Egypt because of earlier Egyptian troop withdrawals to bolster Canal defenses.

An Israeli Foreign Ministry statement Oct. 29 described the attack as "security measures to eliminate the Egyptian *fedayin* [commando] bases in the Sinai Peninsula" from which raids repeatedly had been launched across the Israeli frontier. The ministry said that the decision to strike at Egypt (reportedly made at an Israeli cabinet session Oct. 29) followed persistent declarations by Egyptian Pres. Nasser that "his country remains in a state of war with Israel." Egyptian hopes of "annihilating" Israel, the Israeli statement said, had been "crowned a few days ago by [the formation of] a Syrian-Jordan-Egyptian military command under the Egyptian commander-in-chief. "Israel reported that 24 Israelis had been killed and wounded by *fedayin* mines in "the last week."

Israeli communiqués Oct. 30 said that the attack on Egypt had been widened along a 70-mile front. Israel claimed the capture of Quseima on the northern Sinai frontier and said that Israeli forces were within 20 miles of the Suez Canal west of Nakhl. Israeli dispatches said that the Israeli air force had been unleashed over the Sinai Peninsula following strafing of Israeli ground forces by the Egyptian air force. Israel Oct. 30 reported 3 Egyptian MiG-15 jets destroyed and one Israeli plane damaged.

Britain and France issued a 12-hour ultimatum to Israel and Egypt Oct. 30, demanding that hostilities cease and announcing plans to reoccupy the Suez Canal Zone. The Anglo-French message demanded that Egypt and Israel withdraw their forces from the vicinity of the Canal.

Israeli forces reached the Canal Oct. 31 and then pulled back to the 10-mile limit specified in the Anglo-French ultimatum. Anglo-French military operations opened with air attacks on Egyptian and Suez Canal installations and airfields Oct. 31. They were claimed by commando and paratroop landings at key points of the Canal Nov. 5–6.

After 5 days of fighting, Israel Nov. 3 stood in control of all of the Sinai Peninsula except for several small areas where *fedayin* squads still held out. The Gaza Strip had been cut off with the capture of the towns of El Arish and Rafa and the military post at Khan Yunis. Israel also held Abu Aweigla, the Egyptian divisional headquarters in Sinai, and the military bases of Quseima, Kuntilla and Nakhl. Israeli paratroopers captured Sharm el-Sheikh and the island of Tiran at the mouth of the Gulf of Aqaba the night of Nov. 4–5 and took over the Egyptian batteries that had prevented Eilat-based or Eilat-bound shipping from passing between the Gulf of Aqaba and the Red Sea.

Since half of the Egyptian army had been garrisoned in or near the Sinai Peninsula, Egypt's losses were heavy. Hundreds of Egyptian soldiers died defending Abu Aweigla, and about 5,000 troops surrendered to the Israelis, as did Maj. Gen. Muhammad Fuad el-Digwy, military governor of Sinai, and

Maj. Gen. Yousef Abdullah Agruli, the commander of the 8th Egyptian Division, together with his staff at Khan Yunis. (Several Soviet technicians expert in the use of military equipment reportedly also were captured, as well as 100 or more tanks.)

In the only naval clash between Egyptian and Israeli forces, the 1,200-ton Egyptian destroyer *Ibrahim Awal* (the former H.M.S. *Cottesmore*) was disabled by Israeli warships and aircraft and taken in tow Oct. 31 after it began shelling Haifa. The crew of 250 became prisoners of war.

Meanwhile, Egypt had at once rejected the Anglo-French ultimatum. On behalf of its government, the Egyptian embassy in London Oct. 30 issued a statement in which Egypt claimed "all rights to take the measures to which she is entitled under the UN Charter, including the right to defend herself," and described the Israeli invasion as "nothing but a link in the chain of aggressions extending over the last few years against the Egyptian as well as the Arab borders, the purpose of which is to create a continued state of tension and to endanger peace in the Middle East." (Israel had justified its mobilization Oct. 28 and invasion the next day first of all on a renewal of *fedayin* raids Oct. 21 and 27 in which 4 Israeli soldiers were killed. Israel had expressed a determination to liquidate the *fedayin*'s Sinai bases.)

In a joint communiqué from Nicosia, Cyprus, Oct. 31, Britain and France announced that "an air offensive by bomber aircraft under allied [Anglo-French] command has been launched against military targets in Egypt." The allied forces attacked 4 Egyptian airfields Oct. 31 and Nov. 1 at Abu Suweir, Fayid, Kasfareet and Kabrit in the Suez and Nile Delta areas and at Inchass Airfield 20 miles from Cairo. In dawn-to-dusk bombing-and-strafing raids from British and French carriers, the Anglo-French air armada destroyed approximately 100 Egyptian aircraft—Soviet-made MiG-15 fighters and Ilyushin jet bombers.

The British cruiser H.M.S. *Newfoundland* Nov. 1 sank the

Egyptian frigate *Domiat* near the Red Sea 80 miles south of Suez after the *Domiat*, carrying mines, had refused to heed a call to stop. The cruiser rescued the frigate's crew.

British and French aircraft from the carriers H.M.S. *Albion* *Bulwark*, *Eagle* and the *Arromanches* Nov. 2 destroyed a military barracks near Cairo and the shortwave and regular transmitters of Radio Cairo in the desert outside the city. British and French fliers also attempted to destroy an Egyptian blockship being towed to the southern end of Lake Timsah —apparently so that Egypt could close the Suez Canal—but the craft, though disabled, was maneuvered south and scuttled broadside athwart the channel by the Egyptians, partially blocking the Canal.

The chief targets of Anglo-French air sorties Nov. 3–4 included the military airfield at Luxor, 400 miles south of Cairo, on whose runways 18 Ilyushin bombers were reportedly destroyed, a concentration of tanks near the Pyramids, the Ismailia railroad yards and an Egyptian army barracks at Almaza. British Seahawk naval planes sank 3 Egyptian torpedo boats and damaged a 4th near Alexandria. Meanwhile, the British frigate H.M.S. *Crane* in the Gulf of Suez shot down an Israeli plane that mistakenly interfered with a patrol put ashore by the frigate.

The Anglo-French headquarters in Nicosia announced Nov. 4 that the Egyptian air force had ceased to exist. It also announced that air reconnaissance had shown the Suez Canal blocked by 4 ships sunk at Port Said by the Egyptians and that the El Ferdan Bridge across the Canal had been demolished. 7 foreign ships were reportedly trapped south of Port Said by the Egyptian obstructions.

British Prime Min. Anthony Eden announced Nov. 6 that an Anglo-French ceasefire would take effect at midnight Nov. 6–7, subject to the unconditional acceptance of Egypt and Israel. Anglo-French headquarters Nov. 6 announced the capture of Port Said and Port Fuad by British and French paratroopers dropped over the areas early Nov. 5. Port Fuad fell without resistance, but more that 100 paratroopers and British marine commandos from the carriers H.M.S. *Ocean* and *Theseus* were killed in the fight for Port Said and its Gamil Airfield. The Egyptian commander accepted a cease-fire late Nov. 5 under Anglo-French terms but soon withdrew his acceptance on orders from Cairo, and fighting was resumed for several hours.

The British reappointed the Egyptian commander, Muhammad Riad, as military governor of Port Said. Riad accepted the resumption—as he later put it—only "for the good of the Egyptian population." Riad estimated Nov. 24 that the Anglo-French invasion had cost 3,000 lives and about $28 million in property damage.

Gen. Sir Charles Keightley, commander of the joint Anglo-French forces in Egypt, said Nov. 7 that a (UN-sponsored) cease-fire was in effect in the Suez Canal Zone. Keightley reported that the Port Said area had been secured and that British paratroop patrols had reached to within a mile of Qantara when the cease-fire went into effect. The Anglo-French force, estimated to total 70,000 to 80,000 men, ended its Suez Canal Zone buildup Nov. 9. Egyptian forces reportedly continued their buildup south of the Suez Zone truce line.

The British War Office issued revised casualty lists Nov. 13, reporting 25 Britons killed, 2 missing and 149 wounded during the Suez operation. French losses were not reported. Port Said dispatches Nov. 10 reported at least 360 Egyptians killed and 500 wounded in fighting for the city. Dr. Ezzeldine Hosni, head of the Egyptian General Hospital in Port Said, said Nov. 10 that "not less that 1,000 bodies" of Egyptian soldiers and civilians had been brought to the hospital during the battle. (Photographers David Seymour, president of Magnum Photos [U.S.], and Jean Roy of *Paris-Match* magazine [France] were killed by Egyptian machine-gun fire. Nov. 10 while passing from British to Egyptian lines near Qantara.)

The British War Office said Nov. 13 that 32 vessels had been sunk in the Suez Canal during the Egyptian fighting. 20

craft, many of them Suez Canal Co. tugs and cranes, were reported sunk in Port Said harbor at the waterway's northern
entrance. British naval commander J. R. L. Moore, in charge
of Suez salvage operations, estimated Nov. 11 that it would
take "months" to clear the Canal even though a 17-foot channel was reported still open. Moore said that a 30-vessel salvage
fleet was en route to the Suez Zone from Malta.

Israeli officials had claimed Nov. 10 that about $50 mil-
lion worth of Egyptian equipment had been captured intact
during the brief Sinai and Gaza campaigns, including: 100
tanks (40 to 45 Soviet-made T-34s, the rest U.S.-made Sher-
mans), 100 British-made Bren Gun Carriers, 1,000 military
vehicles, 200 field guns (British 6-lb., 17-lb. and 25-lb.;
30-mm.; Czech recoilless rifles) and large amounts of Russian,
Czech and Swedish small arms, 7,000 tons of ammunition, 3
fuel dumps holding 700,000 gallons of gasoline, and a complete Soviet mobile radar station. Israeli informants had said
Nov. 10 that 3,000 Egyptian soldiers had been killed and
7,000 captured and that several thousand remained at large
but were unarmed.

Egypt, prostrated by its attackers, was rescued by the UN
with the full support of the world's 2 superpowers, the U.S.
and the Soviet Union. According to some observers, the loser
became the winner: Britain, France and Israel were forced to
disgorge their gains; Britain and France let go permanently of
their dominant influence in the Middle East and North Africa;
Israel was stigmatized for a decade, but Gamal Abdel Nasser,
the main target of the campaign, emerged stronger than ever
and ready to promote to the fullest extent his political version
of pan-Arabism.

The pro-Western Baghdad Pact (METO) powers supported
Egypt. The government heads of 4 Baghdad (METO) Pact
powers—Turkey, Pakistan, Iran and Iraq—condemned "Israeli
aggression" against Egypt Nov. 8 and demanded the immediate
withdrawal of British, French and Israeli troops from Egyptian territory. A communiqué issued following talks in Tehe-

ran Nov. 5–8 supported proposals to move a UN force into the ceasefire zone and demand respect for "Egypt's sovereignty." The 4 premiers, whose meeting was called by Pakistani Pres. Iskander Mirza, urged a settlement of the Arab-Israeli dispute on the lines of the 1947 UN partition plan for Palestine.

Iraq Nov. 9 severed diplomatic relations with France and announced that it would boycott any METO meeting attended by Britain, a member of the alliance. Iraqi government spokesmen Nov. 12 urged responsible leaders to avoid any action that could lead to World War III. They cited possible provocation to NATO powers, including Turkey, if Arab states should admit Russian military advisers.

The heads of government of the Colombo Powers (Burma, Ceylon, Indonesia, India and Pakistan) met in Delhi Nov. 12–14 (with the exception of the Pakistani premier who was attending the Baghdad Pact meeting in Teheran) and condemned the attack on Egypt. A joint communiqué said: "The premiers note with satisfaction the impressive expression of world opinion both within and outside the United Nations against the aggression on Egypt. They welcome the resolution of the UN General Assembly . . . directing the cessation of hostilities and the withdrawal of the forces of Israel, the United Kingdom and France from the territory of Egypt. They note also with satisfaction that these resolutions have largely resulted in a ccase-fire in the area of hostilities and in assurances being given on behalf of the governments of the United Kingdom, France and Israel that their armed forces will be withdrawn from Egypt."

The Sinai and Suez campaign was described by some observers as a political windfall for the Soviet Union, whose actions had met with international criticism since Oct. 22, the onset of the Hungarian uprising. The Kremlin, it was said, made a deliberate effort to focus world attention on the Middle Eastern situation, and it championed the Egyptians as helpless underdogs. The U.S., however, was reported to be acutely embarrassed by the behavior of its Western Big-3 allies and Israel and annoyed at being obliged to salvage American prestige and influence with Nasser and his countrymen.

Officially, the Eisenhower Administration took the position that the U.S. had been caught almost completely by surprise. According to Eisenhower Administration sources, it wasn't until late October that American intelligence sources had begun reporting to the Administration on growing evidence of a Franco-Israeli arms arrangement and an increasing Israeli military buildup.

Pres. Eisenhower, campaigning for reelection, had told TV interviewers Oct. 24 that no one could challenge Egypt's legal right to nationalize the Suez Canal. Eisenhower revealed Oct. 28 that he had sent Israeli Premier David Ben-Gurion a message Oct. 27 noting "disturbing reports from the Middle East," including word of "heavy mobilization" of Israeli armed forces, and urging that "no forceful initiative be taken which would endanger the peace." Eisenhower said the U.S. had not heard of "largescale mobilization in countries neighboring Israel which would warrant such Israeli" action. He said he would send "a further urgent message" to Ben-Gurion and similar notes to the Arab states concerned.

Following the Israeli thrust into Sinai, U.S. Amb.-to-Britain Winthrop Aldrich visited Foreign Secy. Selwyn Lloyd at the British Foreign Office in London early Oct. 30 but learned nothing there to prepare him for the Anglo-French move that started a few hours later. Eisenhower appealed to British Prime Min. Eden and French Premier Mollet Oct. 30 to cancel the then projected British-French military action. A White House statement said that Eisenhower's appeal had been sent "as soon as the President received his first knowledge, through press reports of the ultimatum." The statement said Eisenhower had requested that "full opportunity" be given the UN to settle the crisis "by peaceful means." Press reports Oct. 30 said Eisenhower was "disturbed" over the lack of Western coordination of policy on the Egyptian situation.

State Secy. Dulles called in the British and French envoys Oct. 30 to express "extreme displeasure" at the Anglo-French failure to inform the U.S. of the impending ultimatum. British diplomatic sources asserted Oct. 30 that U.S. Amb.-to-Britain Aldrich had been informed of the Anglo-French move at least 7 hours before the first news reports of the ultimatum. (Other sources said the U.S. envoy was not informed.) The British and French envoys reportedly denied State Department suspicions of Israeli-British-French "collusion" to provoke military action against Egypt.

A White House statement issued Oct. 29 had said that the U.S. would refer the Israeli attack on Egypt to the UN Security Council. The decision was said to be based on the Tripartite Declaration of 1950, in which the U.S., Britain and France had pledged to guarantee existing Arab-Israeli borders. The statement disclosed that Eisenhower, at a meeting with State Secy. Dulles, Defense Secy. Charles E. Wilson, Joint Chiefs of Staff Chairman Arthur W. Radford, CIA Director Allen W. Dulles and other Administration leaders Oct. 29, had "recalled that the U.S." had "pledged itself to assist the victim of any aggression in the Middle East." "We shall honor our pledge," the statement said.

Eisenhower Administration officials showed amazement and anger when, in an emergency session of the UN Security Council Oct. 30, Britain and France vetoed a U.S.-authored resolution against the new military activities in Egypt. This was the first time that Britain had used the veto and the first instance of the U.S. and USSR being aligned against Britain and France on a major issue before the council. The action in the Security Council was on an American-sponsored resolution calling for: (1) "Israel and Egypt immediately to cease fire"; (2) Israel to "withdraw its armed forces behind the established armistice lines"; (3) "all members" to "refrain from the use of force or threat of force in the area" and "refrain from giving any military, economic or financial assistance to Israel so long as it has not complied with" the resolution. The vote on the resolution was 7–2 (Australia and Belgium abstaining), but Britain and France—permanent members with veto power—cast the 2 negative votes. British delegate Sir Pierson Dixon held that the UN could not act quickly enough to affect the situation.

U.S. Amb.-to-UN Henry Cabot Lodge Jr. said that the UN had a "clear and unchallenged responsibility" to maintain the Palestine armistice agreements. Soviet delegate Arkady A. Sobolev charged that Britain and France were trying to use "Israeli aggression" as an excuse for seizing the Suez Canal in another act of "aggression against Egypt."

Eisenhower Oct. 31, in the closing days of his 2d Presidential campaign, told Americans in a TV address on the Middle Eastern crisis:

> The Middle East was, as we all know, an area long subject to colonial rule. This rule ended after World War II, when all countries there won full independence. Out of the Palestine mandated territory was born the new state of Israel. These historic changes could not, however, instantly banish animosities born of the ages. Israel and her Arab neighbors soon found themselves at war with one another. And the Arab nations showed continuing anger toward their former colonial rulers, notably France and Britain.

> The United States . . . has labored tirelessly to bring peace and stability to this area. We have considered it a basic matter of U.S. policy to support the state of Israel and at the same time to strengthen our bonds both with Israel and with the Arab countries. But unfortunately, through all these years, passion in the area threatened to prevail over peaceful purpose, and in one form or another there has been almost continuous fighting.

> This situation was recently aggravated by Egyptian policy, including rearmament with Communist weapons. We felt this to be a misguided policy on the part of the Egyptian government. Israel, at the same time, felt increasing anxiety for her safety. And Britain and France feared more and more that Egyptian policies threatened their lifeline of the Suez Canal.

> These matters came to a crisis on July 26 of this year when the Egyptian government seized the Suez Canal Co. For 90 years, ever since the inauguration of the Canal, that company had operated the Canal,

largely under British and French technical supervision. There were some among our allies who urged an immediate reaction to this event by use of force. We insistently urged otherwise, and our wish prevailed, through a long succession of conferences and negotiations, for weeks—even months—with participation by the United Nations. There in the UN only a short while ago, it seemed that an acceptable accord was within our reach on the basis of agreed principles. But the relations of Egypt with both Israel and France kept worsening to a point at which first Israel, and then France and Britain, determined that, in their judgment, there could be no protection of their vital interests without resort to force.

Upon this decision events followed swiftly. On Oct. 28 the Israeli government ordered mobilization. On Oct. 29 their armed forces penetrated deeply into Egypt and to the vicinity of the Suez Canal—nearly 100 miles away. On Oct. 30 the British and French governments delivered a 12-hour ultimatum to Israel and Egypt, now followed up by armed attack against Egypt. The United States was not consulted in any way about any phase of these actions. Nor were we informed of them in advance.

As it is the manifest right of any of those nations to take such decisions and actions, it is likewise our right, if our judgment so dictates, to dissent. We believe these actions to have been taken in error, for we do not accept the use of force as a wise or proper instrument for the settlement of international disputes. To say this, in this particular instance, is in no way to minimize our friendship with these nations nor our determination to maintain those friendships.

We are fully aware of the grave anxieties of Israel, Britain and France. We know that they have been subjected to grave and repeated provocations. The present fact nonetheless seems clear. The action taken can scarcely be reconciled with the principles and purpose of the UN, to which we have all subscribed. . . .

Now we must look to the future. In the circumstances I have described, there will be no U.S. involvement in these hostilities. I have no plan to call Congress in special session. . . . At the same time it is—and will remain—the dedicated purpose of our government to do all in its power to localize the fighting and to end the conflict.

We took our first measure in this action yesterday. We went to the UN with a request that the forces of Israel return to their own lines and that hostilities in the area be brought to a close. This proposal was not adopted because it was vetoed by Britain and France. It is our hope and intent that this matter will be brought before the UN General Assembly. There, with no veto operating, the opinion of the world can be brought to bear in our quest for a just end to this tormenting problem. . . .

. . . I am ever more deeply convinced that the UN represents the soundest hope for peace in the world. For this very reason I believe that the processes of the UN need further to be developed and strengthened. I speak particularly of increasing its ability to secure justice under international law. In all the recent troubles of the Middle East there have been injustices suffered by all nations involved. But I do not believe that another instrument of injustice—war—is a remedy for these wrongs. . . .

James B. Reston of the *N.Y. Times*, said in a *Times* report Oct. 31: "There was no attempt in the official quarters to conceal the disappointment of the U.S. government in the sudden—and what is felt here [in Washington] to be the provocative—action of the British and French governments. . . . So sharp were the feelings here on this question that officials of the U.S. government lent some credence to reports that the Israeli government not only had informed the French and British in advance of the plan to invade Egypt, but that the Israeli officials were encouraged to believe that they would have the support of France and perhaps even of Britain if they did move. . . . Consequently the capital was full tonight of charges of 'collusion' between Israel and France and, to a lesser extent, between Israel and Britain."

The Soviet Union Nov. 1 strongly condemned the Anglo-French military action in Egypt and said that it would urge the "Bandung [Afro-Asian] powers" to demand that British, French and Israeli forces quit Egypt immediately. Soviet Foreign Min. Dmitri Shepilov described the Anglo-French air operations against Egyptian airfields Nov. 1 as an "act of gangsterism." The Kremlin Nov. 2 sent notes to Britain and France in which the Soviet government accused the 2 countries of violating the 1888 Constantinople Convention guaranteeing freedom of navigation in the Suez Canal. Britain and France had set up a "naval blockade" in Egyptian waters of the eastern Mediterranean and the Red Seas and bore full responsibility for "acts of aggression affecting not only Egypt but other states as well," the Soviet note charged.

At the height of the Suez crisis, the USSR Nov. 4 crushed the Hungarian revolution with a massive deployment of Soviet troops to Budapest and other Hungarian centers of rebellion against Soviet control of Hungary.

Soviet Premier Nikolai A. Bulganin warned Britain, France and Israel Nov. 5 that the USSR was fully prepared "to crush the aggressors and restore peace in the East through the use of force." Bulganin the same day proposed in an open letter to Pres. Eisenhower a joint Russo-American military action that would end the fighting and remove the Anglo-French threat to Egyptian sovereignty. Bulganin told Eisenhower that the U.S. and the USSR, as Security Council members and possessors of "all modern types of arms, including the atomic and hydrogen weapons," bore "particular responsibility for stopping war." He proposed that American and Soviet air and naval forces be combined in the Middle East, "backed by a UN decision," as a "sure guarantee of ending the aggression against" Egypt. Bulganin wrote British Prime Min. Eden of his proposal for U.S.-Soviet action and accused the British government of pursuing a colonialist foreign policy. In a 3d note, Bulganin told French Premier Guy Mollet to consider "the position of France if she were attacked" by "states having . . . modern and terrible" weapons. Bulganin also warned Israeli Premier Ben-Gurion that Israel's attack on Egypt was "sowing such hatred" for Israel as to "place in jeopardy" its "very existence." The USSR Nov. 4 had sent Britain and France notes of formal protest against the bombing of Egypt and closure of the Suez Canal. Moscow recalled Amb.-to-Israel Aleksandr N. Abramov; Israeli Amb.-to-USSR Joseph Avidar, visiting Tel Aviv, canceled plans to return to Moscow Nov. 5.

A White House statement Nov. 5 rejected Bulganin's suggestion of joint U.S.-Soviet intervention by force in Egypt as "unthinkable" and "an obvious attempt to divert world attention from the Hungarian tragedy." The statement said further intervention in Egypt would contravene the UN General Assembly's action to establish a UN peace force.

Ben-Gurion replied to Bulganin Nov. 8 that "some of your arguments are based on incomplete and incorrect information." Ben-Gurion added: "In an order dated Feb. 15, 1956,

by the commander of the 3d Egyptian Division in Sinai, Maj.
Gen. Ahmed Salem, . . . it is written *inter alia:* 'Every commander is to prepare himself and his subordinates for the un-
avoidable war with Israel for the purpose of fulfilling our
exalted aim—namely the annihilation of Israel and her extermination in the shortest possible time and by fighting her as
brutally and cruelly as possible.'"

After reiterating Israel's complaints about the resumption
of *fedayin* raids, the Egyptian embargo of the Canal to Israeli shipping, its blockade of the Gulf of Aqaba and the
Egyptian-Jordanian-Syrian military alliance as *casus belli,* Ben-
Gurion said: "Yesterday I stated in the Knesset that we are
willing to enter immediately into direct negotiations with
Egypt to achieve a stable peace without any prior conditions
and without any compulsion. . . . I am constrained, in conclusion, to express my surprise and sorrow at the threat
against Israel's existence contained in your note. . . ."

The Soviet delegation to the UN Nov. 5 put before the
Security Council a resolution proposing that Britain, France
and Israel "immediately, and not later than 12 hours after the
adoption of this resolution, cease all military operations
against Egypt and withdraw their troops from Egyptian territory within 3 days." The resolution also proposed that, acting in conformity with UN Charter Article 42, the U.S., the
Soviet Union and other UN members with "powerful air and
naval forces . . . give armed and other aid to the victim of
aggression—the republic of Egypt—by sending naval and air
forces, military units, volunteers, military equipment and
other types of aid" if Britain, France and Israel failed to comply "by a fixed date" with the terms of the resolution. The
Soviet government, the resolution said, was "ready to make
its contribution toward the task of curbing aggression and
reestablishing peace by sending to Egypt the air and naval
forces needed for that purpose."

U.S. Amb.-to-UN Henry Cabot Lodge told the Security
Council that the Soviet plan "would convert Egypt into a

still larger battlefield" and went counter to "everything the General Assembly and Secretary General are trying to do" to win a UN-policed ceasefire. Lodge attacked Soviet "cynicism and disregard of the values of international morality" in decrying the attack on Egypt while practicing "butchery . . . against the people of Hungary." The Soviet resolution was defeated by a vote of 4 (the U.S., Britain, France, and Australia) to 3 (the USSR, Yugoslavia and Iran), with 4 abstentions (Belgium, Cuba, Nationalist China and Peru).

Pres. Eisenhower ordered a global alert of U.S. armed forces Nov. 6, the U.S. Presidential election day. Israel and Britain Nov. 6 agreed to halt their advance. (Israel had already cut off the northern Sinai and captured Gaza.) The Anglo-French force by then had control of the Suez ports, but ships already sunk in the Canal rendered the occupation futile.

The UN General Assembly had reconvened Nov. 4-5 to hear Hammarskjöld report on a proposed UN emergency force. The Assembly voted 57-0 early Nov. 5 to approve a resolution creating a UN Command Force and naming Maj. Gen. Eedson L. M. Burns of Canada, UN Truce Supervision Organization head, as chief of the UN force. Approval of the resolution, submitted by Canada, Norway and Colombia, came after Hammarskjöld had urged the Assembly late Nov. 4 to act without watiing for his full report on the project. Hammarskjöld reported that Colombia, Norway and New Zealand had pledged participation in the force and that other nations had submitted the question to their parliaments. He urged that Burns be named UN force chief "on an emergency basis" and be authorized to recruit a "small staff" of officers from UN truce supervision teams in the Middle East and additional officers "directly from various member states"—none from the permanent members of the Security Council (U.S., Britain, France, USSR, Nationalist China). U.S. Amb.-to-UN Lodge said Nov. 5 that the U.S. would aid the UN force "as regards airlifts, shipping transport and supplies."

Eisenhower Nov. 7 approved Defense Department orders to tighten U.S. defenses and subject the Atlantic fleet to "readiness" tests. The Navy Department disclosed Nov. 9 that the 60,000-ton carrier *Forrestal* would be transferred to Mediterranean service in Jan. 1957 to be followed by the 45,000-ton carrier *F. D. Roosevelt* in April. The Navy had ordered a submarine "hunter-killer" group to break off a visit to Rotterdam Oct. 30 and sail to reinforce the U.S. 6th Fleet in the Mediterranean.

Well-organized demonstrations took place in Moscow Nov. 5 and 6 outside the British, French and Israeli embassies. The demonstrators, most of them students and factory workers, shouted demands for the withdrawal of the 3 countries' forces from Egypt and submitted petitions to this effect at the British and French embassies, forcing their way into the British embassy to do so.

Britain's and France's determination to keep up their invasion of the Suez had already evoked Soviet threats of intervention on the side of Egypt. The official Soviet news agency Tass reported Nov. 10 that "great numbers of Soviet air force pilots, tank personnel, artillerymen and officers" who were World War II veterans had "asked to be allowed to go to Egypt as volunteers in order to fight together with the Egyptian people to throw the aggressors out of Egypt." "The Soviet people will not stand idly by at the spectacle of international banditry," Tass declared. It quoted "leading Soviet circles" as having warned that "the USSR will raise no obstacle to the departure of Soviet volunteers" for Egypt "if Britain, France and Israel, contrary to UN decisions, do not withdraw . . . and delay the implementation of the decisions."

The Egyptian ambassador in Moscow was reported Nov. 12 to have told journalists that more than 50,000 Soviet reservists had volunteered for duty in Egypt. He also said that Communist China had offered Egypt 250,000 volunteers and that Indonesia was prepared to send Egypt 50,000 fighting men.

Pres. Eisenhower said at a White House press conference

Nov. 14 that "it would be the duty of the UN, including the U.S., to oppose" the introduction of or any intervention by Soviet or Chinese volunteers into the Middle East. Eisenhower said that the UN was "not by any manner of means limited to resolutions" when confronted with such emergencies. He termed the Soviet gesture toward Egypt an attempt to "woo for the moment" a susceptible Arab state.

The Syrian minister to West Germany called attention to the irrelevance of the dispute over potential Soviet volunteers by asserting Nov. 15 that there were no Soviet volunteers in the Middle East, that Egypt no longer saw any need of such volunteers in the light of the existing cease-fire and that he had been authorized by Egypt, Syria, Jordan, Iraq and Yemen to make his statement.

Soviet Premier Bulganin Nov. 15 opposed the stationing of UN forces in the Suez Canal Zone and demanded that Egypt be consulted on the deployment of UN troops elsewhere on Egyptian territory. In notes to British Prime Min. Eden, French Premier Mollet and Israeli Premier Ben-Gurion, Bulganin renewed Soviet demands for the withdrawal of their troops from Egypt. He also urged the payment of compensation to Egypt for the loss of life and property damage inflicted by the invading foreign forces. Bulganin told Eden and Mollet that the continued presence of Anglo-French forces and the planned deployment of UN troops to the Suez Canal Zone "would be contrary to the [Suez] Convention of 1888." Bulganin said that the evacuation of Egypt by British, French and Israeli forces would render the UN troops unnecessary. He conceded that with Egyptian permission, UN forces "could be stationed on the 2 sides" of the 1949 Israeli-Egyptian armistice line. In a harsh note to Ben-Gurion, Bulganin rejected Israeli assertions that the attack on Egypt had come only after provocation. Bulganin said that it was Israel "who was guilty of many armed attacks" on "neighboring Arab countries." Bulganin denounced alleged Israeli plans to annex the Sinai Peninsula and Gaza Strip and warned that Israeli foreign policy had "undermined Israel's international position and aroused deep hatred against her."

Diplomats from NATO countries and Israel walked out when Soviet Communist First Party Secy. Nikita S. Khrushchev denounced their policies during talks at receptions in Moscow Nov. 17–18 in connection with a Polish-Soviet conference. He said Nov. 17 that the Anglo-Egyptian attack on Egypt was "piratic" and that Israel was a "puppet" of "imperialists" in their "hopeless attempt to restore lost colonial bastions." He addressed this warning to capitalists: "History is on our side. We will bury you." He repeated the denunciation at a Polish embassy reception Nov. 18 and said that Egyptian Pres. Nasser, although not a Communist, "he has even put Communists in jail," was "fighting for national independence, . . . is the hero of his nation, and our sympathies are on his side."

The USSR disclosed Nov. 17 that it was sending 15 million rubles [$3¾ million] worth of food and medical supplies to Egypt. British informants reported Nov. 20 that Egypt had begun negotiations with the USSR for the replacement of the tanks, jets and artillery lost to the Israelis. More immediately urgent to U.S. leaders, however, was the necessity of keeping the Soviet Union from obtaining a greater bridgehead in the Middle East than it had already gained with the introduction into Egypt of some 2,000 Soviet-bloc technicians, diplomats and propagandists.

The threat of armed Soviet intervention in the Middle East apparently waned Nov. 15–16 following the warning by Pres. Eisenhower that the U.S. would oppose the dispatch of Russian "volunteers" to aid Egypt. UN Emergency Force units landed in Egypt Nov. 15 and were ordered to take up truce supervision positions in the Port Said area Nov. 20. Acting U.S. State Secy. Herbert Hoover Jr. told the UN General Assembly in New York Nov. 16 that "the UN would be obligated" to take action against the introduction of "so-called volunteers" into the Middle East." Hoover warned that the prohibition on the reinforcement of Egyptian, British, French and Israeli forces applied to "all" powers, including those "engaged in hostilities." The introduction of "external" forces, he said, would be "a threat to the UN Force now entering the area."

Nasser said Nov. 19 that there were no Soviet volunteers in Egypt and that none had been requested from any country. Nasser, in a telephoned interview with *Al Azhar* editor Mustafa Amin, urged that a UN commission be formed to investigate Israeli claims of capturing quantities of Soviet-built Egyptian materiel during the Sinai and Gaza fighting.

Canadian Maj. Gen. E. L. M. Burns arrived in Egypt and took command of the UN Emergency Force (UNEF) Nov. 22. Burns, who set up temporary headquarters for the UNEF in Cairo Nov. 22, met Nov. 25 in Port Said with the Anglo-French commander, Gen. Sir Charles Keightley, and with Adm. Pierre Barjot, deputy commander; Lt. Gen. Sir Hugh Stockwell, field commander; and Maj. Gen. André Beaufre, deputy field commander. The Port Said talks centered on UNEF military and logistic problems and the mission of 190 UNEF infantrymen, who had been confined to camp pending clarification of their functions.

The UN General Assembly Nov. 26 voted 52–9 (13 abstentions) to provide an initial $10 million for UNEF operations. The funds, requested Nov. 22 by Secy. Gen. Hammarskjöld, were approved despite opposition from the USSR. Soviet Deputy Foreign Min. Vassili V. Kuznetsov Nov. 26 protested plans to assess UN members for UNEF costs. He demanded that the "aggressors" against Egypt pay all UNEF and Suez Canal clearance costs. The Assembly agreed to bypass assessments by creating a special account for UNEF finances.

Gen. Burns disclosed Nov. 27 that the UNEF would expand its forces in the Port Said-Port Fuad area to one battalion—800 to 1,000 men. The UNEF Nov. 27 reported its total strength in Egypt as 1,415 men, with an additional 765 Yugoslav troops on board vessels off Port Said awaiting docking space. Burns Nov. 26 revealed plans to base UNEF headquarters in the Canal Zone near El Qantara.

Other Western & Neutral Reactions

Britain's opposition Labor Party, headed by Sir Hugh Gaitskell, bitterly opposed the Eden cabinet's decision to seize the Suez Canal Zone. Laborites in the House of Commons Nov. 7–12 strongly criticized the British attack upon Egypt, but news of the cease-fire and the formation of the UN Emergency Force brought defeat of Laborite censure motions Nov. 8 and Nov. 12.

The Commonwealth countries, with the exceptions of India, Pakistan, Ceylon and the Union of South Africa (which protested that it had not been "consulted"), supported the policy of the British government. (Canada, however, had been among the first countries to advocate moderation and the recourse to negotiation after Nasser's nationalization of the Canal. Canadian External Affairs Min. Lester B. Pearson had told the House of Commons in Ottawa July 28 that Canada, while condemning the Suez seizure, had urged the solution of the dispute through the UN.)

In France, Socialist Premier Guy Mollet defended his government's Mideast policy against the attacks of his most powerful rival, Radical Party ex-Premier Pierre Mendès-France. Speaking at a Radical Party rally Nov. 13, Mendès-France charged that by delaying Western action to counter the seizure of the Suez Canal, the West had raised Nasser's prestige and then had brought on itself the opposition of "the great majority of other nations" when action finally was taken.

In Israel, the policy of the coalition government of Premier Ben-Gurion was in the main unopposed except by the tiny Israel Communist Party.

The Egyptian nationalization of the Suez Canal was landed throughout the Arab world. Even Jordan, which was linked by treaty to Britain, allowed foreign Arab troops on its soil in case of war with Israel.

Nasser's action was also supported by Premier Jawaharlal Nehru of India, who stated Nov. 1 in a note to UN Secy. Gen. Dag Hammarskjöld: "We have been profoundly shocked by recent developments in the Middle East and, more particularly, by the Anglo-French invasion of Egypt after their rejection of the Security Council resolution moved by the United States. It is clear that Israel has committed large-scale aggression against Egypt. Instead of trying to stop this aggression, the United Kingdom and France are themselves invading Egyptian territory. This is not only an affront to the Security Council and a violation of the UN Charter, but also likely to lead to the gravest possible consequences all over the world. Egypt, which has suffered from Israel aggression, has in addition to suffer grievously by the Anglo-French invasion of her territory. The argument that this invasion is meant to protect the Canal and to ensure free traffic has no force, as the first result of this invasion is for this traffic to cease. In view of the disastrous consequences of the invasion of Egyptian territory, I earnestly trust that the UN will take strong steps in this matter to prevent the world plunging into war and demand the immediate withdrawal of all foreign troops from Egypt. The procedures of the UN must be swifter than those of invasion and aggression. In sending you this message I am not only reflecting the unanimous views of my government and people but also, I am sure, a large number of other peoples."

U.S. Pres. Eisenhower asserted Nov. 27 that the Suez crisis had not damaged NATO or the U.S.-British-French alliance. In a statement issued by the temporary White House in Augusta, Ga., Eisenhower stressed that "differences" had arisen "from a particular international incident." He said, however, that "these differences in no way should be construed as a weakening or disrupting of the great bonds" between the U.S., Britain, France and "other allies." The NATO alliance, Eisenhower said, remained "a basic and indispensable element of American defense alliances."

Egypt appeared to be encouraged by the American rift with Britain and France. Egyptian Foreign Min. Mahmoud Fawzi warned Nov. 27 that he would press for UN economic and military sanctions against Britain, Israel and France and possibly for their expulsion from the UN, if they rejected UN demands for evacuation of Egypt "forthwith." Ali Sabry, Nasser's political aide, said Nov. 27 that Egypt was relying on "faith in the UN" and U.S. "pressure" to force Anglo-French withdrawals from the Canal Zone. Sabry expressed hope that the U.S. would withhold "any help on solving the [British-French] oil shortage."

British & French Nationals Expelled

The foreign ministries of Britain and France announced Nov. 24, 1956 that they had learned from the Swiss foreign ministry that the Egyptian government intended to expel all British and French nationals in Egypt as "enemy nationals" within a week to 10 days. British sources estimated at the time that there were then in Egypt about 13,000 British subjects or persons under British protection—among them 5,000 to 6,000 Maltese, 4,500 to 5,000 Cypriots, about 1,700 British nationals and approximately 1,000 others from Gibraltar, Aden and other overseas territories. French sources reported that more than 8,000 French nationals had remained in Egypt at the beginning of November and that Egypt had interned at lease 200 of them.

Swiss diplomats, representing British and French interests in Egypt, protested Nov. 24 against the planned expulsions and Nov. 26 against the confiscation of expellees' property. Dispatches from Paris Nov. 25 had reported that the deportees would be permitted to leave with only £20 ($56) and that 300 Frenchmen and Britons in Egypt had been arrested and interned Nov. 12. Cairo reports Nov. 26 said that Nasser had agreed to consider 5,000 British Cypriots in Egypt as Greek citizens exempt from expulsion.

The Egyptian government Nov. 26 issued a statement denying that it had ever planned the mass expulsion of British and French nationals and saying that British and French citizens in Egypt were free to remain or to leave "at their own discretion."

But Max Koenig, Swiss minister in Egypt, said Dec. 9 that expulsions of individual British and French citizens from Egypt and the sequestration of their property were "continuing relentlessly" on a large scale. Egyptian Interior Min. Zakaria Mohieddin said Dec. 9 that, of some 18,000 British and French citizens in Egypt, 1,452 had been ordered expelled from the country.

472 British technicians of Suez Contractors, Ltd., interned for 51 days, were exchanged Dec. 21 for 357 Egyptian prisoners of the British and French forces at El Cap through the offices of the Swiss legation, and they sailed aboard the troopship *Asturias* for Cyprus. Several interned British journalists and the British embassy and consular staffs had already left Egypt.

Egyptian Amb.-to-UN Omar Loutfi said during a UN General Assembly debate on the matter Dec. 18 that of the 11,000 British nationals in Egypt at the time of the Anglo-French attack, 719 had been expelled for security reasons, 706 had left voluntarily, and 450 technicians had been interned. Of the 7,000 French nationals in Egypt, 2,648 had been ordered to leave, 474 had left voluntarily, and one had been interned, Loutfi said. He stated that the Egyptian government's treatment of foreign nationals had not exceeded recognized measures of security in time of war and had conformed to international law. He asserted that the property of foreign nationals had not been confiscated but sequestrated, as was customary in war time.

Egyptian Foreign Min. Mahmoud Fawzi, speaking before the National Press Club in Washington Dec. 13, had listed 740

French citizens, 713 Britons and 120 Jews as interned by Egypt "for valid reasons of security."

Egypt Expels Foreign & Stateless Jews

Egypt Nov. 23, 1956 ordered the expulsion of 50 of its 100,000 Egyptian Jews for allegedly collaborating with the British, French and Israeli invaders.

The UN General Assembly President, Prince Wan Waitha-yakon of Thailand, disclosed Nov. 27 that he had received a letter from Israeli Foreign Min. Golda Meir charging that Egypt was expelling 30,000 Jews and had closed Jewish hospitals in Cairo and Alexandria.

A. L. Easterman, political director of the World Jewish Congress, quoted in London Nov. 27 from an order by Cairo's military governor that all Jews who had "not succeeded in entering into the Egyptian way of life" would be expelled. The order, published in the Egyptian press Nov. 22, covered 14,000 stateless Jews in Egypt, all Jews naturalized in the past 25 years who had any contacts with Zionism or sympathies for Israel, all Jews naturalized in the past 32 years who could not "prove" their loyalty to Egypt and all Jews naturalized after 1900 whom careful "consideration" showed to be suspect in their loyalties.

Egypt asked the International Red Cross Dec. 9 to help resettle 280 stateless Jews facing expulsion from Egypt for security reasons. Egyptian officials asserted that "no Egyptian Jew" had been "expelled or his property confiscated."

Israeli Foreign Min. Meir had asked the U.S. Dec. 7 to urge Egypt to treat its Jewish residents "in a humane manner," and the U.S. Dec. 11 expressed "deep concern" to Egypt over the reported maltreatment of Egypt's Jewish population. The U.S. State Department disclosed Dec. 22 that U.S. diplomats in the Mideast were investigating reports of Egypt's deportation of Jews. The State Department said that an inquiry by the U.S. embassy in Cairo had produced contradictory results.

Haim Nahum, Egyptian chief rabbi, Dec. 20 denounced the "brutal Anglo-French-Israeli aggression against our dear motherland Egypt." Nahum, 84 and totally blind, asserted that "no foreign government especially Israel, is authorized to speak" for Egypt's Jews. The World Jewish Congress disclosed Nov. 27 that Nahum had resigned in protest against the expulsion of Jewish residents.

The Jewish expulsion orders reportedly were widened Nov. 25 to 30,000–50,000 persons (stateless and foreign Jews and some Egyptian Jews in categories naturalized after 1900, 1925 and 1933.)

It had been reported from Paris Nov. 25, 1956 that 2,000 to 3,000 Jews had been arrested following the Israeli invasion of Sinai Oct. 29.

(More than 11,000 Jews had left Egypt by the beginning of Feb. 1957, their property having been confiscated by the Egyptian government, and the American Jewish Committee reported in Paris Apr. 12, 1958 that 17,000 Jews had left Egypt since the onset of Nasser's "anti-Zionist" campaign.)

AFTERMATH OF SUEZ CRISIS

UNEF Replaces Anglo-French Forces

Under strong pressure from the UN, the British and French governments told UN Secy. Gen. Dag Hammarskjöld Dec. 3, 1956 that they would withdraw all Anglo-French forces from the Suez Canal area without delay. Substantial numbers of troops and vessels had already been withdrawn as a token of good faith. Israel had agreed in principle as early as Nov. 9 to leave most of the territory it had seized, and Israeli forces began withdrawing Dec. 6.

A Soviet statement, issued Dec. 8 through the Tass news agency, said that the British, French and Israeli pledges to withdraw from Egyptian territory "naturally cancels the question of dispatching Soviet volunteers to Egypt." The Soviet people had expressed "satisfaction" that the "fires of war in the Arab East had been extinguished," Tass said. The statement noted that the Soviet Union was counting on the fulfillment of the withdrawal promises despite British, French and Israeli moves "to win some conditions in return for" their observance of UN withdrawal demands. (The Israelis had reportedly won UN agreement to an indefinite control of the Sinai Peninsula by the UN Emergency Force replacing British, French and Israeli troops.)

UN Emergency Force contingents assumed control over most of the invaded sector of the Suez Canal Zone Dec. 16 as British and French troops continued their withdrawals under increased Egyptian harassment. UNEF patrols fired for the first time Dec. 15 to ward off Egyptian guerrilla attacks on UN and Anglo-French forces in Port Said. Maj. Gen. E. L. M. Burns, UNEF commander, charged in a protest to Egypt Dec. 15 that Egyptians had attacked UNEF patrols twice Dec. 14–15. No UNEF casualties were reported.

British and French troops withdrew behind a narrow barbed-wire perimeter adjoining the Port Said docks Dec. 16 to await evacuation from the Suez Canal Zone. 27 Egyptians

were reported killed and 100 wounded in night fighting in
Port Said Dec. 15–16, when British tanks fought off what
was regarded as a final Egyptian guerrilla attack on the withdrawing Anglo-French forces.

350 Egyptian policemen arrived in Port Said Dec. 18
to help UNEF troops maintain order in the city pending its
reoccupation by Egypt. Sir Hugh Stockwell, Anglo-French
field commander, had agreed to their entry Dec. 16 on the
condition that they were "well behaved." (Egyptian officials
had insisted Dec. 16 that UNEF troops leave Port Said as
soon as the Anglo-French withdrawals were completed. UN
officials held that the cease-fire terms envisaged by the UN
General Assembly included extended policing of Port Said
by UNEF and Egyptian police units.)

All British and French forces were evacuated by Dec. 22,
1956.

Egyptian government spokesmen said Dec. 26 that Egypt
would refuse to resume direct negotiations with Britain and
France on a settlement of the Suez Canal dispute. Egypt
they said, continued to accept the "6 principles" for a Suez
settlement approved Oct. 13 by the UN Security Council,
and would insist on negotiating a Suez solution through the
UN.

Pres. Nasser Dec. 27 asked visiting Soviet newsmen to
convey his thanks to the USSR for its offer of "volunteers"
and diplomatic support for Egypt during the current Mideastern crisis. Nasser said that he hoped Egyptian-Soviet friendship would "grow in strength."

(The Soviet newspaper *Izvestia* claimed Dec. 28 that "the
resolute stand taken by the Soviet government" and "all progressive mankind" had brought "ignominious defeat" for the
Anglo-French attack on Egypt. Moscow radio said Dec. 28
that Nasser's postponed visit to the USSR would take place
in 1957.)

Nasser Jan. 1, 1957 abrogated the 1954 Anglo-Egyptian
treaty governing the evacuation of the Suez Canal Zone and

the maintenance of Britain's Suez Zone military bases. The abrogation decree ended the treaty effective Oct. 31, 1956, when British bombers were first known by Cairo to have attacked Egypt. Cairo radio said Jan. 2, 1957 that Britain's Suez Zone base (including equipment and stores valued at $112-$140 million) had been liquidated and "no longer exists in Egypt." The British foreign office said Jan. 2 that it had received no notice of the pact's abrogation and regarded it as still in force.

Israel Quits Sinai

A UN General Assembly resolution Nov. 7, 1956 called for the immediate withdrawal of Israeli troops from Egyptian territory.

Israeli Premier Ben-Gurion addressed the Knesset Nov. 7 and urged that Israel retain captured Egyptian territory as a bargaining position for an eventual peace settlement. Although Ben-Gurion later agreed Nov. 9 to withdraw troops from the Sinai Peninsula, he insisted on the continued Israeli occupation of 2 areas previously under Egyptian administration: the Gaza Strip, sandwiched between Israel and the Mediterranean Sea, and the Strait of Tiran, separating the Gulf of Aqaba (which Israel termed the Gulf of Eilat) from the Red Sea.

Although Israel agreed in principle Nov. 9 to withdraw from Sinai, lengthy negotiations ensued over the future military status of the peninsula. The actual withdrawal began Dec. 6.

Israeli Amb.-to-U.S. Abba Eban conferred with UN Secy. Gen. Dag Hammarskjöld Dec. 5 and, according to Israeli sources, won agreement to indefinite UNEF control of the Sinai Peninsula.

Gen. Burns said Dec. 6, after a meeting in El Arish with the Israeli army chief-of-staff, Gen. Moshe Dayan, that arrangements had been made for UNEF troops to contact

Israeli army units as they retreated from the Sinai Peninsula. Burns said that Yugoslav UNEF units had penetrated 15 miles into the Sinai Peninsula and had found principal roads heavily mined. Israeli forces were reported Dec. 6 to be destroying Sinai road and rail facilities as they withdrew.

Israeli troops withdrew to a line 47 miles east of the Suez Canal Dec. 18. The Israelis had halted UNEF troops 31 miles from the canal Dec. 14. The new withdrawals were carried out according to agreements reached between Gens. Burns and Dayan in Jerusalem Dec. 16. Burns said Dec. 17 that UNEF troops would follow the retreating Israelis "as rapidly as possible up to the [1949 Israeli-Egyptian] armistice line." Burns denied reports that Egyptian units were entering Sinai behind advancing UNEF troops but said that some Egyptians were clearing Israeli minefields for the UN forces.

(Dr. Louis Gailland, International Red Cross Representative, said Dec. 26 that a visit to the 1,600-year-old St. Catharine monastery in Mount Sinai had shown Egyptian reports of Israeli pillage to be "devoid of any foundation." The UN Educational Scientific & Cultural Organization [UNESCO] Dec. 28 assigned an observer to supervise the transfer of the site from Israeli to UN control.)

UN envoys Andrew W. Cordier of the U.S. and Col. Alfred George Katzin of South Africa assured Nasser Dec. 30 that UN Secy. Gen. Hammarskjöld was exerting pressure to force speedy Israeli withdrawals from Egyptian territory. Meeting with Nasser before leaving for UN headquarters in New York Dec. 31, Cordier and Katzin indicated that the UN would continue to press for Israeli withdrawal up to the 1949 armistice line.

Israeli UN delegation sources said Dec. 31 that Israeli Amb.-to-U.S. Abba Eban, in talks with Hammarskjöld and the U.S. State Department, had made clear that Israel regarded its occupation of the Gaza Strip and Gulf of Aqaba areas as "special positions" pending its receipt of firm guarantees against aggression from these areas.

Israeli troops withdrew Jan. 7, 1957 to a line running south through El Arish. Continuing their withdrawal Jan. 10–17, they left El Arish and fell back to within 12 miles of the Israeli border Jan. 15. They ignored UN appeals to halt their scorched earth policy in the Sinai area and destroyed all military installations before leaving El Arish. Incoming UN Emergency Force units were mobbed by cheering Egyptians Jan. 15.

Although the Israeli troops fell back behind the 1949 boundaries of the Sinai Peninsula, they retained control of the Gaza Strip and the Strait of Tiran. The Gaza Strip had been allotted by the 1947 UN partition plan to a future Arab state in Palestine. The Strip, however, was occupied by Egyptian troops in 1948, the remainder of the would-be Arab Palestine being divided by force between Israel and the Hashemite Kingdom of Jordan. Hence, neither Israel nor Egypt possessed recognized sovereignty over the Gaza area. The Strip contained the towns of Gaza and Khan Yunis, as well as about 300,000 Arab inhabitants, most of them Palestinian refugees supported by the UN Relief & Works Agency for Palestine Refugees in the Near East (UNRWA). Before the Israeli occupation, the Egyptians had paid little attention to the area and considered it militarily indefensible. As for the Strait of Tiran, the Egyptian armed forces had 2 tiny garrisons guarding this waterway—in Sharm el-Sheikh on the Sinai Peninsula and on the island of Tiran—both under Egyptian sovereignty. These 2 posts were potentially capable of blockading entry to the Israeli port of Eilat in the Gulf of Aqaba.

UN Secy. Gen. Hammarskjöld had asked Israel Nov. 21, 1956 to report on Gaza Strip conditions and to permit the entry of UNEF observers. Israel, however, refused to yield the area to UNEF troops. Israel ordered military rule relaxed in the Gaza Strip Nov. 25. Ex-Gaza Mayor Rushdi el-Shawa and an Israeli-picked municipal council took limited control of the city Nov. 26. Plans were revealed to resume civil control throughout the Gaza Strip. Israel renewed Gaza Strip postal service Dec. 4 and reopened the area's schools Dec. 10.

A report on Gaza Strip conditions, submitted Dec. 3 to Hammarskjöld by U.S. Lt. Col. Knute R. Nelson of the UNEF and made public Jan. 14, 1957, lauded Israeli administration of the area but cited indications that Israel planned a prolonged occupation.

Israeli Foreign Min. Golda Meir said in Washington Dec. 11, 1956 that an Israeli withdrawal from the Gaza Strip was "a special problem . . . being dealt with in talks" with Hammarskjöld.

Israeli Premier David Ben-Gurion had reaffirmed Dec. 18, 1956, in a *N.Y. Times* interview, that Israel "would not allow the Egyptians to return to the Gaza Strip." He emphasized that "under no conditions can the Egyptians come back" to Gaza. He suggested that "a UN high commissioner" take control of the disputed Gaza area. Ben-Gurion urged that the Sinai Peninsula be demilitarized and that the Strait of Tiran be internationalized, with Israeli troops remaining at the southern tip of the Sinai Peninsula.

Washington sources said Jan. 3, 1957 that the U.S. had rejected an Israeli plea for support in an Israeli attempt to win international guarantees for (a) the passage of Israeli shipping through the Suez Canal and Gulf of Aqaba, (b) the barring of Egyptian *fedayin* from the Sinai Peninsula and (c) the prevention of an Egyptian army reoccupation of the Gaza Strip. U.S. State Secy. John Foster Dulles reportedly told Israeli Foreign Min. Meir that Israel should comply immediately with UN demands for the withdrawal of all Israeli troops behind the 1949 armistice line.

Both Egypt and the UN charged Israel with misrule of the Gaza Strip. Egypt's semiofficial Middle East News Agency charged Jan. 11 that Israeli troops had murdered 8,000 Arab youths in the Strip. A memo from the UN Relief & Works Agency for Palestine asserted Jan. 14 that an estimated 386

Arab refugees had been killed in rioting in Khan Yunis and Rafa in the early days of Israeli occupation.

Israel indicated that it was just as determined to retain military control of the strategic points around its port of Eilat and the Gulf of Aqaba as it was to interdict Egypt from the Gaza Strip. Gen. Burns, UNEF commander, said after a meeting with Israeli Gen. Dayan Jan. 10 that "the Israelis are not withdrawing from Sharm el-Sheikh."

Israel Quits Gaza & Aqaba Under U.S. Pressure

The U.S. government began in early Feb. 1957 an intensive campaign of pressure to persuade Israel to evacuate the Gaza Strip and the territory at the Strait of Tiran between the Gulf of Aqaba and the Red Sea. The Israelis still controlled the small island of Tiran in the Strait as well as the fort of Sharm el-Sheikh in southern Sinai.

U.S. State Secy. Dulles announced at a press conference Feb. 5 that the U.S. government would give "very serious consideration" to UN sanctions against Israel.

Senate Republican leader William F. Knowland (R., Calif.) denounced the sanction proposal on the senate floor Feb. 7 and told an audience at Georgetown University (in Washington, D.C.) Feb. 11 that U.S. foreign policy should "not be tied as a tail to a UN kite." The Senate Democratic leader, Lyndon B. Johnson (D., Tex.), sent Pres. Eisenhower Feb. 19 a letter protesting against any possible U.S. support for UN sanctions.

Despite strong Senate objections, Eisenhower continued to apply pressure on Israel through non-UN diplomatic channels.

The N.Y. Herald Tribune reported Feb. 7 from Tel Aviv that Israeli Premier Ben-Gurion had rejected a personal appeal from Eisenhower that Israel withdraw from the Gaza Strip and Sharm el-Sheikh. A letter from Eisenhower, purportedly delivered to Ben-Gurion Feb. 3–4, was said to have

warned that Israel's continued defiance of UN withdrawal demands "could not be helpful toward undisturbed continuity
of American-Israeli friendship" and that the U.S. would be
bound to support any UN move to impose sanctions on
Israel. White House and U.S. State Department spokesmen
refused Feb. 7 to comment on the existence of the letter, but
Washington informants were openly alluding to its contents
by Feb. 10. Israeli Amb.-to-U.S. Abba Eban had conferred
at the State Department Feb. 8, reportedly to transmit a
tentative rejection of Eisenhower's demand and to clarify
Israel's position.

Director Gen. Walter Eytan of the Israeli Foreign Ministry told newsmen in Tel Aviv Feb. 8 that Israel (a) was "willing to withdraw our army from Gaza if the administration of
that area remains in our hands," (b) would "welcome international observers or [UN] representatives" in the Gaza area
and (c) had "to all intents and purposes" carried out the
rest as soon as we receive guarantees of nonbelligerency from
Egypt."

Public demonstrations called by Israeli political parties
throughout Israel Feb. 9 supported the government's continued refusal to recall troops from Egyptian territory unless
Israel received guarantees of its "right to free navigation, security and peace."

Israeli Foreign Min. Meir told reporters at UN headquar-
ters in New York Feb. 10 that a U.S. guarantee of unimpeded
Israeli shipping through the Gulf of Aqaba "would greatly
influence" Israel's position on withdrawals from Egypt. U.S.
State Secy. Dulles met in Washington with Israeli Amb. Eban
Feb. 11 and reportedly offered a U.S. promise to support
(a) UNEF-protected passage for Israel through the Gulf of
Aqaba and (b) the entry of "the efforts and good offices of
of the UN" into the Gaza Strip on that area's evacuation by
Israel. Washington sources said Feb. 12 that Dulles, in his
talks with Eban, had offered to test Egyptian intentions by
sending U.S. vessels through the Gulf of Aqaba to the Israeli

port of Eilat, thus assuring Western access to a nearly complete trans-Israel 8-inch oil line from Eilat to Ashkelon on the Mediterranean.

The Israeli government, replying in an *aide-memoire* Feb. 15, drew attention to the lack of specific protective guarantees in the U.S. proposal.

A resolution presented to the UN General Assembly Feb. 22 called on the UN to condemn and impose sanctions on Israel for its continued refusals to withdraw its troops from the Gaza Strip and Sharm el-Sheikh. The proposed resolution was read to the assembly by Lebanese Foreign Min. Charles Malik and cosponsored by Iraq, Afghanistan, Indonesia, Pakistan and Sudan. It was not formally introduced for debate. It urged "all states" to "deny all military, economic or financial assistance and facilities to Israel in view of its continued defiance" of UN resolutions.

Assembly debate on the draft resolution and UN Secy. Gen. Hammarskjöld's Feb. 11 report on Israeli-UN withdrawal talks were suspended Feb. 22–26 to let the U.S. government continue its efforts to persuade Israel to accept American and UN security guarantees and withdraw from Egyptian territory.

Eban arrived in Washington Feb. 24 with "new instructions" from the Israeli government and immediately renewed negotiations with State Secy. Dulles. Eban told newsmen after a 3-hour meeting with Dulles that he was "urgently communicating" the results of the exchange to the Israeli government. An American Broadcasting Co. radio report from Jerusalem Feb. 24 said that Eban had been ordered to present modified Israeli withdrawal terms under which Israel would (a) agree to UN control of the Gaza Strip if Egypt did not return there and (b) evacuate Sharm el-Sheikh if the U.S. supported Canadian proposals (circulated in the UN Feb. 20–24) for a UNEF naval police force.

Israeli leaders continued to make clear their opposition to any use of UN sanctions to force withdrawals. Foreign

Min. Meir, in a statement in the *N.Y. Herald Tribune* Feb. 23, denounced the "irony" of the UN's considering sanctions in view of the fact that "Egypt refuses to live in peace with Israel." Director Gen. Walter Eytan of the Israeli Foreign Ministry warned Feb. 24 that a UN sanctions vote against Israel would make it "impossible for the United Nations ever to appear in a mediating role" between Israel and the Arab countries.

But Israeli Premier Ben-Gurion told the Knesset Feb. 25 that recognition of Israel's "right of self-defense under the [UN] Charter," to be invoked if its vessels again were barred from the Gulf of Aqaba, was the "best guarantee" that the gulf would remain open. He thus publicly relinquished Israeli demands for an international safeguarding of the gulf's entrance, but made it clear that Israeli vessels, if stopped, would be justified in shooting their way through to the port of Eilat. Ben-Gurion arrived at this position after various U.S.-Israeli exchanges.

In a radio-TV speech Feb. 20, Eisenhower had offered to drop the threat of UN sanctions if Israel would accept U.S. guarantees of its vital interests. The speech was strongly criticized by some prominent Americans as an attempt to bypass heavy Congressional disapproval of the sanction threat. The U.S. guarantees for Israel's shipping and security, outlined in Eisenhower's speech, were in effect rejected by Ben-Gurion Feb. 21. Ben-Gurion told the Knesset that Israel would withdraw from the Gaza Strip on the receipt of a firm assurance that Egypt "will not return to that area, either directly or indirectly," and from Sharm el-Sheikh if it received guarantees that the UN Emergency Force would occupy the area "until peace is concluded with Egypt" or if an "effective arrangement" were made for Israeli use of the Gulf of Aqaba. Ben-Gurion conceded that "Eisenhower's demand" had "placed me under great moral pressure" and had made clear the "grave meaning" of possible American support for UN sanctions against Israel. He asserted, however, that "any attempt to compel us to accept a miscarriage of justice and a system of discrimination will meet with the unflinching opposition of the people of Israel." He said that Israel would make a further attempt to reach a settlement through negotiations with the U.S. He expressed hopes that "the door is not closed." Ben-Gurion also answered a personal message received from Eisenhower following the President's Feb. 20 broadcast. Israeli spokesmen said Feb. 22 that Ben-Gurion's reply was "constructive."

A White House statement, issued Feb. 22 after Mideast policy discussions between Eisenhower and Dulles, expressed regret that "Israel has not yet found it possible to withdraw." It said that "the door is certainly not closed to further discussion." The statement promised a delay of further U.S. moves until Israeli Amb. Eban returned to the U.S. from talks with Ben-Gurion.

In the final week of February, Israel worked out an agreement with the UN for the replacement of Israelis with UNEF troops. Hammarskjöld said Feb. 22 that Egypt had also agreed to "special and helpful arrangements" with the UN for use of the UNEF, UNRWA and other UN agencies in the Gaza and Aqaba areas. He said that Egypt had recognized the "present special problems and complexities of the Gaza area" and would consider an increased role for the UN during "the period of transition" from UN to Egyptian control of the occupied areas.

The Egyptian government had indicated Feb. 21 its approval of Eisenhower's Feb. 20 speech warning of possible U.S. support for UN sanctions against Israel. Egyptian informants termed the Eisenhower position "positive and just" and said that it would "do much to bring peace to the Middle East." Abdel Kader Hatem, Egyptian government information director, denied Feb. 23 an assertion by Hammarskjöld that Egypt had agreed to an expansion of UN and

UNEF roles in the Gaza and Sharm el-Sheikh areas. He said that the UNEF's presence on Egyptian territory would remain subject to Egyptian permission.

The Eisenhower Administration reportedly softened its position on sanctions Feb. 24–27, as events appeared to fuel its growing hopes for Israeli withdrawals and in response to increased Congressional opposition to any use of sanctions, which U.S. Amb.-to-UN Henry Cabot Lodge Jr. was said to favor. State Secy. Dulles met with Senate Democratic and Republican leaders Feb. 24 to discuss U.S. Mideastern policy. He faced continued opposition on any U.S. support of sanctions from Senate majority leader Lyndon B. Johnson and minority leader William F. Knowland.

The UN General Assembly reconvened Mar. 1, 1957. Israeli Foreign Min. Meir informed the Assembly that Israel was prepared to evacuate "completely" its troops from the Gaza Strip and the Strait of Tiran. The decision was based on the Israeli assumptions that only the UNEF would be allowed to place military forces in Gaza and that Israeli shipping would pass unimpeded into the Gulf of Aqaba.

The Gaza Strip was evacuated by Israel Mar. 6–7. The Strait of Tiran was evacuated Mar. 8. 2 6-inch Egyptian guns in the Sharm el-Sheikh fort were dismantled (there were no permanent installations on the island of Tiran). 2,600 UNEF troops took control of Gaza without incident, and a UNEF rifle battalion occupied Sharm el-Sheikh.

UN Secy. Gen. Hammarskjöld returned to UN headquarters in New York Mar. 28 from talks in Cairo with Egyptian Pres. Nasser. He told newsmen on his arrival that the talks had been "exploratory" and that he hoped they would "prove helpful" in reaching a Mideast settlement. Hammarskjöld met later Mar. 28 with U.S. Amb.-to-UN Lodge, British UN delegate Sir Pierson Dixon, Canadian External Affairs Secy. Lester B. Pearson and members of the 7-nation UN Emergency Force's Advisory Committee to discuss the Cairo talks.

Hammarskjöld, in a report issued Apr. 1, said that Egypt had agreed (a) to inform "the refugees and other inhabitants of the Gaza Strip that it is Egyptian policy to prevent infiltration across the [Gaza-Israel] demarcation line," (b) to reinstate the "Egyptian regulations against infiltration, which include penalties," and (c) to make clear to the local population "the role of the UNEF in assisting the prevention of infiltration."

A message to Egypt from the UNEF Advisory Committee, made public by Hammarskjöld Apr. 1, expressed the hope that the UNEF would continue to be stationed "at the armistice line as a deterrent to incursions." The note urged that it be made clear to Gazans that strict "enforcement of this policy" would be carried out by Egypt, with the UNEF having "the duty to assist in the enforcement." It warned that if the Egyptian-UNEF arrangements "prove insufficient or unsatisfactory," the Advisory Committee "would have to revert to the issue and consider" with Hammarskjöld "further proposals" to assure the proper "functioning of the force."

The Egyptians said Mar. 30 that a Palestine Arab police force was being formed in the Gaza Strip to begin patrols with the UNEF under the "interim agreement" with the UN aimed at giving Egypt responsibility for aiding border security without requiring the presence of large Egyptian forces in the Strip.

The UNEF disclosed Apr. 2 that it had begun moving its supply base from Abu Suweir, in the Suez Canal Zone, to Rafah, in the Gaza Strip. UNEF patrols would be continued in the Sinai Peninsula and a contingent retained near the Great Bitter Lake in the Suez Zone.

Suez Canal Salvage

The Suez Canal remained closed from Nov. 1, 1956 to Mar. 29, 1957. The major reason the Canal could not be navigated was the presence of vessels sunk by the Egyptians in a sabotage operation during the Anglo-French attack.

The British Admiralty said Dec. 3, 1956 that an inspection of the Canal showed 49 vessels and bridges sunk in the waterway, with 11 sunken vessels blocking the main channel. (French UN spokesmen had demanded Nov. 19 that Egypt pay for the removal of 35 ships and 2 bridges sunk in the Canal as "acts of sabotage.") The cost of clearing the Canal was estimated at $40 million.

Salvage operations under Anglo-French auspices already were under way during Nov. 1956. Port Said dispatches indicated Nov. 28 that Anglo-French salvage crews had cleared a channel that would permit 10,000-ton vessels to use the Canal as far as the British lines at El Cap, about 1/3 the way down the Canal from the Mediterranean Sea. Egypt Dec. 1 contracted for the reconstruction of the destroyed El Ferdan railway bridge and announced that the Canal's southern port of Suez had been opened.

Since the Egyptian government regarded the British and French salvage crews as "enemy aliens," the salvage operation was placed under official UN guidance. A UN General Assembly resolution passed by 65–0 vote Nov. 24 had instructed UN Secy. Gen. Hammarskjöld to arrange for the clearance of the Canal, and Hammarskjöld had named this 3-man committee on Canal-clearance problems: technical—U.S. Lt. Gen. Raymond A. Wheeler (ret.), engineering consultant to the World Bank; financial—John J. McCloy, board chairman of the Chase Manhattan Bank and ex-high commissioner for Germany; UN aid—South African Col. Alfred George Katzin, a deputy assistant UN secretary general.

Gen. Wheeler said in Port Said Dec. 11 that the Canal would be reopened as soon as a one-way channel had been cleared. He estimated that full clearance would be accomplished in less than a year. Wheeler had conferred with Egyptian and Anglo-French officials in Cairo and the Canal Zone Dec. 8–11.

British Prime Min. Sir Anthony Eden said in Jamaica

Dec. 14 that "the Canal must be cleared by all available means and without further delay." British Foreign Secy. Selwyn Lloyd told the House of Commons in London Dec. 17 that Hammarskjöld had not replied to British and French offers (a) to continue clearance work in the Suez Canal by the Anglo-French salvage fleet under UN protection, or (b) to release civilian salvage vessels for charter by the UN, or (c) to continue work in the waterway by 6 Anglo-French vessels with civilian crews under the UN flag. Lloyd said that Britain and France had asked for a UN reply by Dec. 17. He warned that if the UN did not meet British-French conditions for the use of their salvage vessels, the entire Anglo-French clearance fleet would be recalled. Lloyd said that Britain and France had rejected UN requests for the use of 6 Anglo-French salvage vessels without their crews.

A spokesman for Hammarskjöld said Dec. 17 that British crews could not be used by a proposed UN salvage fleet because Egypt regarded them as "enemy aliens." Egyptian Foreign Min. Mahmoud Fawzi said in New York Dec. 16 that Egypt would not permit British or French salvage crews to work in the canal "in view of their [the crews'] own safety" after the "ravages" of the Suez area during "the recent agression against Egypt." Egyptian UN envoys suggested that "technicians under UN sponsorship" man Anglo-French salvage vessels.

A tentative clearance agreement between the UN and Britain and France was announced by Wheeler Dec. 21. Wheeler reported that 12 British salvage ships and one French salvage vessel and 7 supply ships would be used by the UN clearance fleet with their own crews. Wheeler said that 2 German salvage ships under UN charter had been sent to El Cap to continue the work started by the Anglo-French fleet. Wheeler, who conferred Dec. 20–25 with Egyptian officials and Col. Mahmoud Yunis, deputy director of the Egyptian Suez Authority, said Dec. 25 that the UN was still awaiting Egyptian acceptance of the clearance program.

Yunis had said Dec. 23 that Egypt had begun salvage work in the Canal and would continue with UN assistance. Egyptian navy crews began clearing mines from the Canal Dec. 24, and Egypt gave 3 Anglo-French vessels permission to continue salvage work in Port Said. But Egyptian Suez Authority spokesmen said Dec. 25 that Egypt would not permit full-scale clearance operations until all Israeli forces had left Egyptian territory.

Hammarskjöld Dec. 25 dispatched an aide, Andrew W. Cordier and Col. Katzin to Egypt for the negotiation of a Canal clearance agreement with the Nasser government. (Hammarskjöld's clearance aide, John J. McCloy, Dec. 20 denied reports appearing Dec. 19 that he was negotiating with major U.S. banks for a $10 million UN loan to finance initial Suez clearance work.)

Initial UN salvage operations were based on an Egyptian-UN canal clearance agreement announced Dec. 26. The implementation of the agreement was delayed until political issues were clarified through talks in Cairo Dec. 27–29 involving Cordier, Katzin and Yunis. A detailed Egyptian-UN agreement was reached Dec. 30 on the deployment of UN salvage ships in the Canal. No accord was reported on the use of Anglo-French salvage vessels within the Canal proper.

Clearance work was extended to the waterway's full length Dec. 31 when Egyptian minesweepers began preceding UN salvage vessels southward through the Canal from El Cap. UN sources said Dec. 29 that the UN clearance fleet would number 36 vessels divided into 3 groups—one working northward from Suez to the sunken Egyptian LST *Akka,* a 2d northward from the *Akka* to El Cap and a 3d southward from Port Said to El Cap. 3 Anglo-French vessels were retained to continue salvage work begun in Port Said.

Gen. Wheeler said Dec. 30 that a 25-foot channel would be open for a limited passage by 10,000-ton vessels (small oil tankers) in March and a full channel by May. Wheeler said that the UN would continue salvage work until Canal facilities were fully restored but that the formal reopening of Canal traffic would be up to Egypt.

The UN salvage crews were soon left the task of removing all obstructions on the waterway between El Cap and Suez, a town on the Red Sea. (The stretch between Port Said on the Mediterranean Sea and El Cap, about 1/3 the way down the Canal, had already been cleared by Anglo-French crews.)

A limited channel from El Ferdan to Port Said was opened when German lifting vessels pulled the wrecked El Ferdan railway bridge from the Canal Jan. 4, 1957. Despite UN objections, Egyptian tugs Jan. 5–6 turned 13 vessels trapped in the Canal near Ismailia and formed them into a northbound convoy. They left the Canal at Port Said Jan. 8. (Col. Mahmoud Yunis had said Jan. 6 that "we [Egypt] will prove to the world that we can run this Canal even after 2 aggressions.")

The U.S. government made $5 million available to the UN from Mutual Security Agency funds Jan. 8 to help meet the UN's initial Canal clearance costs. 8 West European and British Commonwealth countries were said to have agreed Jan. 2 to advance an additional $5–$6 million for the salvage program. The World Bank agreed Jan. 2 to act as UN agent in handling the loans and paying UN-chartered salvage firms.

The single biggest ship in the canal—the Egyptian tanker *Akka*—was removed Feb. 1. The removal of 5 more smaller obstructions in March completed a 25-foot-deep channel through the Canal, permitting the navigation of small ships.

The first regular convoy of ships to pass through the Canal since its closure Nov. 1, 1956, left Suez Mar. 29, 1957 and cleared Port Said Mar. 31. The 9 freighters, ranging up to 7,061 tons, were led into the Mediterranean by the Soviet ship *Krasnador*. The Egyptian Suez Authority Mar. 29 opened the Canal to vessels of up to 11,000 tons and of no more than 25-foot draft. The authority Mar. 29 listed 244 pilots in its Suez force, 99 of them Egyptian.

Egypt Reopens Canal

Egypt reopened the Suez Canal to vessels of all drafts Apr. 10, 1957. The government announced that henceforth, all dues were payable in advance to the Suez Canal Authority or its recognized agents.

The Egyptian government issued a declaration on the Canal Apr. 24. The first 5—and most important—articles stated:

1. *Reaffirmation of 1888 Convention.* It remains the unaltered policy and firm purpose of the government of Egypt to respect the terms and spirit of the Constantinople Convention and the rights and obligations arising therefrom. . . .

2. *Observance of the 1888 Convention & UN Charter.* While reaffirming their determination to respect the terms and spirit of the Constantinople Convention of 1888 and to abide by the principles and purposes of the UN Charter, the government of Egypt are confident that the other signatories of the said Convention, and all others concerned, will be guided by the same resolve.

3. *Freedom of Navigation, Tolls & Development of the Canal.* The government of Egypt . . . [is] determined: (*a*) to afford and maintain free and uninterrupted navigation for all nations within the limits of and in accordance with the provisions of the Constantinople Convention; (*b*) that tolls shall continue to be levied in accordance with the agreement concluded on Apr. 28, 1936, between Egypt and the Suez Canal Maritime Co.; and that any increase in the current rate of tolls within 12 months, if it takes place, shall be limited to one per cent; and that any increase beyond that level shall be made through negotiations and, failing agreement, shall be settled by arbitration according to the procedure set forth below. . . ; (*c*) that the Canal shall be maintained and developed in accordance with the progressive requirements of modern navigation, and that such maintenance and development shall include the 8th and 9th programs of the Suez Canal Maritime Co., with such improvements thereto as are considered necessary.

4. *Operation & Management.* The Canal shall be operated and managed by the autonomous Suez Canal Authority established by the government of Egypt on July 26, 1956. The government of Egypt look forward with confidence to continued cooperation with the nations of the world in advancing the usefulness of the Canal . . . [and] will welcome and encourage cooperation between the Canal Authority and representatives of shipping and trade.

5. *Finance.* (*a*) Tolls shall be payable in advance to the account of the Canal Authority at any bank chosen for this purpose by the

Authority. The Canal Authority has authorized the National Bank of Egypt to undertake this operation, and is also negotiating with the Bank for International Settlements to accept payment of the canal tolls on its behalf. (*b*) The Canal Authority shall pay to the government of Egypt 5% of all gross receipts as royalty. (*c*) The Canal Authority will establish a Suez Canal Capital & Development Fund into which shall be paid 25% of all gross receipts. This Fund will ensure that there shall be available to the Canal Authority adequate resources to meet the needs of development and capital expenditure for the fulfilment of the responsibilities they have assumed and are determined to discharge.

The 15-country Suez Canal Users Association disclosed in London May 9 that member states had been freed from SCUA restrictions against the use of the Suez Canal. A communiqué said that the action did not imply "acceptance of the Egyptian declaration" on Canal operations, which it said had fallen "short" of the "6 principles" for a minimum Suez settlement approved by the UN Security Council in 1956. The communiqué, at French insistence, stated that all SCUA members except France would resume the use of the Canal although the SCUA did not "recommend" its use. (SCUA member states were Britain, U.S., France, Spain, Australia, New Zealand, Norway, Denmark, Sweden, Netherlands, Italy, West Germany, Portugal, Turkey, Iran. Countries maintaining SCUA observers: Japan, Ethiopia, Pakistan.)

Prime Min. Harold Macmillan told the British House of Commons May 13 that his government "can no longer advise British shipowners to refrain from using the Canal." Macmillian said that, following the resumption of Suez traffic by other Western nations, British shippers were being instructed to use the Canal and pay Egyptian Suez Authority tolls into a controlled sterling account. He emphasized that SCUA members had "reserved their rights" on future Canal operations and that Britain did "not accept the Egyptian declaration as a permanent and satisfactory settlement."

Macmillan's statement, greeted in Cairo May 13 as proof of British capitulation to Egypt's control of the Canal, brought Laborite demands for debate on a censure motion attacking the effect of the government's Suez policy on Britain's prestige and economy. 8 Conservative MPs, led by Viscount Hinchingbrooke, broke with the government leadership May 13 and formed an "Independent Conservative" group. Sir Winston Churchill, in an address May 3 to the Conservative Party's Primrose League, had defended ex-Prime Min. Sir Anthony Eden's "resolute action" against Egypt in 1956 and criticized the UN's handling of the Suez dispute.

British government sources said May 13 that talks on a resumption of economic relations with Egypt would begin in Rome May 23. The Egyptian Finance Ministry named a 4-man committee May 14 to represent Egypt at the projected Rome talks. The ministry also issued orders to the Egyptian Suez Authority to accept tolls paid into special British sterling account in lieu of dollar payments required of other Suez users. Representatives of the Bank of England and Egyptian National Bank were reported May 12 to have begun talks in Switzerland on a relaxation of the mutual British-Egyptian fund freeze.

A preliminary agreement was reached in Rome Apr. 29, 1958 on compensation of the Universal Suez Canal Co. for the nationalization of the Suez Canal. A declaration of principles for settlement of the compensation dispute was signed for the United Arab Republic (UAR, as Egypt and Syria were styled following a short-lived union announced Feb. 1, 1958) by Chairman Abdel Guelil el-Emary of the Egyptian Central Bank and for the Suez Co. by Chairman Jacques Georges-Picot, Charles M. Spofford and John Foster. The accord was witnessed by Vice Pres. William A. B. Illif of the World Bank, who, with George D. Wood, a New York banker, had mediated the dispute in extended negotiations in Cairo, Paris and Rome.

The preliminary agreement fixed these terms for compensation: (a) the UAR's waiver of claims to £E5.3 million ($14.8 million) in Canal tolls paid to the Suez firm's Paris and

London accounts after the Canal's seizure; (b) UAR payment, in 6 annual installments ending in 1964, of £E23 million ($66 million) for Egyptian assets of the Suez Canal Co.; (c) the Anglo-French company to retain all Suez Canal Co. assets and liabilities outside of Egypt, including debentures and pensions of retired employes resident outside Egypt. (Assets outside Egypt that were left to the company were estimated at $200 million; liabilities were reported to total $6½ million in outstanding debentures.)

El-Emary told newsmen Apr. 26 that the UAR cash payment to the Suez firm represented the difference between the value of Suez Co. shares and the Anglo-French firm's non-Egyptian assets awarded to Egypt, plus "about £E10 million" ($28.7 million).

Assets of the Egyptian government and of the Universal Suez Canal Co., frozen in the U.S. since the 1956 Suez crisis, were released May 1, 1958 after the signing of the Suez compensation agreement by the United Arab Republic the Suez Co.

A U.S. Treasury Department announcement Apr. 30, 1958 said that was releasing assets worth $26 million to the UAR and $44 million to the Universal Suez Co. $14 million of the $40 million in Egyptian funds originally frozen by the U.S. already had been released for Egyptian government expenses in the U.S. Assets of the Suez Co. were freed in compliance with the provisions of the compensation settlement awarding to the company all non-Egyptian Suez assets. American State Department officials had indicated Apr. 30 that U.S. aid to Egypt would be resumed "after a decent interval."

A UAR pledge to keep the Suez Canal open in wartime to ships of all nations except Israel was reported May 5 to have been given Soviet leaders by visiting UAR Pres. Nasser. Cairo officials said May 5 that Nasser had stressed freedom of shipping through the Canal at all times in talks Apr. 30–May 2

with Soviet Premier Khrushchev.   Other subjects discussed:
unified terms and the repayment of an estimated $500 mil-
lion in Soviet loans to the former Egyptian and Syrian governments—which had merged as the UAR—and cultural and
technical exchanges.

mand Force—219. Relief &
Works Agency for Palestine Refugees in the Near East (UNRWA)—
52, 235-6. Sanctions against Israel—239-43. Security Council—
65-9, 83-5, 87, 96-8, 101, 106,
188-205, 218. Suez—185-205,
213-4, 244, 246
UNITED States—66, 76, 87-8, 93,
144, 152, 155-7, 159, 174-5, 177,
181, 189, 195, 210-3, 219, 242,
249. Aid to Mideast—44, 47, 77,
121, 124; arms & military aid—
36, 77-8, 94, 114, 118-9; Aswan
Dam—119-27, 134. Arab-Israeli
peace efforts—100-6. Baghdad
Pact—76. Egypt—19, 36, 38, 44,
77-8, 142, 161, 183, 251. International Cooperation Administration—77. Israel—88-9, 94, 119,
237-43. Soviet Union—101-2,
126. State Department—38, 93-4,
102-3, 141, 228. Suez—46, 130,
141-4, 170-2, 180, 182-5, 247.
Tripartite Declaration of 1950—
62, 95, 100, 102, 147, 196, 213
UNIVERSAL Suez Canal Co.—See
'Suez Canal Co., Universal,' under
SUEZ Canal
UNIVERSITIES: Closing—19

V

VICTORIOUS (destroyer)—129
VISHINSKY, Andrei Y.—66
Von BRETANO, Heinrich—152

W

WAFD Party—See WAFDISTS
WAFDISTS—7-9, 13, 17, 20, 24,
26, 36-40, 58-9
WAHAB Bey, Ibrahim Abdel—20,
34
WAHHABI Sect—47
WAITHAYAKON, Prince Wan—228
WHEELER, Raymond A.—244-6
WHITE, Lincoln—141, 182
WILSON, Charles E.—147-8, 213
WILSON, Harold—98
WOMEN: Optional voting—131
WOOD, George D.—250
WORLD Bank (International Bank
for Reconstruction & Develop-
ment)—120, 122, 125, 127
WORLD Jewish Congress—229
WORLD War I—7, 9
WORLD War II—13, 20, 30, 47,
136
WORLD Zionist Congress—108

Y

YAFFI, Abdullah—123
YEMEN—70, 73, 192, 221
YOUNG Egypt—13
YOUSSEF, Hassan—39
YOUTH League—150
YUGOSLAVIA—72, 132-4, 150,
174-5, 189, 219
YUNIS, Mahmoud—138, 176, 245-
7

Z

ZAGHLOUL, Saad—7-8
ZEID, Hussein Abou—38, 51